CONCORDE CONSPIRACY

CONCORDE CONSPIRACY

The Battle for American Skies 1962-77

GRAHAM M. SIMONS

The History Press

Cover illustrations: *Front*: *top, left*: flag of the United States at the memorial to President Kennedy in Hyannis, Massachusetts. *(Kelson Collection)*; *top, right*: the flag of the United Kingdom, the right way up, here viewed from behind. *(Stefano Brivio Collection)*; *middle*: Air Aircraft Concorde *(© Trinity Mirror/Mirrorpix/Alamy)*; *bottom*: Manhatten, July 1976. *(Isaac Newton Collection) Back*: The XB-70A was fitted with two sets of 'passenger windows' while with NASA, in order to demonstrate visually the American SST. *(USAF)*

First published 2012

The History Press
The Mill, Brimscombe Port
Stroud, Gloucestershire, GL5 2QG
www.thehistorypress.co.uk

© Graham M. Simons 2012

The right of Graham M. Simons to be identified as the Author of this work has been asserted in accordance with the Copyrights, Designs and Patents Act 1988.

British Library Cataloguing in Publication Data.
A catalogue record for this book is available from the British Library.

ISBN 978 0 7524 6365 0

Typesetting and origination by The History Press
Manufacturing managed by JellyfishPrint Solutions Ltd
Printed in India

Contents

Acknowledgements

A project of this nature could not be undertaken without considerable help from many organisations and individuals. Special thanks must go to Marilyn Phipps of Boeing Archives, Col Richard L. Upstromm and Tom Brewer from the USAF Museum, now the National Museum of the USAF, for the provision of many photographs and details. The archives of the National Advisory Committee for Aeronautics provided access to all their relevant material, as did Lynn Gamma and all in the US Air Force Historical Research Center at Maxwell Air Force Base, Montgomery, Alabama. Much other primary source documentation is also located in the National Archives and Records Administration at College Park, Maryland, the history files of the Central Intelligence Agency and the Presidential Libraries of John F. Kennedy and Lyndon B. Johnson. Thanks must also go to Darryl Cott of British Aerospace, David Lee, the former Deputy Director and Curator of Aircraft at the Imperial War Museum at Duxford, John Hamlin and Vince Hemmings, the former curator of the East Anglian Aviation Society's Tower Museum at Bassingbourn.

The author is indebted to many people and organisations for providing photographs for this book, many of which are in the public domain. In some cases it has not been possible to identify the original photographer so credits are given in the appropriate places to the immediate supplier. If any of the pictures have not been correctly credited, the author apologises.

Introduction

The story of Concorde and the Americans is one of spies, lies, arrogance, dirty tricks and presidential hatred. It is one of deceit, treachery, mistrust and confusion.

The Americans were initially dismissive of Anglo-French efforts – then arrogant to the point that they thought that not only could they do better, but that they were the only ones capable of completing the project. President Kennedy said, 'Make it happen – make it bigger, make it faster.' He might well have added, 'Make it to beat my presidential rival in France.'

The Americans always referred to the aircraft as 'the' Concorde – the Europeans called it simply 'Concorde', although there were initially spelling differences with or without the 'e'.

It is often said that knowledge is power, so the Americans set out to gain knowledge on their competitors – by fair means or foul. They had been comprehensively beaten to the title of being the builders of the world's first jet airliner by the British de Havilland Comet – an aircraft that then went on to beat them to the title of the world's first jet airliner to enter airline service, and the world's first passenger jet to fly on the prestigious transatlantic service. Even the Soviets managed to get their Tu-104 into regular airline service two years before the Boeing 707. Militarily they had also been comprehensively beaten into space, with the first satellite, the first animal and the first man and woman placed into orbit.

For a nation that regarded itself as the world's only superpower and to be technologically more advanced than any other nation, the Americans were determined that they would not be beaten to the next milestone: the builders of the world's first supersonic airliner. The Central Intelligence Agency, the Federal Aviation Authority and other government agencies all came in to play under Presidential Order to spy on the French, the Soviets and the British in order to gain an edge.

Jingoism, blind patriotism and national pride also played their part; but this eventually degenerated into political infighting amongst vested-interest groups. With the assassination of President Kennedy, Lyndon Johnson took over and, as with his predecessor, was very much in favour of an American supersonic transport aircraft (SST) project. Under Presidential Order, he established a President's Advisory Committee on Supersonic Transport (PAC-SST) under the chairmanship of Robert Strange McNamara, the US Secretary of Defense.

By definition, the chairman of any committee is selected to preside over meetings and lead a committee to consensus from the disparate points of view of its members. The chairman is expected to be impartial, fair, a good listener and a good communicator. Nothing could be further from the truth with Robert McNamara. He set out to cold-bloodedly sabotage the project right from the start. In his own words:

> Right at the beginning I thought the project was not justified, because you couldn't fly a large enough payload over a long enough nonstop distance at a low enough cost to make it pay. I'm not an aeronautical engineer or a technical expert or an airline specialist or an aircraft manufacturer but I knew that I could make the calculation on the back of an envelope.
>
> So I approached the SST with that bias. President Johnson was in favor of it. As chairman of the committee I was very skeptical from the beginning. The question, in a sense, was how to kill it. I conceived an approach that said: maybe you're right, maybe there is a commercial market, maybe what we should do is to take it with government funds up to the point where the manufacturers and the airlines can determine the economic viability of the aircraft. We'll draw up a program on that basis.

So the project studies continued, but the steady drip, drip, drip of McNamara's negative attitudes and biased reporting slowly defeated any hopes of an American SST, just as he had killed off the North American B-70 Mach 3 bomber project for the United States Air Force (USAF) and through manipulation of funding with the World Bank also ensured the death of the UK TSR-2 strike aircraft in favour of the US General Dynamics F-111 Aardvark.

McNamara had a track record for political intrigue and manipulation. He may have come to the post of Secretary of Defense from the Ford Motor Corporation, but he moved in the murky world of Cold War spies, so-called 'Black' projects and those who worked on them. This was a highly secret and insular world that had links between the politicians on Capitol Hill, the defence industry and the rarefied atmosphere of research faculties of the Ivy League universities. From this world came the strange saga of Professor William A. Shurcliff's Citizens' League Against the Sonic Boom, which suddenly surfaced just at the time Robert McNamara left public office and went to head the World Bank. Shurcliff, who had worked on the fringes of the atom bomb project, was employed by Polaroid Corporation under Edwin Land of Land Camera fame, who also secretly worked for the Defense Department and the CIA on the cameras for the U-2 and SR-71 spyplanes. Shurcliff was well known in this world and was thus in a good position to express publicly the negative views on the SST held by McNamara. It is doubtful if we will ever know the depth and scope of these links, for apart from much still remaining secret, when Land died on 1 March 1991 at the age of 81, his personal assistant shredded his personal papers and notes.

Shurcliff's Citizens League Against the Sonic Boom was without doubt instrumental in killing off the Boeing 2707, so that hurt American pride and the arrogance of their national ego easily created a mindset of 'if we cannot do it, neither will you'. This collective mindset then set about destroying the Anglo-French Concorde by attempting to block the aircraft's certification to operate into and over the USA and prevent its access to American airports by legal challenges and bans.

This then is that story – a story told using primary source documentation. It is one that has echoes back to the de Havilland Comet and Boeing 707, and resonates forward to today with the recent political battle between Boeing and the European Aeronautic Defence and Space Company over the KC-X replacement for the ageing Eisenhower-generation fleet of KC-135 tankers that were so badly needed for the USAF. This was a battle that was won by Boeing by using partisan political support such as that which came from Senator Patty Murray, who is just the latest in a long line of politicians from Capitol Hill who were prepared to manipulate the facts in favour of 'the company' rather than concentrate on what was really going on.

Graham M. Simons
Peterborough
June 2011

1

In the Beginning

From the late 1940s onwards, it seemed that man's mission was to achieve even greater speed, and this was translated first into subsonic jet aircraft and then into supersonic military aircraft development, with the first major British design being the Miles M.52 – an aircraft design that was well ahead of its nearest rival, the American Bell X-1. According to Miles Aircraft's chief aerodynamicist Dennis Bancroft, in 1944 the Air Ministry signed an agreement with the USA to exchange high-speed research and data. Miles gave their data to Bell Aircraft, but the Americans reneged on the arrangement and no data was forthcoming in return. The M.52 was cancelled in February 1946. The transition to a supersonic commercial transport was to take much longer.

Having led the way with commercial jet transports, it was natural that in order to capitalise on this initial success, Britain's aeronautical design teams should turn their attention to supersonic transport aircraft. By the mid-fifties, the ground lost by the de Havilland DH.106 Comet accidents and Vickers VC-7 cancellation could, it was hoped, be reclaimed with the production of hundreds of aircraft travelling faster than the speed of sound.

Great Britain was not, however, the only country studying supersonic transports; so were the French, the Americans and the Soviets. One design – due to tremendous political infighting – was eventually stillborn; another, although the first to fly, soon gave up; and the two remaining merged into one to carry passengers routinely very quickly and very expensively carry passengers across the Atlantic. That survivor, so scorned by economists, acclaimed by engineers and loathed by environmentalists, was the Anglo-French Concorde.

The British Miles M.52 design that could well have been the world's first supersonic aircraft to fly. Seen here is the mock-up at the Miles Woodley site in 1944. *(Simon Peters Collection)*

Charles E. 'Chuck' Yeager with his Bell X-1 46-062, 'Glamorous Glennis', in which he became the first man in the first aircraft to break the sound barrier officially, on 14 October 1947. *(USAF)*

For any nation to create a supersonic airliner was, and still is, an enormous challenge. Scientists had explored the secrets of aerodynamics during the first half of the twentieth century, translating the theory and experimentation into the design and refinement of a succession of aircraft. Air transport had seen progressive increases in speed, but strange effects appeared when aircraft approached the speed of sound. Air resistance rose dramatically to impose a serious obstacle – the so-called sound barrier – to conventional flight. The changes were sudden as the normally orderly airflow broke down and shock waves, akin to the bow waves of a ship, were generated at the nose and tail of the aircraft.

In 1947, USAF captain Charles E. 'Chuck' Yeager, flying the rocket-powered, air-launched Bell XS-1 research aircraft that bore more than a passing resemblance to the M.52, including the one-piece tailplane, became the first pilot to exceed the speed of sound in level flight. Supersonic speeds, it should be explained, are expressed in terms of Mach number, generally pronounced 'Mak', which is the speed of an object moving through air, or any other fluid substance, divided by the speed of sound in that substance for its particular physical conditions, including those of temperature and pressure. It is commonly used to represent the speed of an object when it is travelling close to or above the speed of sound. Mach 1 varies from about 760mph at sea level to about 660mph at a height of 50,000 to 60,000ft, and gets its name from Austrian physicist and philosopher Ernst Mach (1838–1916), who contributed much to its study. By the end of the 1950s a number of fighter aircraft were in service that could fly brief bursts at supersonic speeds, but they could not cruise supersonically for hours at a time.

The Work of Barnes Wallis

Even before the end of the Second World War, Barnes Wallis recognised that the next big milestone in flight would be a supersonic aircraft, and his main interest became the development of a supersonic airliner. He recognised that the increase in drag at supersonic speeds would require very efficient aerodynamics, and as a leap towards this target – and to reduce weight – Wallis proposed to dispense entirely with the tail for his new aircraft. He also wanted to exploit the idea of laminar flow to produce a fuselage with very low skin drag. The basic form of his new aircraft, which he called an aerodyne, thus had just three structural elements: an egg-shaped fuselage and two wings which had no flaps or ailerons. Although offering efficient flight characteristics, this new form of aircraft presented substantial control problems. To solve these, Wallis used his knowledge as an airship designer. He knew that when an elongated solid body such as an airship or aircraft fuselage travelled through the air at a slight angle, it generated large rotational forces but no substantial linear forces. To balance these rotational forces, Wallis planned to locate the wings towards the rear of the aircraft, giving an inherently stable form. Control was to be effected by pivoting the wings round a vertical axis – sweeping the wings backwards would allow faster speeds, while sweeping them forwards would give greater lift for landing and take-off. To change direction, he proposed to sweep the wings unevenly, the aircraft turning towards the wing that was swept the most. This was the 'wing-controlled aerodyne'.

Wallis developed a series of models under the designation 'Wild Goose', but as the Wild Goose experiments continued, he realised that he was not going to get the range required from the design. By 1953, the 'slender delta' planform was the favourite of designers of supersonic aircraft, and he knew that most of

Sir Barnes Neville Wallis CBE, FRS, RDI, FRAeS (b. 26 September 1887, d. 30 October 1979) with one of his Swallow models. Note the engines above and below the wing. *(Vickers)*

the lift from this shape came from the leading edge. He therefore proposed an arrowhead planform using a delta, but with the non-lifting rear part removed, and with the wings projecting backward from a smaller delta-shaped forebody which also provided lift. Having the wings so far back would make take-off and landing

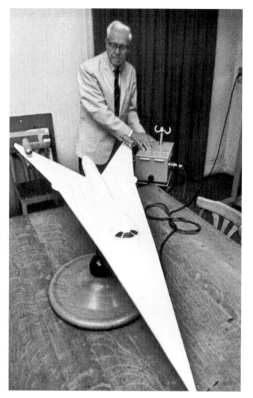

problematic, so he reverted to his variable-geometry wing concept, pivoting the wings at the rear of the forebody, so that they could be swept forward – almost straight – for low-speed manoeuvring and landing. This series of designs became termed 'Swallow'.

An SST variant was proposed long before the Concorde project, with the swing wings having the benefit of reducing landing and take-off speeds, foreshadowing the Boeing 733/2707 of more than a decade later. A unique feature of both versions of the Swallow was the 'elevator cockpit'. The entire flight deck, contained in a circular tub, could be raised above the fuselage to increase vision and lowered to improve aerodynamic streamlining.

By 1960, Wallis realised that Mach 2.5 – which at the time was regarded as the speed limit on the slender delta – was too slow and he produced a new design for an aircraft with a top speed of Mach 4-5.

Contemporary designers exploring speeds in this range were being challenged by the material problems associated with the heat generated by the air friction. Solutions to these used materials like stainless steel and titanium for the airframe. However, Wallis was keen to continue using light alloys, but devised an 'isothermal flight' profile which balanced increasing speed with increasing height, and therefore thinner

Above: Barnes Wallis with another version of the Swallow, showing the 'elevator cockpit' that could be raised to improve the view over the nose.

Right: A possible layout for the civil version of the Swallow. *(Vickers)*

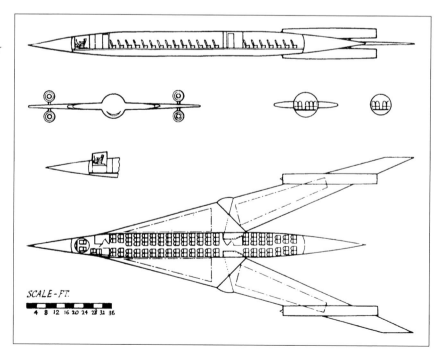

air, allowing the airframe temperature to remain within safe limits. Wallis' experimentation with new forms continued, using one single wing that was still pivoted on a horizontal shaft with large leading- and trailing-edge flaps. This allowed the configuration of the aircraft to be continually altered for the wide range of different flight regimes encountered between take-off and a cruise at above 100,000ft and Mach 4. As the aircraft was in the most efficient configuration at all times, range could be maximised, and a nonstop London–Sydney flight was believed to be achievable with this 'universal' aircraft, with a flight time stated at being around five hours.

A model of the Barnes Wallis Swallow IV with swing wings and a rear fuselage that is split in two directions – one across to give the effect of elevator control, and one down the rear fuselage to provide aileron control. *(Author)*

Enter the Royal Aircraft Establishment

There were serious aerodynamic problems that had to be solved in the design of a supersonic airliner, and not only in shaping the aircraft to give the best possible performance. The study of supersonic airliners in Britain really began in 1954 at the Royal Aircraft Establishment (RAE) at Farnborough, when a working party was set up under noted Welsh aeronautical engineer Morien Morgan, who was later called 'the father of Concorde', to investigate the possibility of a faster-than-sound transatlantic airliner. Its initial design was for an aircraft based around the Avro 730 supersonic bomber, with thin unswept wings and a long slender fuselage, only able to accommodate around fifteen passengers. The aircraft could have travelled at Mach 2 from London to New York, but the all-up weight was estimated at above 300,000lb, with an excessive cost per passenger. It was evident that the development of such an aircraft was not justifiable.

All this changed after the head of supersonic research at the RAE, Philip Hufton, went to America in 1955, and saw developments in supersonic aircraft using the 'area rule' effect. This stated that if the shape of an aircraft's cross-sectional area was the same all along its length, the wave drag would be minimised. Encouraged by this, Hufton filed a report suggesting that a supersonic transport may now be feasible. A further avenue of investigation was an entirely new shape of aircraft based on German wartime research which could be designed for supersonic flight - the delta wing.

Welsh aeronautical
engineer Sir Morien
Bedford Morgan CB
(b. 20 December
1912, d. 4 April
1978)

As a result of this, those back at Farnborough, who just months before had been saying that an SST could not be justified, now had their interest rekindled in a major way. Among those now re-examining supersonic flight at the RAE was a German aerodynamicist, Dr Dietrich Küchemann CBE, FRS, RAeS. Before the war Küchemann joined Ludwig Prandtl in aerodynamics research, publishing his doctoral thesis in 1936. With the war looming, Küchemann volunteered for service in 1938, and as expected was given a non-combatant role in Signals, serving from 1942–45. During this period he continued to research, notably into the problems of high-speed flight, wave drag, swept-wing theory and initial steps on the road to the 'area rule', and designed an aircraft called the 'Küchemann Coke Bottle'. After the war he moved to England as part of Operation Surgeon, a British programme to exploit German aeronautical research and deny German technical skills to the Soviets. Küchemann joined the RAE at Farnborough where he studied aircraft propulsion in depth and became the leading expert on such topics as ducted fans and jet engines. He also began to study delta designs. In order to further research, it was decided that the RAE alone could not look into all the problems that would need to be investigated, especially if Britain was to try to get ahead of the field as it had done with the Comet less than a decade earlier. It was decided that all the major parties in the industry, as well as airlines, government, ministries and the Air Registration Board, should be included.

Under the chairmanship of Morien Morgan, the deputy head of the RAE, the Supersonic Transport Aircraft Committee (STAC) was set up on 1 October 1956. This committee had its first meeting on 30 November 1956. Its two key objectives were to investigate the possible market for an SST and to define an operator's broad requirements so that areas of desirable research could be carried out. Among the representatives were all the major aircraft companies, namely A.V. Roe, Armstrong Whitworth, Bristol Aircraft, de Havilland, Handley Page, Shorts and Vickers-Armstrong. These were joined in November 1957 by English Electric and Fairey. Also represented were the four main engine companies: Armstrong Siddeley, Bristol, de Havilland Engines and, of course, Rolls-Royce. Other representatives came from the British Overseas Airways Corporation (BOAC) and British European Airways (BEA), as well as government departments: the Air Registration Board, the Aircraft Research Association, the National Physical Laboratory, the National Gas Turbine Establishment, RAE, Ministry of Supply and Ministry of Transport and Civil Aviation. The committee foresaw the prestige that a successful SST would bring to Britain, as well as the possible military transport spin-off.

The committee looked at the problems of flying at speeds from Mach 1.2 to Mach 2.6, and the issues that were associated with materials, especially at a higher speed, with detailed research carried out. In the event, two sizes of aircraft were proposed: a medium-range transport carrying 100 passengers over 1,500 miles at Mach 1.2 (800mph) and a Mach 1.8 (1,200mph) or faster long-range airliner carrying 150 passengers. Many different shapes of aircraft were investigated, including swept wings, variable wings, M-wings, slender wings and aircraft capable of vertical take-off. As a result of the research, the committee found that although a Mach 2.6 machine would probably be feasible, its development would take too long.

At the time Morien Morgan commented:

Light alloy construction would be used, and engines could be straightforward developments of present-day large jet units. Long slender shapes, with subsonic leading edges and supersonic trailing edges, can give sufficiently high L/D while the optimum cruise aspect ratio is large enough for a sensible compromise to be visualized between cruising efficiency and reasonable approach speed.

In the early stages, de Havilland concentrated on Mach 1.2 long-range designs with swept wings, the so-called 'M'-wing and delta-wing planforms. The M-wing form was also investigated by Vickers, Bristol and Armstrong Whitworth. Shorts looked at both medium-range and long-range transports with swept and delta wings at Mach 1.5 and Mach 1.8, while Handley Page studies featured delta, cropped-spearhead and swept wings at Mach 1.8. Avro concentrated on a medium-range, straight-wing Mach 1.8 transport.

The committee initially decreed that for the Mach 1.2 airliner, an M-wing or possibly swept wing would be preferable, while for the Mach 1.8 an integrated slender wing or long thin delta should be studied. At the time, total development costs of the Mach 1.2 design were put at £60–80 million, while those for the Mach 1.8 were around £95 million.

Politically, the SST emerged from the research laboratories and entered the political arena when, in May 1958, Derick Heathcoat-Amory, Chancellor of the Exchequer in the Conservative government of the day led by Harold Macmillan, reported the conclusions of an ad hoc inquiry into the future of the British aircraft industry to a Cabinet meeting in 10 Downing Street. The report concluded that fewer aircraft manufacturing companies were needed – and also warned that the development of the next generation of aircraft, such as supersonic transports, would almost certainly only be possible with substantial government assistance.

The first jet airliner in the world – the de Havilland Comet – seen in early July 1949, just before it flew for the first time. *(BAe Hatfield/ Darryl Cott)*

Left: Conservative Prime Minister Maurice Harold Macmillan, 1st Earl of Stockton (b.10 February 1894, d. 29 December 1986).

Right: Conservative politician Aubrey Jones (b. 20 November 1911, d. 10 April 2003).

Left: Derick Heathcoat-Amory, 1st Viscount Amory KG, GCMG, TD, PC, DL (b. 26 December 1899, d. 20 January 1981) served as Chancellor of the Exchequer from 1958 to 1960.

This arose again in December when Jones, the Minister of Supply, reported that the country's aircraft industry was in a bad way. He suggested that one way to strengthen it would be to resume the immediate post-war practice of providing government support for the development of selected aircraft, even those for which there was no immediate requirement. The largest project was likely to be the supersonic civil transport. The prime minister agreed, and said the Ministerial Committee on Civil Aviation should be reconvened to give further consideration to this suggestion.

At first the supersonic transport was regarded purely as a possible national venture, and Britain believed it had a head start in this race, just as it had a decade or so earlier with the DH.106 Comet jet airliner. Initial technical studies into the prospects for transport aircraft that would fly faster than sound had already begun. Then the idea that Britain might collaborate with the USA to develop and build a supersonic transport began to take shape in 1959. Both countries had SST research under way and were thinking about the possible development of supersonic civil airliners. The initiative for collaboration came from the British government.

One has to be careful in reading some of these contemporary reports, no matter how authoritative, for in some cases there are aspects of wishful thinking associated with them, in that what was reported never came even close to fruition, even to this day. For example, in the 12 December 1958 edition of *The Aeroplane*, Dr Robin R. Jamieson, chief ramjet engineer of Bristol Aero-Engines Ltd, emphasised the advantages of ramjets for supersonic airliners in a recent lecture before the Bristol branch of the Royal Aeronautical Society. After discussing the applications of ramjet power for propulsion at speeds up to Mach 5, he gave consideration to the types of ramjet which might be suitable for hypersonic flight up to Mach 12. He went on to say, 'The superiority of the ramjet for flight speeds greater than Mach 2.5 led to Bristol studies of the use of ramjets for supersonic transports.'

American Developments

The American dimension was developed in a note Macmillan received from Harold Watkinson, his Minister of Transport and Civil Aviation. Watkinson had been talking supersonics with Lieutenant General Elwood Richard 'Pete' Quesada, chosen by US President Dwight D. Eisenhower to be the first administrator of the Federal Aviation Agency (FAA). Both men agreed that the airlines should have at least eight to ten years' use of the existing subsonic jets before they were forced to buy supersonic machines, but they recognised that this would not necessarily happen.

Watkinson also reported that at the International Civil Aviation Organization (ICAO) conference in San Diego, Britain had called attention to the big problems that would face civil aviation authorities if an SST was to come into operation within the next ten years, and had proposed that ICAO staff examine these matters. This suggestion had been supported by most of the other nations at the meeting but had been opposed by the United States. The US attitude made sense, the minister concluded, only if the Americans had already decided to proceed with a supersonic transport project of their own. This conclusion by Watkinson was coupled with the assumption that the American SST would begin life

Harold Watkinson PC, CH (b. 25 January 1910, d. 19 December 1995), British Minister of Transport and Civil Aviation.

America's answer to the Comet was the Boeing 367-80, seen at roll-out on 14 May 1954. Despite popular claims to the contrary, this was not the prototype Boeing 707 – although looking somewhat like it, it is in fact at least two stages away, having undergone two increases in fuselage diameter and other changes. *(David Lee Collection)*

as a military project – as had the subsonic Boeing 707 airliner, which had 'rode on the back' of the KC-135 tanker, itself derived from the Boeing Model 367-80 – and would almost certainly come from the North American Aviation B-70 Mach 3 bomber wanted by Strategic Air Command, which would breed a civil version.

Harold Watkinson thought that the cost of an all-British supersonic project would be enormous, and that it was doubtful if Britain could match the United States in straight competition. He suggested that the government should encourage British firms to set up a joint project with whichever US company won the SST contract.

Indeed, it was soon clear that Watkinson's assumptions were correct, for by November 1960 the civil version of the B-70 was common knowledge. The British aeronautical magazine *The Aeroplane and Astronautics* ran a four-page article on the design, stating:

Transport versions of the B-70 have been studied and three different versions proposed. The first, which could be available by late 1963, represents the minimum conversion of the bomber.

By 1966 a more extensively modified version could be produced for operation by the Military Air Transport Service as a cargo and passenger transport. This aircraft would retain J93 engines, but would have a fuselage of greater diameter to improve volume, loading and operation. It would carry 107 military passengers. In the cargo role it would carry 75,000lb. for 2,470 naut. miles or 36,000lb. for 2,930 naut. miles. A commercial version could carry 80 first-class or 108 tourist-class passengers.

By mid-1967 it is considered that a competitive commercial transport could be produced. It would be powered by a turbo-fan version of the J93, and its fuselage and systems would be modified to permit FAA certification. Equipped with thrust reversers this supersonic airliner could operate from airports with a runway length equivalent to 10,500ft. at sea level. It would cruise at Mach 3 (1,980mph) at 70,000ft.

Operating costs have been calculated for transport B-70 operations during 1968. Assuming 3,000 hours utilization a year, and extrapolated currency inflation factors the cost will be 2.5 cents per seat mile for a typical transcontinental flight and 2.75 cents per seat mile for a transoceanic flight, assuming 90 passengers are carried.

Lieutenant General Elwood 'Pete' Quesada (b. 13 April 1904, d. 9 February 1993), first head of the FAA in the US. *(USAF)*

When STAC's 300-page report was submitted in March 1959, it recommended the design studies for two supersonic airliners: one to fly at a speed of Mach 1.2 and the other at Mach 2.0. The Ministry of Aviation acted quickly, with feasibility studies being commissioned for three aircraft types from the Hawker Siddeley Group and Bristol Aircraft in September of that year. A major change was that the proposed speed had now increased to Mach 2.2. The Hawker Siddeley Group was chosen to study an integrated wing, which was to be handled by its Advanced Projects Group, and resulted in a design with an all-up weight of 320,000lb and a wing area of 6,000sq. ft.

Concurrent with this, Hawker Siddeley also undertook joint studies with Handley Page into Mach 2.2 airliners. Bristol Aircraft were to study a slender-shape wing design with a distinct fuselage. Both companies were also asked to investigate a Mach 2.7 aircraft.

A Flight by Boeing ...

In early 1959, M.L. Rennell, the chief engineer of Boeing's Transport Division, provided an insight into a typical Mach 3 flight from Paris to New York by a Boeing SST at a presentation given to the Institute of Aeronautical Sciences:

> The flight takes off from Orly at 11.00hrs giving a local arrival time at Idlewild of 07.30hrs. The supersonic transport will be able to load, taxi-out and take-off in much the same manner as the subsonic jet. Near-capacity loads of about 150 passengers are carried.
>
> Flight Planning: The optimum flight plan from the long-range cruise standpoint would require a climb to 65,000ft followed by a climbing cruise as fuel is consumed, reaching an altitude of 75,000ft just prior to descent. However, at the request of air traffic control the plan approximates the optimum cruise path by two constant-altitude segments, using an altitude of 68,000ft initially and 72,000ft for the second half of the cruise. The fuel load has to be increased by 0.8% of the take-off weight to cover this 'step-cruise' operation.

Climbing along the path for minimum fuel consumption, the aircraft would reach sonic velocity at 20,000ft about halfway to the coast of France, and the sonic boom heard on the ground would be objectionable over a considerable area. The climb-path will therefore be selected to reach sonic velocity over the English Channel, and the aircraft will be at 30,000ft when this velocity is attained; the intensity of the 'boom', therefore, will be substantially reduced. Fuel loading has to be increased by 0.4% for this off-optimum climb path.

Headwinds at cruising altitude are reported to be 50 knots, somewhat lower than the winds at the cruising altitudes for the subsonic jets. A 50-knot wind is fairly typical of winter weather at 60,000 to 80,000ft. The effect of wind is quite small for an aircraft of this type because of the short mission time. In this case the dispatcher has increased the fuel load by 0.7% to allow for headwinds, which prolong the trip time by only three minutes.

Reserve fuel requirements are based on CAR Regulation SR-427, effective October 1958, and provide sufficient fuel to fly an additional 10% of the normal trip time, plus diversion to the most distant alternate, plus 30 minutes' holding at 1,500ft above the alternate. The alternate for this flight is Washington, D.C., and the reserve fuel required is about 8% of the take-off weight (compared with 5% for current subsonic jet transports).

Other possibilities to be taken into account are emergencies such as a cabin decompression, which would force the aircraft to descend to an altitude of, say, 15,000ft, where the cruise would be continued at a subsonic speed. If such a failure occurs more than 1,400 miles from the point of origin, with 8% reserve fuel, the aircraft cannot return to take-off point, and unless it has reached the 2,100-mile mark it will not have sufficient fuel to complete the trip.

However, should decompression occur halfway between Paris and New York the aircraft would still have a 1.100-nautical-mile range capability, sufficient to reach alternates such as Gander or Goose Bay. A similar situation exists with two engines failed.

Automatic Controls: Up to this point, the crew has encountered no problems different from those they experienced back in the 1950s. But, after take-off, they will experience a greatly compressed time in which to accomplish their jobs.

Designers and operators, therefore, are going to have to decide which jobs to give to the crews of supersonic transports and which to delegate to automatic devices. Greatest use can be made of the pilot's analytical ability, memory and experience when he is used to monitor the general situation. The complete use of automatic controls must be approached with caution, however, and the pilot must be left with acceptable means of taking over and of practicing during regular airline operation.

The supersonic transport will undoubtedly have more automatic controls. However, it is believed that back-up manual controls, which meet the requirements for pilot proficiency, can and will be developed. Past experience must not be discarded by statements that a new era of control automaticity will accompany the advent of the supersonic transport.

Take-off and Climb: Take-off clearance is obtained prior to engine start. Take-off ground run is comparable to that of the subsonic jets, but somewhat greater due to the higher thrust-to-weight ratio of the supersonic airplane (0.35 as compared to 0.20 for the Boeing 707).

Long-range radar in the Paris air traffic control area will monitor the climb-out. The danger of collision with an intruder in the climb-out corridor is virtually eliminated because all aircraft will be required by law to maintain an illuminating radar beacon. The flight crew now have area surveillance in the cockpit as well as direct communication with the ATC long-range surveillance radar.

The pilot may elect to accomplish his climb by pre-programmed tape operating through the autopilot. Time to climb to the initial cruise altitude of 68,000ft and to accelerate to Mach 3 is about 15 minutes. In order not to exceed the cabin differential-pressure limit of 10.5psi, the cabin altitude is increased at a rate of about 500ft/min. During the climb and acceleration the relative slant of the cabin floor is about 12°.

En Route: The constant-altitude, constant-Mach-number cruise is easily handled by the autopilot. The pilot monitors cruise conditions and fuel consumption and, when the aircraft reaches the halfway check point, he initiates the climb to the second segment altitude.

Navigation equipment includes the best of that available on the subsonic jets, plus digital computers which avoid the necessity of the pilot solving a mathematical problem to arrive at his position, which is changing by about 30 miles each minute. Present position is automatically reported in code to recording equipment on the ground. Only occasionally is it necessary to use vocal radio contacts. All ground-to-air messages are received on the airborne radio-teletype, virtually eliminating the need for the pilots to take notes.

Of the emergencies with which the crew might have to contend, high-altitude decompression, as already noted, would require a rapid decrease in altitude to normal breathing levels. Pressurization of the cabin during descent would be accomplished by ram-air cooled with water spray. Oxygen service would be provided in addition to the ram pressurization.

During the cruise, collision avoidance will be partially achieved by night-plan separation. The high altitude at which the supersonic jet cruises will keep it above other types. As a further protection against other supersonic aircraft an infra-red detector would be of use at the high cruise altitude, or a complete

One of the many versions of the early Boeing SST designs, this one being the Model 733. Again, the artist gives the impression that it is almost 'above the atmosphere'. *(Simon Peters Collection)*

collision avoidance system such as that on which Boeing has been working for two years.

Terminal Clearance: At 700–800 miles out from destination the pilot will turn his attention to the terminal traffic and landing clearance problem. The pilot is faced with two possibilities in the terminal area which may alter his flight plan: re-routing to an alternate, or delays due to traffic or runway congestion.

The normal descent path is illustrated below. Fuel required to go to the alternate increases rapidly if re-routing is delayed until the descent has begun, so speedy Air-Traffic Control (ATC) approval or revised instructions are essential. Two descent paths could be used for programmed delays due to terminal congestion – 'race-track' orbiting on the normal descent path or earlier descent to a lower altitude followed by a subsonic cruise.

Before descending, the pilot will observe that his automatic computer has the intended descent path set into it, along with the aircraft's position. He will mentally check that the computed time-of-arrival seems reasonable. This information will be automatically transmitted to the ground traffic-control receiving station, with a coded request for confirmation, if acceptable, or if not, for the minimum delay time which can then be programmed into the remaining cruise and descent.

Priority over other local slower flights would be desirable. The ground computer could recognise this priority from the coded identification in predicting the traffic and landing time.

The process of approach control could be carried out by a system whereby each aeroplane has its own self-contained navigation and code transmitting radio system, or by a long-range ground radar system utilising coded beacons in each

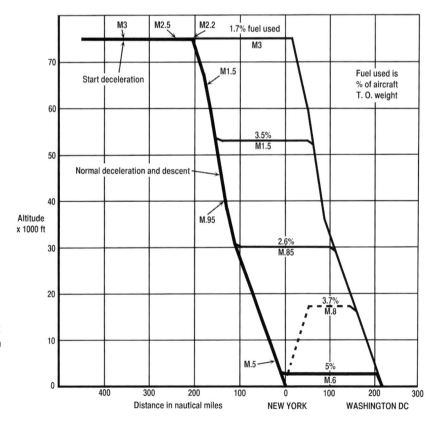

The normal descent into New York, with a series of possible diversions into Washington DC. (Dulles)

aeroplane. The essential feature is that service from the ground traffic-control centre must be rapid. The report continued:

> Descent: In order to eliminate any passenger discomfort, the rate of change of cabin altitude on the descent will be limited to 300ft/min. Since the cabin is at 8,000ft, this establishes minimum descent time at 27 minutes. Within this time, limitation of descent is scheduled so that minimum fuel will be burned, in order to be operating near maximum lift-drag ratio.

> The speed schedule will be approximately as follows: first, the aeroplane is decelerated to Mach 2.2 at cruise altitude because the change in altitude for maximum lift-drag ratio is relatively small in this Mach number range. Next, an approximately linear variation of Mach number with altitude is followed until Mach 0.95 at 55,000ft is reached. Mach 0.95 is maintained down to the altitude for 300 knots EAS, and the final part of the descent is at 300 knots constant EAS.

> In addition to the altitude/speed schedule, the pilot will fly in a definite corridor in the high-traffic-density areas near New York. Since the flight crew will have little time to work with paper maps and instrument procedure books the desired map will be projected on a screen in the cockpit, together with the aircraft's position, determined from the navigation computer.

> During the deceleration and descent the cabin floor will not exceed an angle of 5° nose down, which is comparable to that for a normal descent on the Boeing 707.

> Landing: The best path to a straight-in approach will be used. If the weather is good the pilot will probably do the job manually, as this is a good time to practice. If the weather is bad, he may fly manually down the glide beam, but will probably put it on automatic so he can carefully monitor the overall situation. Automatic approach and landing will be handled by slaving ILS and autopilot to a ground computer which receives intelligence by looking at the aeroplane with K-band radar.

> Scheduling: A possible flight schedule for a fleet of four supersonic transports would provide six Paris–New York round trips a day, with departures from Paris at intervals from 11.00hrs to 01.30hrs, and departures from New York between 07.00hrs and 16.00hrs, plus one at midnight. Arrivals at both ends are at reasonable local times.

> Turn-around time is at least 2.5 hours for all but one flight on the New York–Paris run. Maintenance can be performed at either end of the line. Also, adequate time is available in either New York or Paris to accomplish overhaul on a progressive basis, and it should not be necessary to withdraw aircraft from scheduled operation for periodic overhaul.

> This schedule would provide an average fleet utilization of 7.5hr a day. Long lay-overs by three aircraft at New York during the evening hours might be utilized for short north–south flights. For instance, three New York–Miami services each evening, for which the block time is 1hr each way, would increase fleet utilization to 9hr per day.

> It appears that the supersonic transport can be scheduled to provide good daily utilization even with the small fleets which may be used when it first goes into service. As air traffic continues to expand, the larger fleet sizes which can be supported will provide more flexibility of scheduling.

Others had different ideas. Convair's Vice-President of Engineering, R.C. Sebold, provided alternatives. A Mach 2 transport could be offered in 1965, but Convair favoured a Mach 3 to 5 transport for 1970. They saw no need for a major technological breakthrough:

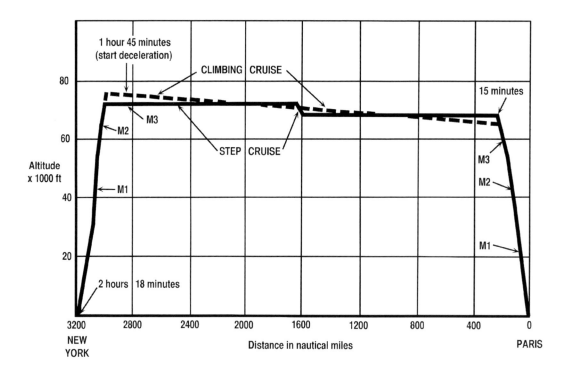

The flight profile for the Paris–New York service as described by Boeing's Transport Division.

Supersonic operation below about 35,000ft is impossible because of sonic boom effects. The faster the aeroplane, the smaller the percentage of trip distance that can be flown at supersonic cruising speed; speeds much above Mach 5, therefore, give small improvements on transcontinental or even transatlantic flights.

Based on 100% load factor, 3,000 hours' utilization and 10 years' depreciation, the direct operating cost of a Mach-3 transport, flown over 3,000n mile stages would be 1.63 cents/seat-mile.

In general, the smallest aeroplane that will do the job will carry the least fuel and have the lowest cost, although the larger the aeroplane, the lower its specific structure-weight. Broadly, the size might be: Span, 70–120ft; length, 170–230ft; and height, 30–50ft for a 135-passenger transcontinental transport. Powerplants are already in the design stage and will be conventional.

Temperature of the inside cabin wall must not exceed 90°F, requiring a 12in thickness of Fiberglass at Mach 4. Cooling by water-cooled air would reduce the weight of insulation by half, with a further reduction by using water directly to cool the cabin. A water-jacketed cabin might be possible, with the inner skin as the primary load-carrying structure in aluminium.

Rates of climb of 6,000ft/min are required to minimize fuel consumption, but the cabin rate of change is limited to 300ft/min. Cabins must be pressurized to 3,000ft or sea-level equivalent and a completely reliable pressurized vessel must be provided.

A closed-circuit TV system, with individual viewing screens, fed from an adjustable external camera, would probably weigh less than windows, which could be omitted with benefit to the pressure-cabin integrity.

Throughout 1959 a series of discussions took place between the British and the French at governmental level on the possibility of collaboration. Aubrey Jones held discussions with the French at the June 1959 Le Bourget Air Show. By September meetings had taken place between the Ministry of Supply and representatives of Bristol and Hawker Siddeley, both of whom argued against US involvement at that time, but they did feel something was possible with a European or Canadian collaboration. Later that year the industrialists suggested that while possibly more financially rewarding, a deal with the Americans would probably be more difficult than with the French.

The Spectre of a Soviet Threat

Over in the USA, pressure was being applied to the government to support the development of a commercial supersonic transport. The aviation press reported that the question of a subsidy for this development was being considered by the Aviation Sub-Committee of the Senate Interstate and Foreign Commerce Committee, under the chairmanship of Senator Almer Stillwell 'Mike' Monroney. To this committee, James Durfee, chairman of the Civil Aeronautics Board (CAB), had addressed a letter claiming that Britain and Russia '... are known to be subsidizing the development of supersonic transport aeroplanes' and that US manufacturers 'may lose to foreign competition unless they receive prompt help and money from the Government'.

According to Durfee, a delay of one to three years in development by US manufacturers 'might mean that some time in the early or mid-1960s the US long-range carriers may be forced by competitive reasons to place orders for supersonic aircraft in other countries. If this happens, the favored position enjoyed by US civil aircraft manufacturers might be lost for decades.'

Durfee went on to say that Boeing, Convair, Douglas and Lockheed could each turn out a supersonic model 'given proper financial encouragement'. He stated that one of these manufacturers could have a prototype flying in about three years – given adequate assurances – and could deliver standard production models by about 1967.

Senator Magnuson said that Durfee's letter confirmed his worst fears that America's leadership in commercial passenger and cargo jet aeroplanes was in grave jeopardy.

There can be no doubt that it was the possibility of a Russian supersonic transport being developed which really worried the US industry and politicians alike – and the press suspected that this would almost certainly result in some form of subsidy being agreed upon.

The USA was still reeling from the shock of the Soviet satellite *Sputnik*, launched into an elliptical low earth orbit on 4 October 1957, and the first in a series of satellites that cumulated in the launch of Soviet cosmonaut Yuri Gagarin, who was the first man in space on 12 April 1961. The unanticipated announcement of *Sputnik 1*'s success – determined by anyone with a radio able to pick up the metronomic 'beep beep beep' of the satellite's radio as it passed overhead – precipitated what became known as the Sputnik Crisis in the USA and ignited the space race within the Cold War. It fuelled American paranoia and fanned the flames of determination to show that America was 'better' than the rest of the world. The launch created a crash programme of political, military, technological and scientific developments.

That Russia, rather than Britain, was the nation's concern, revealed itself in papers presented at the Second Supersonic Transport Symposium held in New York at the end of January 1960. Two of the four papers dealt specifically with the question of national prestige and the threat of competition; both mentioned Russia and neither mentioned Britain. 'Unless as a nation we want to risk lagging

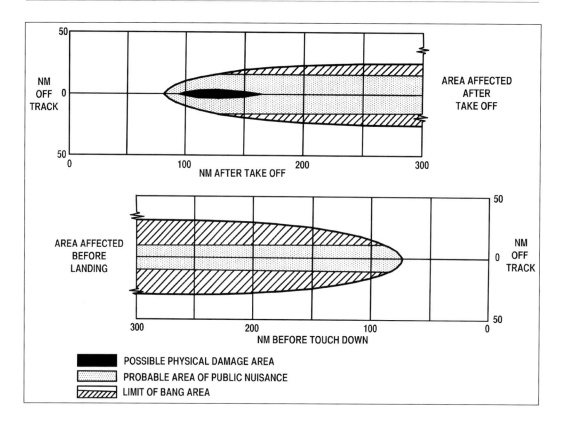

The 1960 perception
of the noise
nuisance created by
an SST on take-off
and landing as
demonstrated by
Peter L. Sutcliffe of
Hawker Siddeley.
This was regarded as
broadly accurate by
all in the industry at
the time.

behind the USSR in the introduction of supersonic transport ... we must start an aggressive development programme without further delay,' said P.J.B. Pearson and James Pfeiffer of North American Aviation.

The other paper – this time from B.C. Monesmith and Robert Bailey of the Lockheed Corporation – stated, 'In the supersonic transport, the US has an opportunity to demonstrate to the World its technological leadership over the Soviet Union. In our opinion, the Government would be justified in supporting the development of a supersonic transport simply for national prestige.'

The American manufacturers, while waiting hopefully for a benevolent government to disgorge a few hundred million dollars, were not standing still. The extent of design studies and wind-tunnel research undertaken by Boeing, Convair, Douglas, Lockheed and North American was enormous: 14,000 wind-tunnel hours on Mach 3 configurations had been accumulated by the last-named company alone, to mention but one spot figure.

It is also worth underlining just one fact: in the considered view of North American Aviation, a prototype US Mach 3 airliner could be flying in 1963.

The view of North American's Corporate Director of Development Planning J.B. Pearson Jr and R. James, manager of Commercial Aircraft Marketing, was contained in 'Supersonic Transports – Considerations of Design, Powerplants and Performance':

> To provide a framework in which to consider the design, powerplant and performance of a supersonic transport, the authors of this paper postulated the following design requirements: range, 3,500 nautical miles with fuel reserves; cruising speed, Mach 2 to 3; cruising altitude, above adverse weather; passenger loads as dictated by economic factors; operating costs less than 3 cents per

seat-mile; noise limitations comparable with present jet transport levels; take-off requirements, equivalent to a 10,500ft runway length at sea level.

A low-aspect-ratio (or narrow) delta-wing planform is suggested, with a fuselage length greater than that of present subsonic jet transports, in order to keep down the cross-sectional area and therefore the aerodynamic drag. A canard (forward tail) arrangement provides for the least drag at supersonic cruising speeds and results in the highest trimmed lift for take-off and landing.

A variable geometry windshield may be necessary, but there is a possibility that a low-drag fixed canopy can be designed to satisfy the FAA and SAE. Doors, escape hatches and windows can be designed to permit reliable supersonic operation at 80,000ft, but the windows in a typical 100-passenger transport would cause an increase of 4% in the gross weight (at a growth factor of 6) and might not be justified.

A choice is made in favour of buried engines, for reduced drag and reduced structural weight. Engines submerged in the fuselage, with tail pipes extending to the rear of the fuselage, offer the best solution. The layout thus described is, in fact, exactly similar to that of the B-70 and confirms that North American designs for a supersonic transport are based on this Mach 3 bomber.

A study of structural considerations shows that, up to speeds of about Mach 2.3, aluminium alloys may be used, but steel or titanium has to be introduced in various structural components above this speed and, by about Mach 2.6, must replace aluminium in virtually all parts of the airframe structure. The use of honeycomb sandwich is indicated by requirements arising from aerodynamic heating of fuel, low-aspect-ratio delta-wing planform, acoustical fatigue, and the employment of higher density materials.

Concerns Over Noise ...

In a paper 'Supersonic Transports – Noise Aspects with Emphasis on Sonic Boom' by Lindsay J. Lina, Domenic J. Maglieri and Harvey A. Hubbard, of the Langley Research Center, it was clear that globally the airlines, manufacturers and research establishments were well aware of the problem of noise:

Three sources of noise – shock waves, aerodynamic boundary layer and engines – are of significance to designers and operators of supersonic transports, and the first and third of these are important also to the public at large. Tests to date indicate that a Mach 3 transport flying at 70,000ft may be audible on the ground over an area 70 miles wide along its flight path.

The sonic boom problem is the newest and probably the least understood. The boom (sometimes heard as a double boom) is produced by shock waves from the nose and the tail of the aircraft, and its intensity is influenced by several factors: Mach number, fineness ratio, body length, altitude (distance and pressure gradient), wind direction and velocity gradient, temperature gradient and a few others of minor importance.

Mach number is of small significance once the point has been exceeded where the boom is first produced; doubling the Mach number from 1.5 to 3.0 increases intensity by only about 26%. Much more significant is the distance between the observer and the flight path, both vertically and laterally; doubling the altitude from 30,000ft to 60,000ft reduces intensity by two-thirds. In tests with military aircraft the lateral spread of the sonic boom from 40,000ft at Mach 1.5 was found to be about 20 miles on each side.

Although sonic booms occur at Mach numbers slightly above 1.0, atmospheric refraction causes the shock wave to be curved sufficiently to miss the ground completely over a small range of speeds above this value. The exact 'cut-off Mach number' varies with temperature gradient, wind gradient, altitude and flight-path angle, and accurate atmospheric sounding or predictions will be essential for supersonic flight planning if advantage is to be taken of this cut-off point.

Changing the flight-path angle (i.e., climb or descent) rotates the whole shock-wave pattern in a manner equivalent to changing the shock-wave angle by changes in speed. Therefore, comparatively high Mach numbers can be achieved in a climb with no boom problems, but speed must be reduced in the descent to eliminate it. In tests, the boom produced by an aircraft climbing at 10° was only one-eighth the intensity for the same altitude and Mach number in level flight.

Some theoretical calculations (based on test results with military aircraft) have been made for a jet transport 200ft long, with a fineness ratio of 13, flying at speeds between Mach 1.2 and 2.0 between 20,000ft and 70,000ft. The damage threshold for noise pressures is assumed to be 2lb/sq ft, which is, therefore, the highest acceptable value for boom disturbance.

The calculations suggest that level-flight cruise above 60,000ft will be satisfactory, but that the climb and descent phases will need careful attention. This is an operating problem, as it is assumed that the aircraft will have been designed for minimum drag and no further aerodynamic refinements will be possible to reduce shock-wave noise.

A steep angle of climb will make possible acceleration to supersonic speeds at a lower altitude than would be the case for level acceleration (for reasons already explained). However, this technique brings the aircraft closer to the Mach cut-off number, which must therefore be assessed accurately for every flight.

Boundary-layer noise is important as a possible source of induced damage to the skin structure, as well as a nuisance to passengers. Surface pressure levels are significantly higher for the supersonic transport than for a Mach 0.8 transport, and noise damage could occur over the rear portion of the airframe surface.

A study of the possible engine-noise levels of a supersonic transport shows a danger of the present-day subsonic jet noise levels being exceeded, even though a 10° climb-out angle is assumed (double the present value). The turbofan engine does, however, promise to keep the perceived noise levels below the arbitrary figure of 112PNdB [perceived noise, in decibels].

Certainly it was not just the Americans who were aware of the noise problems – sonic booms and operating costs were the two key items on the agenda of an all-day symposium held at the Royal Aeronautical Society in London on 8 December 1960, as reported by *The Aeroplane and Astronautics*:

Noise problems are clearly exerting a tremendous influence on the design of the supersonic airliner. Noise produced during ground running and the take-off and climb affects the choice of powerplant, but nowadays this is not expected to be as much of a problem as the supersonic boom during the cruise. In the extreme this may compel countries to ban supersonic flying over land. If this happened, aircraft would probably need to be designed differently to cope with flying long distances subsonically.

Certainly it would have a very bad effect on operating costs which, even without this drawback, are unlikely to be competitive with operating costs of subsonic transports in 1970 when supersonic airliners are expected to enter service.

Members of Hawker Siddeley, the company which has not received a follow-on design study, made a particular point of this problem. It was introduced by Mr Sutcliffe [chief technician, advance projects group, Hawker Siddeley Aviation Ltd] in his talk.

He indicated that, even when cruising at 80,000ft, a supersonic airliner would produce a boom intensity pressure at ground level of between 1 and 2lb/sq ft. This is considered an objectionable noise, equivalent to close-range thunder and likely to cause some window damage. It would probably be unacceptable.

Messrs Morris and Stratford, also of Hawker Siddeley, took this point further by showing the effect on operating costs if supersonic flight over land were not permissible – for example, direct operating costs between London and Johannesburg would go up by about 50%. It was also shown how many airline routes, potentially suitable for supersonic operation, would be excluded, with consequent reduction in prospective sales for supersonic transports.

This problem is taken seriously by the airlines, as Mr C.H. Jackson of BOAC indicated. He showed a map of BOAC routes with operation limited to subsonic speed over all land which had a population density greater than 50 persons per square mile. This greatly curtailed supersonic operation and he felt that a decision on boom effect was vital, as it might decide which type of aircraft should be produced. The implications of this problem should, he thought, be decided before starting design work.

The suggested drastic influence of supersonic boom did not go unchallenged; both its magnitude and effect on people were questioned. Boeings have been very worried by this problem and their calculations of pressure rise and its effect tally with those of Mr Sutcliffe. But their studies show that 75% of air traffic for ranges above 2,000nm is over ocean routes or land areas with low populations, and they expect a demand for 50 supersonic airliners a year from 1968–70 onwards may be possible.

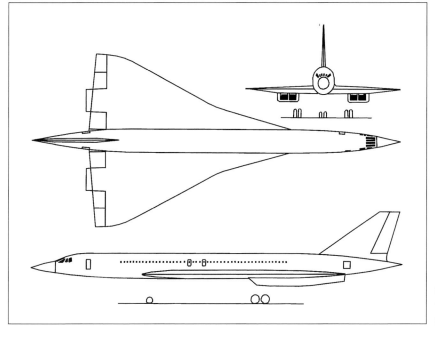

Sud-Aviation's 'Super Caravelle' design.

Changes Within the UK

In a departmental reshuffle following the British general election of October 1959, the Ministry of Supply and the aviation part of the Ministry of Transport were combined to form the Ministry of Aviation (MoA) under Duncan Sandys as minister.

Edwin Duncan Sandys was a British politician and a minister in successive Conservative governments in the 1950s and 1960s. Sandys was responsible for establishing the so-called European Movement in Britain in 1947 and served as a member of the European Consultative Assembly in 1950–51. He was elected to Parliament once again in 1950 and, when the Conservatives regained power, he became Minister of Supply in 1951. Minister of Housing from 1954, he was later appointed Minister of Defence in 1957 and quickly produced the 1957 Defence White Paper that proposed a radical shift in the Royal Air Force by ending the use of fighter aircraft in favour of missile technology. Though later ministers reversed the policy, the lost orders and cuts in research were responsible for several aircraft manufacturers going out of business. As Minister of Defence he oversaw the 'rationalisation' – that is forced mergers – of much of the British military aircraft and engine industry. After becoming Minister of Aviation he caused the failure of Fairey Aviation's concept-breaking Rotodyne vertical take-off and landing machine.

Officials from Sandys' new ministry met their French counterparts in February 1960 to discuss the possibilities of SST collaboration. Morien Morgan disclosed that the UK government was interested in contacting the US government to explore the possibility of a co-operative project. General Jean Gerardin said that the French government might contact the USA but would first consult West Germany. Would the British consider a co-operation that included Germany? The UK officials replied that they thought that SST co-operation would be difficult enough between two countries; it would be impossible between four!

After reporting their feasibility studies in March 1960, it was announced in October that the British Aircraft Corporation (BAC) – into which Bristol Aircraft had now been absorbed – had won the contract to further the design with a Ministry of Aviation contract of £350,000. The Bristol design was submitted in August 1961 as transatlantic Type 198, powered by six Olympus engines and accommodating 130 passengers, with an all-up weight of 380,000lb. It is interesting that in early government documents, questions had been raised about awarding the SST contract to Bristol, except in association with Hawker Siddeley, and under the latter company's leadership. Obviously these misgivings had later been dealt with.

However, a further design was later authorised from BAC for a smaller four-engined aircraft which became the Bristol 223. It could accommodate 100 passengers and had an all-up weight of 250,000lb. At around the same time, the French company Sud-Aviation exhibited a model of their own SST at the 1961 Paris Air Show. Known as the Super Caravelle, it bore a striking likeness to the 223. It seems that minds on both sides of the English Channel were obviously thinking along the same lines.

Edwin Duncan Sandys (b. 24 January 1908, d. 26 November 1987) British Minister of Aviation.

Anglo-French collaboration was raised again at the ministerial level in April 1960, when Duncan Sandys was in typically abrasive form at an Anglo-French meeting. He was pushing for immediate collaboration: 'If we see no possibility of quick collaboration with France, we shall turn to the USA.'

Contacts at the governmental level in the USA also were being explored. In Washington, Roy MacGregor, civil air attaché at the British Embassy held exploratory talks with FAA administrator Quesada. At the end of March he reported back to Sir George Gardner, controller of aircraft at the Ministry of Aviation in London, saying that Quesada was among those who seriously doubted the desirability of the SST, but he might respond to the idea of collaborating with Britain. He suggested that the time was ripe for such an approach to be made.

In July 1960 the 'supersonic airliner' was again considered in Cabinet when the three key ministers – the Chancellor of the Exchequer Heathcoat-Amory, Minister of Aviation Duncan Sandys and Minister of Defence Harold Watkinson – stated the deal they had in mind:

> The object would be to create a negotiating position from which the United Kingdom should attempt to secure United States collaboration in a joint project – since the Americans would only be likely to be interested in collaboration with us if they thought that, without it, the United Kingdom would develop a supersonic airliner which would compete in a limited market with any airliner which they might produce themselves.

A meeting in London during September appeared to offer the ideal opportunity to try to translate this possibility into agreed joint action. This was the first in a series of Anglo-American policy review meetings on civil aviation co-operation, to be attended by officials from the Ministry of Aviation and a US team led by Elwood Quesada. The second item on the five-point agenda was the supersonic transport aircraft. Ministry of Aviation briefing documents for the meeting reviewed the prospects for SST collaboration, making note that West Germany was not interested in SST development.

Discussion of the supersonic transport was thorough but inconclusive in terms of any firm commitment to Anglo-American collaboration. The FAA chief described supersonic transport aircraft as the next major step for the civil air transport industry. The general discussion included a debate on the technical factors that had led Britain to favour an aluminium-alloy Mach 2.2 aircraft, and the USA, drawing on the military B-70 experience, to favour Mach 3 or thereabouts. Sir William Strath, permanent secretary at the Ministry of Aviation and leader of the British team, said that Britain was keen to avoid duplication of the high costs of developing an SST for a very limited market, and was suggesting a full collaboration between the two countries in development and production. If the US government intended to hold a design competition, a full discussion of arrangements for collaboration might have to wait until that competition had been concluded.

The FAA head agreed in principle that collaboration would be of mutual benefit, but he had given no thought to methods of achieving such, and competitive factors might make a mutually acceptable joint project difficult. An American airframe powered by a British engine might be feasible, he suggested. That was not at all what the British team had in mind.

Implications of the meeting were analysed in a follow-up discussion in Sir George Gardner's office at the Ministry of Aviation. He decreed that the link with the US must be maintained and that the UK should proceed with the design study contract but should not give the impression of 'going it alone':

> Mr Morgan said that we must keep the momentum of the project up. We could not afford to wait for the Americans to make up their minds. Sir George Gardner agreed and said that we must declare our policy, pick our firm and say exactly what was to be done. He stressed however that nobody could now predict our

Six examples of
American SST
configurations
as published in
the FAA report
of 1960, some of
which use variable
geometry to
improve take-off,
landing and
low-speed handling
performance.

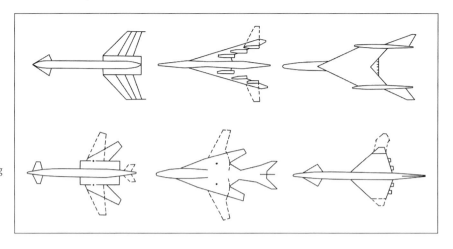

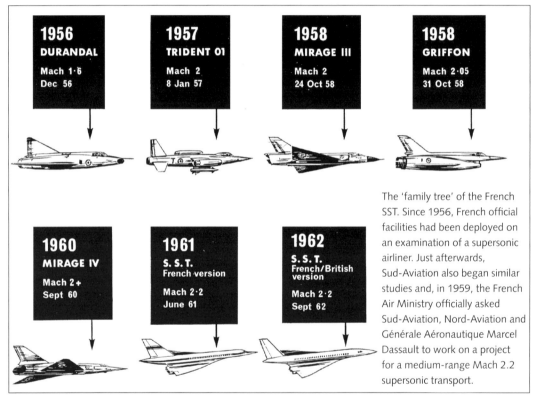

1956
DURANDAL
Mach 1·6
Dec 56

1957
TRIDENT 01
Mach 2
8 Jan 57

1958
MIRAGE III
Mach 2
24 Oct 58

1958
GRIFFON
Mach 2·05
31 Oct 58

1960
MIRAGE IV
Mach 2+
Sept 60

1961
S. S. T.
French version
Mach 2·2
June 61

1962
S. S. T.
French/British version
Mach 2·2
Sept 62

The 'family tree' of the French
SST. Since 1956, French official
facilities had been deployed on
an examination of a supersonic
airliner. Just afterwards,
Sud-Aviation also began similar
studies and, in 1959, the French
Air Ministry officially asked
Sud-Aviation, Nord-Aviation and
Générale Aéronautique Marcel
Dassault to work on a project
for a medium-range Mach 2.2
supersonic transport.

attitude in a year's time and we should therefore still maintain our collaboration
with Mr Quesada. Mr Meeres [N.V. Meeres, an MoA under-secretary] said that
any announcement on the design study contract would need to be qualified by
the statement that no decision had yet been taken to build prototypes. Sir George
Gardner thought this was too negative and would not generate the enthusiasm
we wanted nor would the management put the best men on the job if they
thought there was no future in it. He recognised that there was at present a stop
at the end of a year but maintained we must paint as rosy a picture as possible.
He thought 'we are proceeding to the next stage' was the right tone.

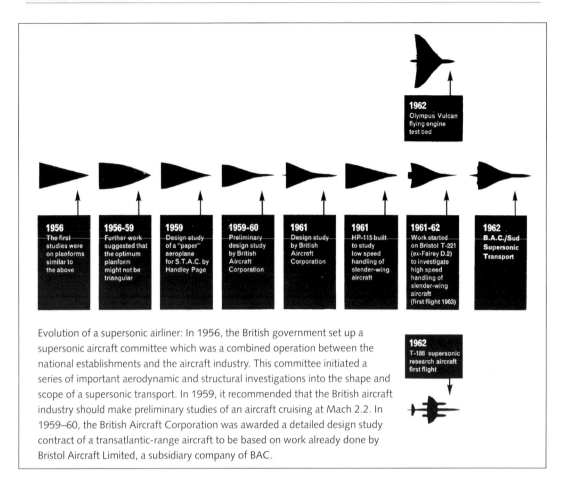

1962 Olympus Vulcan flying engine test bed

1956	1956-59	1959	1959-60	1961	1961	1961-62	1962
The first studies were on planforms similar to the above	Further work suggested that the optimum planform might not be triangular	Design study of a "paper" aeroplane for S.T.A.C. by Handley Page	Preliminary design study by British Aircraft Corporation	Design study by British Aircraft Corporation	HP-115 built to study low speed handling of slender-wing aircraft	Work started on Bristol T-221 (ex-Fairey D.2) to investigate high speed handling of slender-wing aircraft (first flight 1963)	B.A.C./Sud Supersonic Transport

Evolution of a supersonic airliner: In 1956, the British government set up a supersonic aircraft committee which was a combined operation between the national establishments and the aircraft industry. This committee initiated a series of important aerodynamic and structural investigations into the shape and scope of a supersonic transport. In 1959, it recommended that the British aircraft industry should make preliminary studies of an aircraft cruising at Mach 2.2. In 1959–60, the British Aircraft Corporation was awarded a detailed design study contract of a transatlantic-range aircraft to be based on work already done by Bristol Aircraft Limited, a subsidiary company of BAC.

1962 T-188 supersonic research aircraft first flight

On 12 October 1960, Morien Morgan, then the deputy controller of aircraft research and development at the Ministry of Aviation, presented a wide range of points in a report, which explained the current thinking:

1. A wide body of opinion believes that in two or three decades from now the bulk of long distance passenger travel will be at supersonic speeds. If Britain is to retain its position as a leading aeronautical power, we cannot let ourselves be edged right out of the supersonic transport field by America and Russia.

2. At the moment we have a two or three year lead on the USA in hard thought and supporting research on supersonic transport (not bomber) problems. They are in effect just considering setting up the equivalent of our STAC to steer research and project work. We did this over three years ago.

3. In this country, even if adequately financed, we really couldn't cope by ourselves with a Mach 3 steel design except on a very extended time scale with years of preparatory R&D assessment. So this can be dismissed. On the other hand, if properly financed, we could deal by ourselves with a Mach 2 design in light alloy without seriously unbalancing our industry. It would only mop up a portion of the resources of one of our large groups.

4. All the present indications are that the Americans will, for prestige reasons, go for a Mach 3 steel machine. However, technical sense may in the end prevail, and they may veer round to a Mach 2 light alloy aircraft. According

to Quesada they will not be in a position to go to industry and select firms for a specific task for another two years.

5. DGSR(A)'s curves [produced by the Director General for Scientific Research (Aircraft)] illustrating the influence of numbers built on direct operating costs suggest to me that once you have built about 30 light alloy machines the whole venture may be commercially viable even if you amortise fully your development charges. It would be nicer to build 80, but the variation of direct operating costs as between a build of 30 and 80 is quite comparable to the result of possible variation in the technical parameters such as structure weight, L/D [lift/drag ratio] and engine efficiency. I suggest that we should be able to sell 30 to BOAC, Transport Command, and a few friends, and that 'going it alone' on a light alloy machine is not necessarily ludicrous. Anglo-American (and Anglo-French) co-operation can of course be explored. My point is that we would not be sunk if such co-operation was not achieved.

6. If the Americans went ahead vigorously with a steel machine, I suggest that it would come out on the routes at least three years later than our light alloy machine; that its direct operating costs would be higher than ours, even if no development charges were included, and that its initial cost would be considerably higher. Very substantial subsidy would be needed for it to compete with ours. We will not know the precise form here for several years, but my estimate is that we could successfully 'go it alone' on our light alloy machine even if the Americans settled on steel; provided, and only provided, we get moving quickly and don't abandon our lead time.

7. If, after two years study, the Americans settle on Mach 2 light alloy, then will be the time for a straightforward commercial deal between our firm and the American firm to share the market, split design responsibility, and split production. This is bound to lead to inefficiency, but this may be the price to pay for not being forced right out by strong arm methods. If, as I suspect, there is a market for well over 100 aircraft, then it by no means follows that such co-operation is essential; but the case for it can be seen, although I do not think it is as strong as many people at present believe.

    One fact is inescapable, however. Our bargaining position will be immeasurably increased if, during the next two years, we really have made substantial and sustained progress with an actual design. Resting on our STAC laurels would cut no ice at all.

8. The moral of all this is that, even with the present policy thoughts on co-operation with the USA, not much detailed planning on co-operation can be done for the next two years until the Americans have completed their STAC type work and selected a firm; and that there is everything to be gained by really getting a move on at this end with our local Mach 2 project. In this context the £500,000 for the first year is on the thin side, but it will at least enable us to start getting up steam.

9. Co-operation on such matters as certification, background research on airfield standards, noise, harmonisation of safety requirements, and so on is obviously desirable; it may well be appropriate for our people to get together with the FAA chaps on this, as a follow-up to Quesada's visit, in the spring of next year.

It was not just the politicians who were talking to each other. Top management of British and American aircraft companies had begun to explore possible SST collaboration. At the Farnborough Air Show in September 1959, Hall L. Hibbard, senior Vice-President of Lockheed Aircraft Corporation, Burbank, California, called in at the Hawker Siddeley chalet with a novel proposition to put to John

Kay and Stuart Davies. Lockheed had already spent $3.5 million in preliminary design work on a Mach 2 supersonic transport to carry about ninety passengers; Hibbard reported that the company was ready to go ahead with detailed engineering but was seeking additional finance. Lockheed did not expect the US government to put up any SST funds for some time but believed that the British government might welcome US co-operation. In return for UK investment, Lockheed proposed that Hawker Siddeley could share in detailed design and engineering of the SST – and indeed could build the envisaged two prototypes in Britain and go on to share the production. Lockheed estimated the market at about 300 SSTs.

Stuart Davies of Hawker Siddeley had also been discussing collaboration with Boeing, which was keen to establish exactly what type of agreement might be feasible: a joint company, sharing the development of a common design, or a technology-pooling arrangement. The Seattle firm envisaged SST competition with at least one other US firm and appeared 'profoundly distrustful of trying to conduct this battle with hands tied by some prior agreement with a British company and indirectly with the UK government'.

Boeing had been working on a number of small-scale SST studies since 1952. In 1958, it established a permanent research committee, which grew to a $1 million effort by 1960. The committee proposed a variety of alternative designs, all under their Model 733 name. Most featured a large delta wing, but in 1959 another design was offered as an offshoot of Boeing's efforts in the swing-wing TF-X project. In 1960, an internal 'competition' was run on a baseline 150-seat aircraft for transatlantic routes, and the swing-wing version won.

Peter Thorneycroft, the new Minister of Aviation, continued talks with Elwood Quesada. In a letter dated 27 October 1960, Thorneycroft brought the American up to date on UK developments, and then went on to propose something more than just another round of talks:

Hall Livingston Hibbard (b. 25 July 1903, d. 6 June 1996), engineer and administrator of Lockheed Aircraft Corporation.

George Edward Peter Thorneycroft, Baron Thorneycroft CH, PC (b. 26 July 1909, d. 4 June 1994), one of a number of British politicians who occupied the post of Minister of Aviation during the years of the SST programme.

Join with us in our studies, or if you prefer it, ask us to join with you, in a study of the Mach 2.2 aircraft. There is no commitment to make it but no one can judge it until they have really studied it and at the moment it looks to us by far the best bet from an economic point of view. If we agree that the study shows this to be the best approach, then in the event of either of us deciding to go ahead we will find ways to enable the other to have an opportunity if he so desired to share in the development and production of it. If either of us prefer the Mach 3 or higher we will give the other a chance to join in going ahead with that.

Quesada's reply was non-committal in the extreme. The FAA head promised, 'Your proposal for cooperation will certainly be given our fullest consideration. A specific reply will not be easy but please be assured I will communicate with you on this matter as soon as I am able.'

Given that Quesada signed his letter to the British minister on the day the US presidential election was won by John F. Kennedy, the tone was not surprising – the winds of change were blowing through Washington DC, and the following January a new administrator was appointed to head the FAA, with Quesada moving on to sit on the Board of American Airlines.

The FAA Report

In October, a report signed off by FAA administrator Quesada, NASA administrator T. Keith Glennan and Secretary of Defense Thomas S. Gates recommended 'that the executive and legislative branches of out government give prompt and immediate initiation of an orderly national program for the development of a commercial supersonic transport aircraft'. It seems that the trio retained open minds on the merits of international co-operation; they accepted that co-operation could be of mutual benefit but disliked the idea of inter-governmental agreements, which might impose unacceptable constraints on, as they said, 'the best engineering and economic courses of action'.

These thoughts were expanded upon in December when the FAA-sponsored 'Commercial Supersonic Transport Aircraft Report' spelled out the key issues surrounding the case for an American SST.

According to *Aviation Week*, the Defense Department and Budget Bureau had earmarked $5 million of 1961 fiscal-year funds for the FAA programme outlined. This was a cut from the $17.5 million requested by Quesada and the retiring NASA administrator, Keith Glennan. The future of the proposed programme would depend on the views of the incoming Kennedy administration.

As a result of the B-58 and B-70 programmes and earlier supersonic research, the FAA report concluded that the US had 'a unique capability of developing a safe and economically competitive supersonic transport. The magnitude of the development task and the current financial situation of the United States aviation industry preclude its accomplishment on a timely basis solely by private enterprise.' Elsewhere in the report the cost of development was put at above $500 million. The report considered that it was technically feasible to develop a commercially competitive supersonic transport of intercontinental range and that 'flight efficiency and direct operating costs comparable to those of current subsonic jet transports are indicated'. It acknowledged that not all the technical problems had been solved, but that a solution was possible by a vigorous national effort combining the work of industry and the appropriate government agencies.

The report quoted a range of arguments in favour of a US supersonic airliner programme. These included maintaining the US position as the major supplier of transport aircraft; the economic effect (at the time aeronautical exports by the US were worth over $500 million annually and made up 12 per cent of exports of all manufactured goods); maintenance of national prestige and the advantage to national security of having supersonic airliners as potential troop transports; and the threat caused by the likelihood of Britain and Russia producing supersonic airliners.

A US programme was considered urgent if supersonic airliners were to be available in 1968–70. The potential market in the western world then was put at

200 aircraft. The report was somewhat lukewarm on international co-operation in development, although it recognised that it could be mutually advantageous:

> The supersonic transport presents problems of such scope and complexity that it cannot be developed successfully at any reasonable price without complete freedom from restraints on the best engineering and economic courses of action. This fact must be kept firmly in mind in any consideration of co-operation between governments.

A well-organised national effort was proposed. Considering the report was published by the FAA, it is not surprising that they would lead the programme and provide fiscal support. The Department of Defense (USAF) would be responsible for managing development and NASA would provide basic research and technical support.

Certain basic points were emphasised. The programme would cover government assistance to industry for the development of a commercial aircraft. The principle of competition should be used to maximum advantage. Direct government financial assistance should be provided only to the point in development where the aviation industry could carry on in accordance with their normal business practices.

The report was not dogmatic about cruising speed, saying that it would probably lie 'in the Mach number range 2 to 3', but it stated: 'The economic benefit of higher speeds, along with technical considerations of speed-altitude effects on the sonic-boom intensity, tends to dictate flight at the higher speed and altitude. Accordingly, considerable emphasis has been placed on the structural design problems of M-3 flight.'

Discussing a typical transport in detail, the report considered that take-off weight would be in the 350,000 to 400,000lb range and take-off distances within then current runway requirements. Cruise would be at Mach 3 between 65,000 and 75,000ft. If present take-off and landing speeds were to be retained, the aircraft might well have a variable-geometry wing. On the propulsion side, turbofans were favoured although turbojets could also be used. Despite more time and money being necessary for turbofan development, the turbofan 'appears to offer sufficient advantage in the areas of take-off noise, flexibility and off-design efficiency to make its development appear highly desirable'.

Noise was considered to be the major operating problem, both during take-off and in cruising flight. On take-off the turbofan could give an improvement over present noise levels, but the afterburning turbojet would be unacceptable. Sonic-boom noise when cruising at 65,000 to 75,000ft was considered tolerable. The report said that a major flight, wind-tunnel and theoretical programme was now under way to define the significant parameters of the sonic boom.

On 18 January 1961, Roy MacGregor was again in London reporting on the US aviation scene. 'Experience with the B-70 bomber, other technical arguments and an American desire to outdo other nations all pointed to Mach 3,' he suggested. This was making any collaboration with the Americans on a Mach 2 project look more and more unlikely.

Europe Investigates Mach 3 and Other Concerns

The need for more data about ultra-high speed in the mid-1950s led both the UK and France to acquire extensive experience of supersonic aircraft design and operations at speeds over Mach 2. French supersonic experience began in 1956 and included the Sud 212 Durandal, the Sud 9000 Trident, the Nord Griffon and the Dassault Mirage III and IV. The UK's experience was derived from the Fairey Delta 2 and the English Electric Lightning .

In order to conduct kinetic-heating research, the Bristol T.188 supersonic research aircraft was built. The specification called for a single-seat aircraft which would carry a large load of recording instruments. It was required to take off under its own power, climb to operating height, fly a research flight pattern and return to base.

The new aircraft was intended to fly at speeds approaching Mach 3 and was thus to have a steel structure to withstand the kinetic heating involved. Flight duration was to be sufficient for the study of steady-state conditions in aerodynamics and kinetic heating as well as transient phenomena. The project was expected to provide for as much versatility in the research role as possible.

Regarded by many as being ultimately unsuccessful, the project suffered a number of problems, the main being that the fuel consumption of the engines did not allow the aircraft to fly at high speeds long enough to evaluate the 'thermal soaking' of the airframe, which was one of the main research areas it was built to investigate. It also suffered from fuel leaks in a manner that a number of other Mach 3 machines did, such as the B-70 and SR-71. If anything, the problems encountered just reinforced the idea that a Mach 2 machine built from conventional aluminium alloys was the right way to go.

Experience was also needed in low- and high-speed flight, so the Handley Page HP.115 was used to study low-speed handling of slender-wing aircraft while high-speed characteristics of such aircraft were investigated with the Bristol T.221, which was a modified Fairey Delta 2.

The ultimately unsuccessful Bristol Type-188 research aircraft. *(Bristol Aircraft)*

There also was a need to gain as much experience of the military supersonic Bristol Siddeley Olympus jet turbine that was being developed in conjunction with the French aero-engine company SNECMA. Much of this could be done on the test beds, but there was no substitute for 'air time' and this was done by installing an Olympus 593 engine in the bomb bay of Avro Vulcan XA894.

Top: The Handley Page HP.115 was used to test the low-speed handling of the Concorde-type delta wing.

Above: Avro Vulcan XA894 with the Olympus engine in the bomb bay with full reheat on. This test aircraft started flying in February 1962. *(Avro)*

Right: WG774, the first of a pair of Fairey Delta 2 research aircraft built – and seen as the top aeroplane in this formation with sister aircraft WG777 – was later almost completely restructured with the ogee wing form as the BAC 221.

An IATA Conference in Montreal

On 17 April 1961, the International Air Transport Association (IATA) Symposium on Supersonic Transport Aircraft opened in Montreal, Canada, in order to gauge opinions. It was attended by 650 delegates representing thirty-two airlines, nineteen airframe and engine manufacturers and numerous other organisations.

In his opening remarks at the start of the first closed session, Walter Binaghi, President of the Council of the International Civil Aviation Organization, firmly pointed out that supersonic transport aircraft would have to be capable of operation from existing airports; neither carriers nor manufacturers could expect major runway extensions. It would also take time for governments to design and install the new equipment needed for communications and air-traffic control. In this context he made the point that although subsonic jet equipment had been introduced before many of the proper facilities were available, albeit at some loss of efficiency, it was probable that carriers would be prohibited from operating supersonic aircraft until the authorities were satisfied that the necessary facilities did exist.

He also made the point that the competitive position could not be overlooked, and that certain governments might well adopt a restrictive attitude to protect their own national operators if they themselves could not join in the race. Indeed, surviving documents from the symposium suggest that although this technical conference seems to have attracted more interest than any previous one, the amount of real enthusiasm for the project under discussion was strictly limited. The exceptionally large attendance may well have been due to nervousness rather than a basic desire to bring in supersonic transport as quickly as possible. The airlines generally appeared to be somewhat like children on the way to school: hoping that something will happen to prevent it, but feeling that it is ultimately inevitable.

One of the most interesting discussions took place in connection with the noise problem. It was undoubtedly extremely important because it would not only determine the type of powerplant to be used, dependent as it was on the altitude at which the aircraft was permitted to go transonic, but also because, unless solved, it could prevent the use of supersonic transport aircraft altogether.

From surviving documents there seems to have been a lack of precise knowledge on two counts: first, the maximum tolerable figure which could be accepted for a 'sonic boom' and, secondly, what sized boom a supersonic transport aircraft was likely to make. On the first count a figure of 1lb/sq. ft or 128dB was quoted; it was described, somewhat quaintly, as the noise heard if one held one's head approximately 2ft from a bass drum. Certain representatives felt that it might not be possible to hold the sonic boom even to these dimensions and mentioned figures in the region of 1.5lb/sq. ft; others felt that even a figure of 128dB was too high. It is clear that the airlines were sensitive on the subject of sound and were wholly unwilling to let themselves in for a vehicle which may be very restricted in its use.

On the subject of aircraft 'life', most of the airlines said they expected an aircraft to last at least 30,000 hours, but hoped for more and a utilisation figure of about 3,600 hours per annum for a Mach 2 aircraft and 3,200 hours per annum for Mach 3. Those who spoke were clearly insistent that any supersonic aircraft would have to show the same costs per seat-mile as for current subsonic jet equipment – or lower.

The size of aircraft presented considerable problems, because some manufacturers indicated that the general rule was 'the bigger the aircraft the lower the seat mile cost', which might prove even more true of supersonic aircraft than in the case of subsonic equipment, and this would immediately conflict with the need for high utilisation and the general principle that the shorter the duration of the journey the greater the desirable frequency.

Discussions centred on aircraft with a passenger capacity between 100 and 130 and an all-up weight between 300,000 and 350,000lb. The idea of having two different sizes of aircraft was not well received by the manufacturers.

The airlines were almost unanimous in wanting to retain the ability to sell two different classes of service on the same aircraft and were also insistent that the seating in first class should be four abreast. It was clear from the manufacturers' comments that, because of the need to adopt a fineness ratio of 14 to 1, the maximum number of seats which could be fitted abreast, in the type of aircraft being considered, would be five, even for coach or economy class. It was, of course, only the inherent width of the big jets which made it necessary for six-abreast seating to be adopted to accommodate the load. Volume was going to be even more valuable on the supersonic aircraft, but some carriers at least were fairly insistent that space should be made available for mail and cargo at premium rates.

In considering range, the carriers appeared to take the view that they should continue to be able to fly the nonstop services which they operated at the time and some were ready to settle for a requirement of 3,500 nautical miles. Longer ranges might not only add appreciably to cost but could also penalise the aircraft when used over shorter sectors. Most of the studies made by manufacturers seem to have been based on average sectors of 2,000 miles, but one at least felt that a few shorter sectors of about 1,000 miles might be included in a route network, though not too many. One manufacturer said that in his opinion an aircraft could be built to operate over ranges between 600 and 1,800 miles, but did not describe how.

In discussing speed, a good deal of attention was intelligently directed to the considerable difference between supersonic cruising speed and effective 'block' speed. One unnamed carrier pointed out that with a Mach 3 aircraft the 'block' speed on a transcontinental flight was in fact 1,200mph. This, of course, was quite apart from the time taken by the passenger in travelling from the city to the airport and vice versa, and being ground slowly through the formalities of Customs and Immigration; a most worthwhile point, which raised the usual plea for improvement but was, of course, just as valid with the then current generation of aircraft as it would be when supersonic aircraft were introduced.

In September 1962, French President Charles de Gaulle made a plea for Britain and France to co-operate in building a civil aircraft to concentrate on speed rather than increased passenger capacity, and he wanted this aircraft to fly at supersonic speed. It would need to be built using both countries' aircraft industries as the building of such an aircraft would be too expensive for Britain or France to fund alone. Thus Britain and France decided to pool their individual studies, the Sud Super Caravelle and the BAC (Bristol) T.223, into a new joint project which was to become Concorde. The projected costs of the project were so great that the British government made it a requirement that BAC look for international co-operation. Approaches were made to a number of countries, but only France showed real interest. The development project was negotiated as an international treaty between the two countries rather than a commercial agreement between companies and included a clause, originally asked for by the UK, imposing heavy penalties for cancellation.

British Minister of Aviation Julian Amery and French Ambassador Jouffroy de Courcel signed a draft treaty on 29 November 1962 for collaboration in building a supersonic aircraft. The treaty stipulated that Great Britain and France 'must in all aspects of the project make an equal contribution regarding both the costs to be taken on and the work to be carried out, and to share equally proceeds from sales'.

A large model
of the proposed
European SST
that became
Concorde was
displayed at the
1962 Farnborough
Air Show. *(Simon
Peters Collection)*

Later that day, in a joint statement that was news embargoed until 1630hrs GMT, Sir George Edwards, managing Director of BAC, and General André Puget, chairman and Managing Director of Sud-Aviation, said:

We are delighted that the joint supersonic transport aircraft is now to go ahead. We are particularly pleased that our two companies are working together on this venture. We have both been doing preliminary work on this project for over a year and already personal friendships have been formed between many members of the two companies. They quickly discovered that there was a considerable identity of views as to the nature of any practicable supersonic airliner and that the work which had already been separately done on both sides of the Channel showed a remarkable measure of agreement.

We have no doubt that a supersonic transport is the next logical step in civil aviation. We are equally certain that the decision of our two Governments to order an aircraft capable of cruising at twice the speed of sound is the correct one. Such an aeroplane can be built with conventional materials, about whose properties we have much knowledge, and will fly at speeds of which we already have practical experience. It will be powered by engines which, in basic form, are already flying and will use ordinary fuels. When it comes into service in about 1970 the supersonic transport will have built into it the fruits of a research programme already well under way; in France with the work jointly done by Sud, Dassault and the Etablissements de la Direction Technique et Industrielle de l'Air and in Great Britain by that of the Royal Aircraft Establishment, Farnborough. British Aircraft Corporation has supersonic flying experience on Lightning and T-188, and will soon have more with T-221 and TSR-2. There is also the HP.115 programme. The French have experience with the supersonic Trident, Mirage III and Mirage IV.

The supersonic transport will, of course, only be worth while if it offers its enormous speed advantage at acceptable economics. We are fully satisfied that it will take its proper place on the classic curve of aviation progress by providing this increase in speed while also producing a thoroughly economical and competitive aircraft.

Construction was entrusted to four companies: BAC (Britain) and Sud-Aviation (France) were to be responsible for building the airframe, and the Olympus 593 jet engines would be manufactured by Bristol Siddeley (Britain) and the Société Nationale d'Étude et de Construction de Moteurs d'Aviation – commonly called SNECMA (France).

The news release went on to give the first details available:

The proposed Anglo/French Mach 2.2 supersonic airliner will have a slender delta planform and will be powered by four large turbojets (four developed Bristol Siddeley Olympus turbojets).

Its cruising speed of 1,450mph (2,540kph) will enable it to make a Transatlantic flight in about three hours against the seven hours flight time by current big jets. A flight from London to Sydney will take about thirteen hours against the present schedule of more than twenty-five hours.

The aircraft will accommodate about 100 passengers and the passenger cabin will have a normal complement of windows. The overall length of the aircraft will be 170 feet (51.8 metres) and the wingspan 77 feet (25.5 metres).

The Mach 2.2 airliner will be built mainly in aluminium alloy with localised use of titanium or stainless steel in areas subject to high thermal stresses. A retractable visor will be raised in supersonic cruise to reduce aerodynamic drag and lowered in subsonic flight to provide normal vision for the crew.

The engines proposed for the supersonic airliner will be civil versions of the supersonic Bristol Siddeley Olympus being developed for the British Aircraft Corporation TSR-2 strike/reconnaissance aircraft. Mounted in pairs in two nacelles beneath the wings, the engines will exhaust at the wing trailing edge.

His Excellency Jouffroy de Courcel and Julian Amery sign the draft treaty that set the manufacture of Concorde in motion. *(Simon Peters Collection)*

Sir George Robert Freeman Edwards CBE,
DSc, Hon FRAeS, DL (b. 9 July 1908,
d. 2 March 2003), Managing Director
of BAC.

General André Puget (b. 29 January 1911),
President of Sud-Aviation.

Choice of Cruising Speed – Before they began co-operating on this project, the French and British designers had independently reached the conclusion that the best practicable cruising speed for the supersonic airliner was Mach 2.2. This choice was determined by a combination of economic and technical factors.

If, for the next generation of airliners, only a moderate increase were made over present high-subsonic cruising speeds, the aircraft would have to operate largely in the transonic regime where, owing to the onset of 'wave drag', a serious falling-off in aerodynamic efficiency occurs. Such an airliner could not compete economically with the present highly developed and highly efficient subsonic jets.

However, as Mach number increases, two favourable factors are introduced: the effects of the falling-off in aerodynamic efficiency become more and more gradual and the efficiency of the turbine engine is progressively increased.

Good economy, in terms of seat-mile costs, can therefore best be achieved by operating at the highest practicable supersonic speed in order to exploit the increasing propulsive efficiency to the fullest advantage.

British Aircraft Corporation and Sud-Aviation designers decided on a Mach 2.2 cruising speed because techniques and materials used for an airliner operating in this environment need not be radically different from current practice. Beyond this speed aluminium alloy structures begin to suffer rapid deterioration and a complete switch to costly new materials and construction methods is necessary.

Operating Costs – The first cost of the projected supersonic airliner will not be greatly in excess of that of current large subsonic airliners. Fuel costs and some hourly direct costs, such as depreciation and insurance, will also be higher. But the greatly increased operating speed will increase aircraft productivity, and will have the effect of reducing these charges per aircraft mile.

The total aircraft mile costs for a Mach 2.2 airliner should therefore be lower than those of the best subsonic airliner. Its greater annual carrying capacity will enable the operator to meet given traffic requirements with a smaller fleet.

Sonic Boom – This problem has a great influence on the characteristics of a supersonic airliner and the Anglo-French airliner is being designed to take account of the extensive research in both countries and the United States into the problem. In addition, it is expected that by adopting special operational techniques and by not flying at supersonic speeds below certain altitudes, disturbance can be reduced to a minimum.

Airfield Noise – On the runway, noise produced by the supersonic airliner is expected to be little more than that from current subsonic jets. Beyond the runways, whore the noise caused by present big jets is monitored, the supersonic airliner should be quieter because the greater engine power available will enable higher speed and altitude to be attained in the initial phase of the climb and permit a proportionately greater throttling back.

What was of interest to everyone was how this dual-nationality project was to be managed:

British Aircraft Corporation and Sud-Aviation have agreed on plans for full co-operation to implement the joint programme of the British and French Governments for the development of a supersonic transport aircraft.

The distribution of the work between the companies is based on a fifty-fifty sharing of cost covering the whole project – airframe, engines, systems and equipment.

The central direction of the venture will be in the hands of a Board of Directors responsible for the whole industrial programme. The positions of President and Vice-President of this Board will be rotated every two years between France and Great Britain. The Board is as follows:

President and Director General	General A. Puget
Vice-President	Sir George Edwards
Technical Director	Monsieur P. Satre
Deputy Technical Director	Dr A.E. Russell
General Manager & Director of Production, Finance and Contracts	Mr J.F. Harper
Deputy General Manager	Monsieur L. Giusta
Co-Sales Directors	Monsieur J.W. Jakimiuk, Mr A.H.C. Greenwood
Directors	Monsieur B.C. Vallieres, Mr G.E. Knight

Central Control – The design and engineering organisation will organise full interchange of information and will ensure the best possible deployment of the resources of the two companies under one central control.

Prototypes – The organisation for the building of prototypes and of production aircraft will be on similar lines. It has been decided that each country will assemble one prototype and one preproduction aircraft. There will, however, be no duplication of the main production jigs. The manufacture of the various assemblies and sub-assemblies will be divided between the two countries and these components will then be transported to the final assembly lines in France or Britain as appropriate.

This system (each country building its part of the aeroplane and then bringing the components together in two final assembly lines) will also be followed with the production aircraft. This will, in effect, give two centres of production but both will be fed from the same main jigs, some of which will be in France and others in England. Each company will thus be responsible for one general assembly line and for the flight and acceptance tests of the aircraft it assembles.

All production aircraft will be designed to comply with the airworthiness requirements for supersonic transports as established by both the French and British airworthiness authorities.

Deliveries – It is planned that the aircraft should enter service in 1970 or thereabouts.

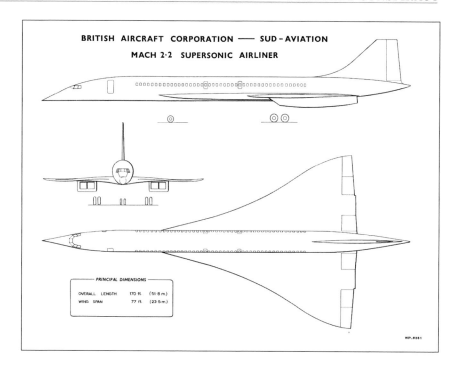

Then there was the matter of a name – of which there are many variations of explanations. When the collaboration began, the design was being referred to by the British as the 'SST' or '223', a reference to the Bristol type number. The French used the terms 'TSS' (*transport supersonique*) or, quite frequently, 'Super Caravelle'. There were those in Britain who felt that they could not accept that.

The suggestion that the aircraft should be called 'Concorde' emerged from an informal family conference at the home of a BAC executive. It was arrived at by the simple process of thumbing through *Roget's Thesaurus*. When the suggestion was put forward officially, the British side approved it tentatively and then submitted it to the French. There were some preliminary murmurs of approval but the subject was regarded as a matter for decision by 'higher authority'.

It was not until 13 January 1963 that French President General de Gaulle made use of the word 'Concorde' with reference to the Anglo-French supersonic aircraft project during a speech he gave. By this time, both companies had been merged into new ones; thus, the Concorde project was between the British Aircraft Corporation and Aérospatiale. The consortium secured 'orders' – which in reality were little more than 'indications of interest' – for over 100 machines from the major airlines of the day: Pan Am, BOAC and Air France were the launch customers, with six Concordes each. Other airlines in the order book included Panair do Brasil, Continental Airlines, Japan Airlines, Lufthansa, American Airlines, United Airlines, Air India, Air Canada, Braniff, Singapore Airlines, Iran Air, Olympic Airways, Qantas, CAAC, Middle East Airlines and TWA.

So ended the reasonably well-mannered and civil prologue. It would soon be time for the main act.

2

'First in the World in Air Transportation'

Concorde came as no surprise to American SST advocates in the Federal Aviation Agency, which had been sponsoring SST research and feasibility studies since 1960.

As Richard Nixon – then vice-president – said at the All States Picnic in Long Beach, California, on 12 October 1960:

> We've got to take a complete new look at what the Government is doing in this field, so that America can move into the supersonic age and continue to be first in the world in air transportation.
>
> That's why I've issued a statement today to the press, a statement indicating what America must do, setting up an air policy commission which will make recommendations as to how in this new area we can see to it that America stays ahead.

Quite exactly where Nixon got this rhetoric about 'being first' from is not clear, but it was almost certainly a 'sound bite' for domestic consumption. What was clear was that the US and the Soviet Union were also considering developing SST aircraft. Andrei Tupolev's experimental design bureau was thought to have begun SST design studies in 1961. Tupolev, who had been jailed by Stalin and then favoured by Khrushchev, was a veteran Russian designer whose many aircraft had included the impressive Tu-l04 and Tu-114 airliners, both of which had been developed from military types. His son Alexei became chief designer of the supersonic Tu-144, which was given the NATO reporting name of 'Charger'.

In 1963 a top-level delegation of British aviation officials and industrialists visited Moscow and were shown a model of a possible Soviet SST. They were surprised by its resemblance to Concorde. The shape and the designation Tu-144 were confirmed at the 1965 Paris Air Show, with a larger model on display. The obvious nickname of 'Concordski' was grabbed by the headline writers of the western world: the shapes were similar, and the quoted speed of the Soviet machine was only slightly higher than that of Concorde. At the 1967 Paris Air Show the Tu-144 model showed changes, and on 31 December 1968 the prototype took to the skies from the Zhukovsky factory runway and into aviation history as the world's first supersonic transport aircraft to fly. The production version was designed to carry 140 passengers at about the same normal cruising speed as Concorde, though it reportedly reached Mach 2.4.

The prototype
Tupolev Tu-144
is rolled out
at Zhukovsky.
*(Tupolev Design
Bureau)*

The Soviet SST prototype made its first public appearance at Sheremetyevo Airport in Moscow, in May 1970, and its first appearance outside the Soviet Union was at the 1971 Paris Air Show. Two years later at the same Paris show, a production Tu-144 – serial number 77102 – demonstrated that major design changes had been made. While in the air on the final day of the show, the Tu-144 executed a violent downwards manoeuvre. Trying to pull out of the subsequent dive, it broke up and crashed, destroying fifteen houses and killing all six people on board, as well as eight more on the ground. A Franco-Soviet investigating board concluded that the accident was not caused by any technical fault of the aircraft.

The causes of this incident remain controversial to this day A popular theory was that the Tu-144 tried to avoid a French Mirage chase aircraft that was attempting to photograph its canards, which were very advanced for the time, and that the French and Soviet governments colluded with each other to cover up such details. The flight of the Mirage was denied in the original French report of the incident. More recent reports have admitted the existence of the Mirage and the fact that the Russian crew were not told about its flight, though not its role in the crash. The official press release did state: 'though the inquiry established that there was no real risk of collision between the two aircraft, the Soviet pilot was likely to have been surprised.'

Another theory claims that the black box was recovered by the Soviets and decoded. The cause of this accident is now thought to be due to changes made by the ground-engineering team to the auto-stabilisation input controls prior to the second day of display flights. These changes were intended to allow the Tu-144 to outperform Concorde in the display circuit. The changes inadvertently connected some factory-test wiring which resulted in an excessive rate of climb, leading to the stall and subsequent crash.

One myth that grew up around the Tu-144 – possibly as a result of the implication of the 'Concordski' tag – was that it was a copy of the Anglo-French machine. While this as a statement is untrue, there was some evidence that the Soviet Union were undertaking industrial espionage against the British and the French, gaining the entire technical documentation for the Concorde prototype. Indeed, the head of the Soviet airline Aeroflot's office in Paris was arrested and expelled from France for Concorde espionage in 1965.

The Results of Studies

Within two months of each other, a pair of reports were published, one on each side of the Atlantic. In June 1961, British MoA officials briefed their minister that 'the situation appears to be hardening against collaboration with the USA, whereas on the other hand the French possibilities seem increasingly worthy of consideration'.

This was the view of industry, also. The results of BAC's further exploration of international SST collaboration were spelled out in their report 'Supersonic Transport Aircraft: International Collaboration', issued on 6 July to the Ministry of Aviation. Approaches to American companies had produced only negative responses, BAC reported, and the US authorities saw little benefit from British involvement in SST development or production. Collaboration with France appeared more promising. There were two options. First, if Britain and France decided to proceed with their respective long-range and medium-range machines, BAC and Sud had agreed, subject to official approval, to collaborate in all possible areas, including the adoption of a common, British, engine. The second option was to join with France in developing a single, medium-range aircraft, which implied leaving the development of a transatlantic aircraft to the US.

Across the pond, on 7 July 1961, North American released the results of a study into possible development plans for an early American SST. The internally funded study had been conducted to aid the Federal Aviation Agency (it became an administration later) in establishing the development plan for an eventual SST. The study assumed that the primary goal would be to develop a supersonic aircraft suitable for general airline passenger service and economically competitive with existing transport aircraft.

The North American study concentrated on the best way to develop the infrastructure necessary to support an SST, not necessarily on a definitive design for a production aircraft. The company realised that the development of an SST involved a broad spectrum of technical, economic and practical problems. Many of these problems could be solved by incorporating the proper qualities and characteristics into the aircraft, but others required operational solutions – such as research into sonic booms, air-traffic control, airports and terminal facilities, and operating policies, procedures and regulations.

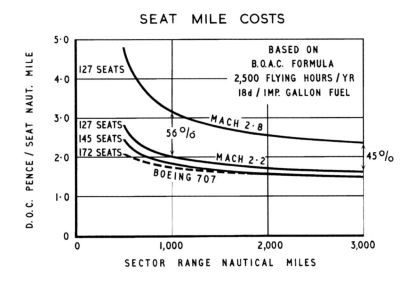

BAC did a number of confidential design and economic studies that resulted in a pair of direct operating cost comparisons, this being seat-mile costs.

This is the
aircraft mile costs
comparison for a
Mach 2.8 SST, a
Mach 2.2 SST and
the Boeing 707.

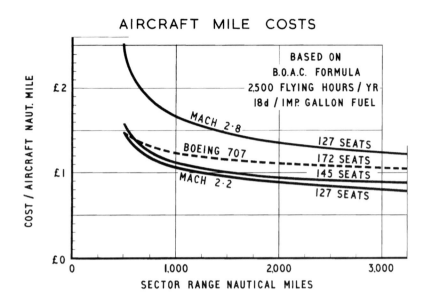

North American felt that the national investment in a commercial SST had
already progressed considerably. They cited, as examples, the research necessary
to produce supersonic fighters and the development of the Convair B-58 Hustler
medium bomber, which was the first long-range supersonic aircraft developed
in the US. The B-58's fuel consumption at supersonic speeds was considerably
better than previous aircraft, but the basic design was 'essentially a compromise
between efficient subsonic and supersonic performance'. An aircraft designed for
an all-supersonic mission could do better. This was the same conclusion reached
during the early WS-110A split-mission studies.

The concept of achieving efficient supersonic cruise by eliminating
compromises for subsonic performance was first applied to the design of the B-70.
Supersonic cruise efficiency was improved to the extent that the range of the
aircraft at Mach 3 speeds was comparable to subsonic aircraft of similar gross
weights. North American believed that the B-70 would provide a basis for a useful
research aircraft, while admitting that it was a less than ideal configuration for
any eventual production SST. After all, it was the only sustained Mach 3-capable
aircraft in the free world.

They were quick to point out that the US government had already invested over
$500 million in technology to support the B-70 programme, an amount that could
be quickly leveraged to develop an SST technology demonstrator.

North American wanted a cautious approach, recognising that it would not
result in an operational aircraft in the immediate future:

> This position pre-supposes that the primary objective is a profitable commercial
> transport, and that a plan is desired which balances urgency, risk, and cost to
> the extent that undue risk and excessive development costs are avoided. If any
> national objectives, such as prestige or military desirability, should shift the
> balance so that urgency became the dominant consideration, with cost and
> risk being minor factors, then obviously it would be possible to develop an SST
> somewhat earlier than the plans presented in this report.

The report went on to describe three possible approaches to achieve the primary
objective of a safe, profitable, supersonic transport for commercial airline service.

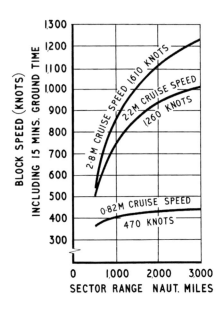

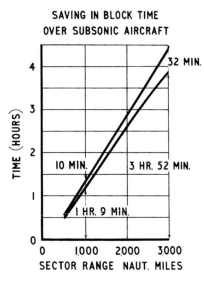

BAC's studies on the effect of supersonic cruise on block speed and time. Block speed is defined as true airspeed in knots under zero wind conditions adjusted in relation to length of sortie to compensate for take-off, climb-out, letdown, instrument approach and landing.

The approaches were called: (1) production prototype; (2) experimental prototype; and (3) military or civil cargo prototype. Also described were two B-70 operational test vehicle programmes that could be implemented.

North American proposed to build two additional XB-70 airframes, modified for use as SST development aircraft. These machines could have flown, according to North American estimates, four years earlier than any purpose-designed SST prototype, allowing a great deal of time to evaluate areas of interest to the SST designers with modification and design changes 'fed back' to the purpose-built SST designs.

One of the modified XB-70s would be used to provide a flying test bed for new SST engines. Although the General Electric J93 turbojet used in the B-70 was one of the keys to its great performance, it would not be sufficiently reliable or economical for commercial service. Due to this, the government had begun financing the advanced lightweight gas generator programme and had awarded contracts to both General Electric and Pratt & Whitney. The supersonic gas generator being developed could be adapted to several different engine cycles – turbofan, fan with duct burning, turbo-ramjet, etc.

North American believed it was essential to gain flight experience with the new engine before the first prototype SST was completed – an excellent idea given the problems encountered with the JTD9 turbofan on the subsonic 747 a few years later. To accomplish this, they proposed modifying one of the additional XB-70 airframes to carry a single SST engine in place of two of the regular J93s. This would leave three J93s on one side and the outboard J93 on the other side, allowing the aircraft to fly under any conditions without the use of the SST engine. Modifications would be needed to the internal ducting to accommodate the increased mass flow required by the new SST engine; minor modifications to the external mould line would also be necessary to accommodate the increased diameter expected of the new engine.

Alternatively, one of the SST engines could be mounted underneath the fuselage. This was essential if the final design required externally mounting the engines – much like the eventual Boeing SST design. In this case, flight testing the inlet configurations and nacelle shapes would be necessary. The engine would be mounted on a pylon that could be partially retracted into what had been designed

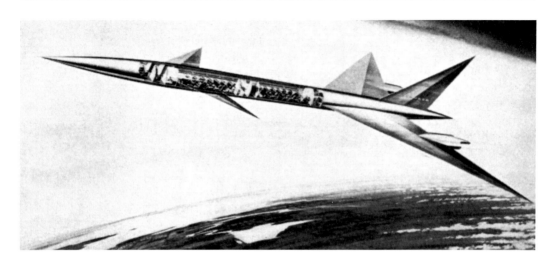

In March 1960,
Lockheed were
promoting their
Mach 3/Mach
3.5 airliner design
that would weigh
around 250,000lb
and cost some
$160 million to
develop. *(The
Aeroplane and
Astronautics)*

as the weapons bay to minimise clearance problems during take-off and landing. The engine would be equipped with a particular inlet design to evaluate engine performance at a certain design point speed. Alternative inlet designs could be tested, but not during a single flight.

The second XB-70 airframe would be modified to a limited passenger configuration by removing the military electronics and fuel from the upper fuselage and replacing them with a small passenger compartment. The fuel would either be moved into the area previously occupied by the weapons bay in the lower fuselage, or just simply be deleted and the range penalty accepted for the demonstration vehicle.

Without changing the line of the upper fuselage, a total of thirty-six passengers could be accommodated in four-abreast seating. The internal diameter of the fuselage was only 100in – 4ft narrower than the contemporary Boeing 707. A single lavatory would be located at the extreme rear of the passenger compartment. A galley was not included, partly because of a lack of room, and partly because all flights were expected to be so short as to eliminate the need for one. Two versions of this design were proposed. The first simply eliminated the fuel normally carried in the upper fuselage. This version had a gross take-off weight of 337,000lb and a range of 2,900 miles. The second version moved 47,400lb of fuel into the weapons bay (for a total of 185,000lb) and resulted in an aircraft weighing 384,500lb, with a range of just over 4,000 miles. Passenger entry and exit, as well as emergency evacuation, would be complicated by the height of the XB-70 fuselage.

Two other configurations were also proposed that slightly changed the outer mould line but provided more realistic passenger counts. Both included the weapons bay fuel. The first extended the internal passenger compartment by 240in, resulting in seating for forty-eight passengers. This version had a gross take-off weight of 427,000lb and could fly 3,850 miles while cruising at Mach 3. The other version increased the passenger compartment another 264in (for a total stretch of 504in) to seat seventy-six passengers. The gross take-off weight increased to 461,000lb, but range was reduced to only 3,600 miles at Mach 3. Neither modification changed the overall length of the fuselage but resulted in a more pronounced change in line of the rear part of the neck. The expected effect on stability was thought to be negligible, but given the marginal directional stability of the XB-70 anyway, the modifications would probably have necessitated an increase in vertical stabiliser area.

North American's rationale for using an XB-70 as a precursor SST demonstrator was highly valid. The primary contribution was the early identification of problems associated with the operation of an SST, made possible by limited passenger flights as early as 1965. Since the FAA would not have certificated the aircraft, they would have been limited to military or government operations, but that did not create any great problems The expected 'areas of concern' included air-traffic control, airport operations, maintenance, scheduling and possible noise complaints from sonic booms. Sufficient lead time was available to resolve these problems in an efficient and orderly manner before large numbers of SSTs were produced. Regulations and systems could be developed to monitor and control the operations of supersonic aircraft by the time production aircraft were introduced into airline service. The FAA could use the early service experience to write new Federal Air Regulations covering the certification process and design criteria for supersonic transports.

There was a great difference between what the Europeans and the Americans were attempting. In the UK it had been widely accepted that the BAC design was for an aircraft that cruised around Mach 2. With an aim of Mach 2 to 2.2, the Europeans, although coming close to the so-called 'thermal barrier' of airframe aerodynamic heating generated by shock waves, were at least in an area where this could be dealt with by making use of more-or-less conventional aluminium alloys. The Americans, however, set themselves a much higher mountain to climb. Mach 3+ would need exotic materials such as titanium of stainless-steel honeycomb structures.

On 6 October 1961, Peter Thorneycroft presented yet another paper to his Cabinet colleagues, in which he stated that the future of the British aviation industry depended largely on supersonic air transport, as well as on international co-operation – not only with Europe but also with the USA. Thorneycroft stated that the Americans' Mach 3, all-steel aircraft was 'an extremely ambitious project, even for them', while with a Mach 2, light-alloy aircraft, Britain had an opportunity

An American SST – North American style! The plan and side views reveal a four-man flight crew, seating for 170 passengers, three lavatories and a small galley but very little space for luggage or fuel! *(NAA)*

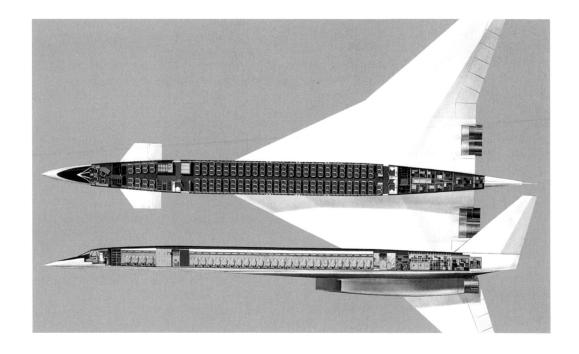

President John
Fitzgerald
'Jack' Kennedy
(b. 29 May 1917,
d. 22 November
1963).

to gain 'the leadership we so narrowly missed with the Comet'. The Mach 2 aircraft could be first in the field, and it promised to be the more economical design.

At this Cabinet meeting Thorneycroft disclosed that he had already met Robert Buron, the French Minister of Transport, to explore possible Anglo-French collaboration on such a project. Interestingly, the Thorneycroft-Buron meeting was of interest to the US also. In the files of the FAA History Office lies a Foreign Service Dispatch, 'American Embassy in Paris, to the Department of State, Washington DC', dated 9 October 1961 and tagged 'Civil Aviation: Supersonic Transport: Buron–Thorneycroft meeting and other recent developments'. It is a full appraisal of the meeting and its outcome in some detail, including that if the Anglo-French venture did not materialise and the French decided to go it alone, they might be interested in using a US Pratt & Whitney engine for their SST. The dispatch reported that Sud-Aviation was giving serious thought to an intermediate short-range SST based on the subsonic Caravelle, which would cruise at about Mach 1.2. One has to wonder, though, how did they know all this?

The FAA Plays an Increasing Role

When FAA administrator Najeeb Halaby assumed office in early 1961 he immediately began lobbying for an American SST development project. He also rejected numerous European, especially British, overtures for a joint SST programme and never had any intention of becoming partners with the British or the French. As he testified on Capitol Hill in April 1961, 'We want to be there ahead of our competitors'. This American posture helped drive the British and French into each other's arms.

FAA administrator
Najeeb Elias Halaby
Jr (b. 1915, d. 2
July 2003).

Soon after moving into his office at the FAA, Halaby accepted an invitation from Sir Harold Caccia, the British Ambassador, to lunch at the embassy in Washington DC. Sir Harold raised the question of co-ordinating the British and American SST efforts, suggesting that there was not enough room in the market for two SSTs. Halaby had no choice but to stonewall: intra-American co-operation was difficult enough, he suggested, let alone an Anglo-American joint venture. Clearly the embassy lunch had been designed to prepare the ground for an approach from the British Minister of Aviation, and in March Peter Thorneycroft duly renewed his efforts at collaboration with a letter to Halaby: 'I am anxious that no time should be lost in pursuing the possibilities of collaboration between our two countries on a supersonic transport project.' Halaby's reply was non-committal on the question of possible joint projects – and, indeed, on any possible US government-funded SST studies.

Peter Thorneycroft refused to give up hope for an Anglo-American project, and went to Washington DC for meetings with Halaby over 6–8 November. In preparation for this, in an internal briefing document FAA officials conveyed the contents of the October dispatch to Halaby, concluding, 'Since there appears to be no basis for a US accommodation with the British on a Mach 2 aircraft, nor they with the US on a Mach 3 aircraft, it is recommended that we inform the British that a government-to-government agreement for the joint development of a supersonic transport can serve no useful purpose.'

Najeeb Elias Halaby Jr was a US businessman, government official and the father of Queen Noor of Jordan. Born in Dallas, Texas, he was a graduate of the Leelanau School, a boarding school in Glen Arbor, Michigan, and is enshrined in that school's hall of fame. An alumnus of Stanford University (1937) and Yale Law School (1940), he served as a US navy test pilot in the Second World War. After the war he served as the US State Department's civil aviation adviser to King Ibn Saud of Saudi Arabia, helping the king to develop Saudi Arabian Airlines. Next he worked as an aide to Secretary of Defense James Forrestal in the late 1940s. He joined Laurance Rockefeller's family office in 1953, reviewing investments in civil aviation. From 1961 to 1965, Halaby served as the second administrator of the FAA, appointed by President John F. Kennedy. Halaby was a proponent of the creation of the US Department of Transportation, which occurred during his time in the Johnson administration.

From all the documentation located, Halaby appears almost obsessively patriotic to the cause of American-built supersonic passenger airliners. His comments appear to suggest that he was single-mindedly pushing for an all-American SST at all costs – and that to allow any Anglo-French design to pose even the slightest of threat would be like letting in the devil incarnate!

The American SST studies were being co-ordinated by a high-level committee of FAA, NASA and Department of Defense (DoD) officials known as the Supersonic Transport Advisory Group (STAG). Within the FAA, a small management office had been created for the supersonic transport programme, headed by Colonel Lucian S. Rochte. One member of the advisory group, Dr Theodore P. Wright, an internationally respected aeronautical scientist, wrote to both Rochte and Halaby in the first half of 1962 to argue the case for SST collaboration between NATO nations in an Atlantic Union approach in the face of the perceived threat from the Soviet Union. Wright's argument, written in terms of the Cold War 'east-west conflict', also related to the market for supersonic airliners. French and British SSTs could usurp the world market by the time a US machine appeared, hence a three-nation consortium approach should be considered, he suggested. The first approach should be on the political level, with the US inviting Britain and France to an exchange of views on possible SST collaboration. 'The mere fact of calling the conference would be important from the standpoint of advancing the cause of NATO or Atlantic community solidarity.'

By mid-1962, it was becoming clear that the tentative talks earlier that year between the UK and France on a merger of their SST projects were more serious than were first believed – and therefore much more of a threat to the American aviation industry than was originally thought. This set off something of a wave of panic, as it was widely believed that almost all future commercial aircraft would be supersonic, and it looked like the Europeans would start off with a huge lead.

Arnold Kotz, a policy planning officer in the FAA, raised the issue again. He argued that SST economic and market uncertainties were such that a three-nation consortium might prove the most economical solution in meeting US objectives. National commercial jealousies would inhibit an efficient joint venture, he said, and there would be many technical, management and economic problems, but:

> ... if the obstacles can be overcome, the west will preserve its prestige vis-a-vis the Soviet bloc; uneconomic competition for a very small market among the

western allies will be reduced or precluded; the claim on US public funds will be substantially reduced; the strain on the US private aircraft industry will be lightened while they would still achieve the largest share of the market since US airlines would presumably order the largest number of aircraft; all western participating countries would share in the advanced technology, and there would be a definite political gain in having key western nations work closely together on a program of this magnitude.

Raymond B. Malloy, international aviation services director, responded with an argument that began with Anglo-French disagreements and led to a different conclusion. There were obstacles to a tripartite SST programme: the timing was out of phase and the practical difficulties of jointly designing or producing anything as complex as an SST were tremendous. The US should concentrate on a long-range SST, leaving Britain and France to build a medium-range machine.

The creation of the Concorde programme provided Halaby with a formidable promotional weapon. By November 1962 the danger posed by the Anglo-French project had become his main lobbying theme. In a report to President Kennedy, Halaby portrayed a successful Concorde as forcing the US to 'relinquish world civil transport leadership' that would cost over 50,000 American jobs and potentially lead to US dependence on foreign suppliers for supersonic military aircraft. It would, Halaby said, force the US to 'spend as much as $3 billion for UK/French imports, with consequent balance of payments deficits and forgo exports as much as $4 billion if we could capture all of the foreign market'. Halaby clinched his appeal by jingoistically warning that 'conceivably' an American president would some day be forced to fly in a foreign aircraft.

The Concorde announcement was a crucial factor in mobilising support within the administration for an American SST programme. As Halaby recalled years later:

> When de Gaulle embraced the joint [Anglo-French] Concorde project, it seemed to trigger competitiveness in John Fitzgerald Kennedy. In fact, I think JFK associated the Concorde most with de Gaulle; on more than one occasion, he said, 'We'll beat that bastard de Gaulle.' Every time I saw the President, from the day de Gaulle made his announcement, he would press me on how our studies were going – and how the British and French were doing.

This rivalry – or was it a personality clash – between Kennedy and de Gaulle seems to have been ongoing. In an internal memo on 31 January 1963, Najeeb Halaby wrote, 'In a conversation with the President on Tuesday, January 29, it became clear that he is much more nearly in favor of going ahead with the procurement of an SST prototype. One of the factors is the desire to out-do de Gaulle'.

Clearly the B-70 could be used as a serious research tool and provided an incredible foundation that was already in place for the Americans to use – and that starting point was Mach 3 speeds. Going through all the US material, one gets the distinct impression that the Americans were being 'driven' by Concorde. Their aims were to better it in both speed and size, and therefore win the commercial battle. They were determined that what had happened a decade or so earlier – when the de Havilland Comet had given all the American manufacturers a bloody nose in beating them by a country mile to the commercial jet market – was not going to occur again.

In November 1962 the NASA Research Center initiated a programme called SCAT – Supersonic Commercial Air Transport – in order to evolve a configuration that could cater for unique requirements for a commercial SST over the entire spectrum from take-off to landing. Their studies came down to two approaches: SCAT-4, a fixed-wing proposal that integrated wing, fuselage, engines and tail into a highly swept, cambered and twisted aircraft design aimed at minimising wave drag due to lift; and the variable-sweep SCAT-15. By early 1963, two other geometries were also being pursued: the SCAT-16 variable-sweep proposal that had evolved from -15, and SCAT-17, a fixed delta-wing layout with a forward canard surface – in other words, a modified B-70 design.

The Influence of President Kennedy

On 21 January 1963, Kennedy sent out the following memorandum:

> Memorandum for: The Secretary of Defense; The Secretary of Commerce; The Administrator, National Aeronautics and Space Administration; The Chairman, Civil Aeronautics Board; The Administrator, Federal Aviation Agency; The Director, Office of Science and Technology.

The XB-70A was fitted with two sets of 'passenger windows' while with NASA, in order to demonstrate the American SST visually. They were, in reality, just stickers. *(USAF)*

In my budget message I stated that studies on the economic and technical feasibility of a commercial supersonic transport should be expedited and the results evaluated as soon as practicable.

As you know, the Federal Aviation Agency is conducting a two-year research and development program to determine the technical and economic feasibility of a supersonic aircraft. The Congress appropriated a total of $31 million in 1962 and 1963 for this effort which I understand is progressing satisfactorily under the direction of the Federal Aviation Administrator. The National Aeronautics and Space Administration and the Department of Defense are also doing research and development that will yield useful information on problems of supersonic flight.

It is desirable that we hold to or better the schedule laid down in 1961, and reach firm decisions as soon as practicable in 1963 on future actions concerning the development of a supersonic aircraft.

At the same time, because of the potential importance of this project, it is essential that these decisions be made only after the most thorough evaluation of all the probable benefits and costs to the Government and to the national economy.

Accordingly, I am requesting by this memorandum that the Federal Aviation Administrator take the lead in preparing as soon as practicable a report summarizing and evaluating all relevant research results and including firm recommendations for possible further action.

I shall expect the Administrator to consult with you from time to time in the preparation of this report, and I request that you extend to him whatever technical or other assistance he may require. I ask that each of you give this matter his personal attention and that your recommendations reflect your considered judgment on this important matter. Finally, I suggest that arrangements be made for the Director of the Budget and Chairman of the Council of Economic Advisers to participate, as appropriate, during the course of the study.

William McPherson 'Bill' Allen (b. 1 September 1900, d. 28 October 1985), President of the Boeing Aircraft Company from 1945 until 1970, seen here with a model of the B-52 bomber.

The American aviation industry was also becoming concerned about the foreign threat to the US. Following the visit of Georges Hereil, the President of Sud-Aviation, to Seattle for talks with Wellwood Beall and others at Boeing Aircraft, William 'Bill' Allen of Boeing told Roswell Gilpatric, Deputy Secretary of Defense, of his concern about the serious threat of subsidised foreign competition. Allen drafted a letter to President Kennedy stressing that 'our present evaluation of their [Britain and France's] proposed airplane and its potential usefulness to our airline customers, both domestic and foreign, causes us deep concern'.

Allen had previously been briefed by Beall, who told him that the French had suggested two options for the US. First, join with France and Britain on the Mach 2.2 aircraft and forget about Mach 3.5. Second, act as sales agent for the European aircraft, with France and Britain providing both sales and technical assistance on the Mach 3.5 machine later. 'This means to me that the race for the supersonic transport has started and we are going to be faced with competition in the United States from foreign manufacturers ...

I believe the foreign threat, particularly that of the French, to our air transport image and our national prestige is so great that an effort much more vigorous than our present national supersonic transport program must be organized.'

One of Beall's associates was even more blunt. Vernon Crunge of Boeing wrote a note that concluded: 'It may be that the British and French will be left to do this thing on the philosophy that is a stupidity of their own and will lead them nowhere, and we shall ultimately overtake them with something more versatile, more economical and better suited to solve the problem.'

In an even more direct way Concorde was a major factor forcing the president to announce an American SST programme. During the spring of 1963, Pan American Airlines – the 'flagship' of all the American airlines, flying many international routes, including the crucial transatlantic run, and which traditionally led the way in ordering new aircraft – made sure that the FAA and the White House knew that the airline was considering ordering a number of Concordes, although it really wanted to purchase a fleet of larger and faster American Mach 3 SSTs. Juan Trippe, President of Pan American, informed high-level US officials, including Halaby, Civil Aeronautics Board chairman Alan Boyd and Secretary of the Treasury C. Douglas Dillon, that he intended to place what he termed as a 'protective order' for six Concordes.

Juan Terry Trippe (b. 27 June 1899, d. 3 April 1981), founder of Pan American World Airways and the person who stole the thunder of Kennedy's SST announcement.

It is interesting to note how much sway Halaby had at this time within the White House. For example, on 1 March 1963, Lyndon Johnson's daily White House diary has a single-line entry showing that the president took a call from Halaby regarding the SST that lasted twenty minutes; that same day the president only accorded the same amount of time to meet Prince Peter of Greece!

Halaby developed his proposed plans for an SST programme in a memorandum to the president on 3 June. Yet again the first topic addressed was 'national considerations'. The first point within this topic was the Anglo-French programme's challenge to US world leadership in civil aviation. According to Halaby, US industry could and should develop a safe and economically feasible SST that was superior to 'de Gaulle's and Macmillan's Concorde'.

Trippe's actions had the desired effect. Vice-President Lyndon B. Johnson, who was chairing a Cabinet-level SST review committee at that time and who had already recommended an SST go-ahead to President Kennedy, became extremely worried over the impact of the Pan American Concorde decision. Armed with Johnson's recommendation and the knowledge of Trippe's move to order Concordes, Kennedy quickly decided to establish an SST programme. However, to Kennedy's great anger and Halaby's shock, Pan American announced its order for six Concordes on 4 June 1963, one day before Kennedy's SST declaration.

The President Announces ...

On 5 June 1963, in a speech before the graduating class of the USAF Academy, President John F. Kennedy committed the US to a supersonic transport programme by saying that he was:

> ... announcing today that the United States will commit itself to an important new program in civilian aviation. Civilian aviation, long both the beneficiary and the benefactor of military aviation, is of necessity equally dynamic. Neither the

economics nor the politics of international air competition permits us to stand still in this area. Today the challenging new frontier in commercial aviation and in military aviation is a frontier already crossed by the military-supersonic flight. Leading members of the administration under the chairmanship of the Vice-President have been considering carefully the role to be played by the National Government in determining the economic and technical feasibility of an American commercial supersonic aircraft, and in the development of such an aircraft if it be feasible.

Having reviewed their recommendations, it is my judgment that this Government should immediately commence a new program in partnership with private industry to develop at the earliest practical date the prototype of a commercially successful supersonic transport superior to that being built in any other country of the world. An open, preliminary design competition will be initiated immediately among American airframe and powerplant manufacturers with a more detailed design phase to follow. If these initial phases do not produce an aircraft capable of transporting people and goods safely, swiftly, and at prices the traveler can afford and the airlines find profitable, we shall not go further.

But if we can build the best operational plane of this type – and I believe we can – then the Congress and the country should be prepared to invest the funds and effort necessary to maintain this Nation's lead in long-range aircraft, a lead we have held since the end of the Second World War, a lead we should make every responsible effort to maintain. Spurred by competition from across the Atlantic and by the productivity of our own companies, the Federal Government must pledge funds to supplement the risk capital to be contributed by private companies. It must then rely heavily on the flexibility and ingenuity of private enterprise to make the detailed decisions and to introduce successfully this new jet-age transport into worldwide service, and we are talking about a plane in the end of the 60s that will move ahead at a speed faster than Mach 2 to all corners of the globe. This commitment, I believe, is essential to a strong and forward-looking nation, and indicates the future of the manned aircraft as we move into a missile age as well.

The entire Kennedy family were all about calculation. John F. Kennedy in particular was a ruthless tactician and he knew exactly how to manipulate the media by telling them precisely what they wanted to hear. Like much that was said in Kennedy's earlier presidential campaign, the Air Academy speech was a triumph of style over substance, but America got the point.

In the summer of 1963, Halaby was at the peak of his power. He had achieved his long-sought goal: an SST programme under FAA direction. However, he soon suffered a dramatic decline in authority from which he would never recover. His fall from grace was partly due to the change in administrations that occurred as a result of the assassination of Kennedy on 22 November 1963. Halaby, a Kennedy appointee, was never close to Lyndon Johnson and did not particularly get along with him. Although an SST supporter, Johnson also wanted to put his own stamp on what had been a Kennedy programme.

If the Pan American motive had partly been to inject more urgency into the American SST project, it had had the desired effect. Within a day or so Kennedy had proclaimed his government's intention to support the American aircraft industry in developing and building a supersonic transport that would be bigger and faster than Concorde. An options list was opened and many of the world's leading airlines, including all those on the Concorde option list, put their names

One of the many 'maybe' colour schemes from Pan American, this one showing the later Boeing 2707. Sir George Edwards of BAC had first-hand experience of this style of Pan American's tactics: 'The Pan American executives came over here and negotiated these options. The French were very keen on allocating them. I didn't want to do it because I knew what would happen. I knew that everybody all over the world would then come and plant down their $100,000 or whatever it was; we would then have an absolutely phoney set of "orders", as the French kept on calling them, and this was really sticking our head in a noose.'

down for the American aircraft. The aim was to get it into service within two or three years after Concorde, and, in view of the American industry's great reputation for getting things done on time, this announcement caused some concern in Britain and France.

This concern was not fully shared by the Anglo-French design team. If the Americans really were going for a Mach 3 SST built in titanium, the Concorde men were convinced that, even with the USA's immense resources and enormous drive, it would take at least a decade to get the aircraft into service. To carry the 75,000lb payload being spoken of would mean a take-off weight of not less than 1 million pounds. The aircraft would be at least 300ft long – the length of a football field – and the structural problems of building an airframe of that length in titanium were mind-boggling. At the very least, Concorde would have a five-year lead over the American aircraft.

What really concerned Concorde's makers, in 1963 and later when the American SST was cancelled, was that the Americans might change their minds about cruise speed and elect to build a Mach 2.2 airliner. This would have been a much more worrying prospect.

In their predictions about the American SST problems, the Concorde designers were right. In their predictions about their own entry into service date, they were years out. The design problems that lay ahead for them might not be of the same magnitude as those which brought the American SST to a halt, but they were still sufficiently formidable to throw an optimistic timetable well out of gear. To get the required greater passenger-carrying capacity in the long-range version meant carrying more fuel, and that meant increased take-off weight, which, in turn, meant more engine power.

Four views showing
the simulated
operation of the
nose visor on the
Concorde mock-up
at Filton, near
Bristol. *(BAC)*

... and Sets Out his Case

On 14 June, Kennedy wrote to the President of the Senate and the speaker of the House:

The Congress has laid down national aviation objectives in the Federal Aviation Act of 1958. These include the development of an air transportation system which will further our domestic and international commerce and the national defense. These objectives, when viewed in the light of today's aviation challenges, clearly require the commencement of a national program to support the development of a commercial supersonic transport aircraft which is safe for the passenger, economically sound for the world's airlines, and whose operating performance is superior to that of any comparable aircraft.

Our determination that the national interest requires such a program is based on a number of factors of varying weight and importance:

A successful supersonic transport can be an efficient, productive commercial vehicle which provides swift travel for the passenger and shows promise of developing a market which will prove profitable to the manufacturer and operator.

It will advance the frontiers of technical knowledge – not as a byproduct of military procurement, but in the pursuit of commercial objectives.

It will maintain the historic United States leadership in aircraft development.

It will enable this country to demonstrate the technological accomplishments which can be achieved under a democratic, free enterprise system.

Its manufacture and operation will expand our international trade.

It will strengthen the United States aircraft manufacturing industry – a valuable national asset – and provide employment to thousands of Americans.

The cost of such a program is large – it could be as great as one billion dollars for a development program of about six years. This is beyond the financial capability of our aircraft manufacturers. We cannot, however, permit this high cost, nor the difficulties and risks of such an ambitious program to preclude this country from participating in the logical next development of a commercial aircraft. In order to permit this participation, the United States, through the Federal Aviation Agency, must proceed at once with a program of assistance to industry to develop an aircraft.

The proposed program, though it will yield much technological knowledge, is principally a commercial venture. Its aim is to serve, in competition with others, a substantial segment of the world market for such an aircraft. While the magnitude of the development task requires substantial Government financial participation, it is unwise and unnecessary for the Government to bear all of the costs and risks. Consequently, I propose a program in which (1) manufacturers of the aircraft will be expected to pay a minimum of 25% of the development costs, and, in addition, (2) airlines that purchase the aircraft will be expected to pay a further portion of the Government's development costs through royalty payments.

The requirement for cost sharing by the manufacturers will assure that the cost of the program will be held to the absolute minimum. In no event will the Government investment be permitted to exceed $750 million. Moreover, the Government does not intend to pay any production, purchase, or operating subsidies to manufacturers or airlines. On the other hand, this will not exclude consideration by the Government of credit assistance to manufacturers during the production process.

Although the Government will initially bear the principal financial burden in the development phase, participation by industry as a risk-taking partner is an essential of this undertaking. First, the development of civil aircraft should be a private enterprise effort, a product of the interaction of aircraft manufacturers and their prospective customers. We wish to change this relationship as little as possible, and then only temporarily. If the Government were the full risk-taker, the degree of control and direction which it would have to give to the program, to the expenditure of funds, to the selection of designs, to the making of technical decisions, would of necessity be too great. If however, private industry bears a substantial portion of the risk, the degree of Government control and the size of the Government staff required to monitor the program can be held to a minimum.

Second, our objective is to build a commercially sound aircraft, as well as one with superior performance characteristics. This will require, at a relatively early stage, a determination whether the aircraft's cost and characteristics are such that it will find a commercial market. This is a difficult task, and our decision that we have succeeded in developing such a commercially sound aircraft will, in large measure, be attested to by industry's willingness to participate in the risk-taking.

If at any point in the development program, it appears that the aircraft will not be economically sound, or if there is not adequate financial participation by industry in this venture, we must be prepared to postpone, terminate, or substantially redirect this program.

Our first concern, however, must be to get the program launched. I am convinced that our national interest requires that we move ahead in this vital area with a sound program which will develop this aircraft in an efficient manner. For that reason I commend this proposal to your early attention. I will shortly submit to the Congress a request for funds to meet the immediate requirements of this program, such as the detailed design competition. Then we will be started on the task of marshaling the funds of Government and the ingenuity and management skills, as well as funds, of American industry to usher in a new era of commercial flight.

The Black-Osborne Report and the Assassination

Just as important in promoting a power shift were complaints from the manufacturers. They objected to Kennedy's original cost-sharing requirements. In August 1963, Kennedy asked Eugene Black, former head of the World Bank, to review the SST financing issue. Black brought in a fellow industrialist and

financier, Stanley de J. Osborne, the chairman of the Olin Mathieson Chemical Corporation. The Black-Osborne Report may have been commissioned by Kennedy, but due to his assassination on 22 November 1963, it was submitted to Johnson in December 1963, and the report – plus the change of president – quickened Halaby's decline.

Black and Osborne sided with industry in deciding that the 75-25 cost-sharing ratio was too much, recommending that 90 per cent of the development cost be assumed by the government and 10 per cent by the manufacturers. Black and Osborne went beyond their charter and offered proposals that were the opposite of what Halaby advocated. They recommended that the SST programme be taken from the FAA and be made an independent 'authority', reflecting a growing opinion by informed persons in government and industry that the FAA lacked the managerial skills and experience to run a complex effort like the SST programme. They also saw no

Eugene 'Gene' Robert Black Sr (b. 1 May 1898, d. 20 February 1992). He was President of the World Bank from 1949 to 1963.

necessity for a crash programme, noting that the British and French were already encountering major problems of their own.

The report raised a number of points that needed addressing, including asking the question: 'Should the United States now join the Concorde consortium?'

While the possibility may have existed some years ago that we could have joined, at least the British, in a joint supersonic transport development, this possibility does not seem to exist today, although from time to time there have been intimations that conversations might be renewed.

1. The Europeans feel that they are well on their way towards production, and that their designs for air frame and engines are sufficiently frozen to make United States technical collaboration somewhat too late and the possible input too complicated to be feasible.
2. The 'Concorde' producers seem confident that their technology and production schedules are well enough in advance of ours so that, at least in the Mach 2.2 regime, they will be able to capture the market. This aircraft has been intended to be the tool in making Europe the dominant force in air transportation during the 1970s and beyond.

3. Our own manufacturers, wary of committee management inherent in consortiums, are even more hesitant of participating in one with foreign producers who have different technological systems and goals.

4. The only present feasible merging of interests would be through the contribution of funds to the 'Concorde' development, and having one or more of our manufacturers acquire manufacturing licenses from the Europeans. This course would result in the necessary division of future markets, compromises on the part of the United States airlines on the first (and probably the next) generation of aircraft, and a marked slowing down of supersonic technological development within the United States. It would also probably make it impossible to proceed with any advanced aircraft, and might well freeze all supersonic transport development to a tripartite consortium for the foreseeable future.

    Unless technological or time factors change current postures, we see neither an efficient nor a commercially possible way of forming a tripartite consortium.

5. The ideal solution for the Europeans would be for the United States to concede the first generation of supersonic transports to the 'Concorde,' and to proceed now with the development of a larger and faster, Mach 3.5 or upward, hypersonic plane, which would follow the 'Concorde' by seven to ten years. This we do not consider sound nor feasible, from an economic and technological point of view, and we will discuss this more fully later.

6. We are not that far behind our European friends to force us to trade money and market limitations for possible advanced technology, which we might think we do not possess. Nor will we lose the whole market if we complete a superior aircraft within a reasonable time after the 'Concorde' is aloft in commercial service.

7. On the other hand, we should like to caution that under no circumstances should the United States assess its own future course by the conclusion that the 'Concorde' will fail to be a good airplane, that it will not live up to its design characteristics, nor that it will not reasonably meet its time schedules. Advanced technology is not the property of any one nation as has been so vividly demonstrated in the past 20 years, and we are therefore confident that Great Britain's and France's technologists are knowledgeable, expert, and able to deliver on their promises.

    It is our conclusion that it is not feasible to join the 'Concorde' consortium and that we must 'go it alone' or abandon the supersonic transport to Europe.

The report also posed the question as to how much delay in deliveries could a US supersonic transport afford, compared with Concorde:

While probably this subject should be discussed as part of the important discussion of 'Program' below, we feel it is important enough to merit separate identification. Based on the conviction that the United States should not race into a supersonic program just to be first or nearly so, at the cost of not having a sound, long-lived, and economic aircraft, we have studied the effect of a delayed delivery of a United States supersonic transport on its potential market.

The two most important factors in this situation are the rate of construction which the competitive plane will have, and the degree of obsolescence which a United States supersonic transport will bring upon the 'Concorde'.

    a. Even if the United States were only to produce a similar plane to the 'Concorde', but with enough improvements to offset the cost/price differential, the projected construction rate of the European plane and the need of competitive airlines to get aircraft would permit the United States to lag behind on its first deliveries by about six months to a year and still have more than a reasonable chance to share the total estimated market of 200-400 aircraft in the 1970s.

    b. On the other hand, if the United States produces a definitely superior plane which incorporates greater range, higher speed, and better airline operating economics, plus the potentiality of 'growth and development', we are persuaded that the United States can be as far back as two to three years and still capture the bulk of the supersonic transport market.

1. The airline industry will probably not permit itself again to suffer the overnight obsolescence such as it had to undertake with the DC-7, and other advanced piston aircraft, when the subsonic jets became operative. Therefore, if the United States can fly and demonstrate a prototype that answers the characteristics mentioned above, before orders have to be placed for the 'Concorde', then no airline will permit more than an absolute minimum of planes to become obsolete.

2. Unlike other planes, the United States supersonic transport will have a price of two to three times that of current jets, and should have a depreciable life of 12 to 15 years. This involves huge investments for the airline industry, and therefore the airlines cannot buy a fleet of an inferior plane, only to have it assuredly and rapidly obsoleted by a superior growth aircraft within the first 10%-20% of the fleet's expected life.

    Therefore we conclude that with assurance that they can have distinctly superior aircraft available within two to three years, the airlines may buy a few 'Concordes' to stay competitive on 'blue-ribbon' runs, but will defer their major purchases for the United States supersonic transport. These facts therefore lead us directly to the conclusions that:

1. The timing of the United States program need not be tied too closely to that of the 'Concorde';

2. The United States program must be able to demonstrate to the airlines a qualified prototype at about the same time in which the 'Concorde' is being demonstrated;

3. The United States cannot afford to build a copy of the 'Concorde' but must, if it is going into the supersonic transport business, build a superior plane;

4. If a superior craft is built, the delay is not only agreeable to the United States airlines, but may even be for most others, including those airlines most closely related to the Governments of Britain and France.

A Change of Power

The Black-Osborne Report triggered a series of internal administration reviews of the whole SST effort in early 1964 that finally led to the formation of the President's Advisory Committee on Supersonic Transport (PAC-SST) on 1 April 1964 under Executive Order No 11149.

President Lyndon Johnson said at a news conference at his ranch on 28 March 1964:

I am drafting an Executive order setting up an advisory board that will report to me in connection with the supersonic transport, which is a very important development. We are making substantial progress on it. We now have a development cost estimate and we have the estimated unit selling prices. We have a number of orders. We have a number of proposals that have already been submitted. We believe the technical challenge of the supersonic transport is manageable. We think the main problem lies in the financial area. We believe that Government and industry participating is the key issue and we have to work that out.

The men I expect to name in that Executive order which is now on the drafting board are: Secretary McNamara – we hope we can get the benefit of his experience not only in production, not only his personal experience, but the entire experience of the Defense Department in giving me counsel; Mr Halaby, of the FAA, the FAA Administrator; Mr Eugene Black, who made the report, former head of the World Bank; Secretary Dillon – we have a good deal involved in the balance of payments; Mr John McCone, Secretary Hodges, and Space Administrator Webb.

The sections of the wooden mock-up of Concorde come together at Filton, near Bristol. (Simon Peters Collection)

The PAC was chaired by probably the most powerful and influential official in the government at that time, next to the president, Secretary of Defense Robert S. McNamara, and was made up of Cabinet-level officials, including the secretaries of Treasury and Commerce, the CIA Director, the administrators of NASA and the FAA, as well as civilians Black and Osborne. A massive power shift had taken place. McNamara was now the most important decision-maker in the SST programme and major policy decisions were now made in the PAC rather than the FAA.

Not long after that, Lyndon B. Johnson said in a statement on 21 May 1964:

> The supersonic transport program is a vast national undertaking and will require the closest cooperation not only among the various Government departments and agencies involved, but also among industry and the American people. If we all work together, I am confident that this country will produce a supersonic transport that will continue to maintain American world leadership in the air.

The statement was part of a White House release announcing that the president had received the first interim report of the President's Advisory Committee on Supersonic Transport and that he had also received a memorandum on the programme from the administrator of the FAA. The statement added that the president had approved the committee's recommendations and the contractors proposed by the administrator.

The previous day, 20 May, the White House daily diary records an enlarged version of the previous statement:

> The President announced approval of 'a program of action designed to move the Supersonic Transport closer to realization'. He ordered federal agencies to 'implement the recommended program immediately' and speed development of a commercial airliner travelling at more than two and a half times the speed of sound. President Johnson said he accepted the suggestions of a recently established President's Advisory Committee on Supersonic Transport headed by Secretary McNamara. He called the SST 'a vast national undertaking' that will require the closest co-operation among agencies, industry and the American people ... so that this country will produce a supersonic transport that will continue to maintain American world leadership in the air.

The committee recommended that the FAA be authorised to place contracts for component development and performance demonstration with manufacturers; that economic studies be made to determine the size and type of plane that would be most profitable; and that sonic-boom studies be carried out under the guidance of the National Academy of Sciences.

In making its recommendations the committee noted that the project was one of high technical risk, and that financing the supersonic transport would require huge sums, involving unusually heavy commercial risks and necessitating major participation by the government.

From the surviving documents, it appears that the US national SST programme was driven by a mindset that was almost like a nation preparing to go to war. If that was the case, then there was a traitor in its midst.

Robert McNamara had set out cold-bloodedly to sabotage the project right from the start.

3

Mack the Knife

Robert Strange McNamara, born in San Francisco, California, in 1916, was a business executive and the eighth Secretary of Defense. He was to serve under Presidents John F. Kennedy and Lyndon B. Johnson from 1961 to 1968.

He graduated in 1937 from the University of California, Berkeley, with a Bachelor of Arts in economics with minors in mathematics and philosophy, later earning an MBA from the Harvard Business School in 1939. McNamara then worked a year for the accountants Price Waterhouse in San Francisco before returning to Harvard in August 1940 to teach accounting in the business school, becoming the highest paid and youngest assistant professor at that time. Following his involvement there in a programme to teach analytical approaches used in business to officers of the army air forces (USAAF) he entered the armed forces as a captain in early 1943, serving most of the war with the USAAF's Office of Statistical Control. One major responsibility was the analysis of US bombers' efficiency and effectiveness, especially the B-29 forces commanded by Major General Curtis LeMay in China and the Mariana Islands.

In 1946, McNamara joined the Ford Motor Company owing to the influence of Charles 'Tex' Thornton, a colonel for whom he had worked while in the military.

Robert S. McNamara (b. 9 June 1916, d. 6 July 2009), seated on the left with President Lyndon Johnson, who made McNamara chairman of the President's Advisory Committee on Supersonic Transport aircraft (PAC-SST).

Above: Alain Enthoven (b. 10 September 1930). He was a Deputy Assistant Secretary of Defense from 1961 to 1965, when he became the Assistant Secretary of Defense for Systems Analysis until 1969.

Right: Secretary of the Air Force Harold Brown (b. 19 September 1927). He worked as Director of Defense Research and Engineering from 1961 to 1965, and then as Secretary of the Air Force from October 1965 to February 1969.

Thornton had read an article in *Life* magazine which reported the company was in dire need of reform. McNamara was one of ten former Second World War officers known within Ford as the 'Whiz Kids', who helped the company to stop its losses and administrative chaos by implementing modern planning, organisation and management-control systems. Starting as manager of planning and financial analysis, he advanced rapidly through a series of top-level management positions. Opponents argued that McNamara's embrace of rationalism – his seeming fetish for numbers and charts – impeded rather than enhanced his ability to apprehend reality.

In 1960, President-Elect John F. Kennedy first offered the post of Secretary of Defense to former secretary Robert A. Lovett; he declined but recommended McNamara. Kennedy sent Sargent Shriver to approach him regarding either the Treasury or the Defense Cabinet post – this was just after McNamara had become president at Ford. McNamara immediately rejected the Treasury position but accepted Kennedy's invitation to serve as Secretary of Defense as long as the president gave assurances that he would have complete control of the Department of Defense, subject only to the higher authority of the president as commander in chief.

McNamara was known to have no fondness of the military in general, or the air force in particular – and especially for his former boss, General LeMay. He frowned upon LeMay's statistical accounting methods and found fault with all the weapons systems favoured by LeMay. This immediately put him in direct confrontation over the B-70 project. McNamara often said that too much money was being spent on such weapons systems, and greatly preferred the neatness and apparent economy of the Intercontinental Ballistic Missile (ICBM) with its attendant theory of mutually assured destruction.

Although not knowledgeable about defence matters, McNamara immersed himself in the subject, learned quickly, and soon began to apply an 'active role' management philosophy, which in his own words was about 'providing aggressive leadership questioning, suggesting alternatives, proposing objectives and stimulating progress'. He rejected radical organisational changes, as proposed by a group Kennedy had appointed, headed by Senator W. Stuart Symington, which would have abolished the military departments, replaced the joint chiefs of staff (JCS) with a single chief of staff, and established three functional unified commands. McNamara accepted the need for separate services but was determined to overhaul the US Department of Defense, arguing that 'at the end we must have one defense policy, not three conflicting defense policies. And it is the job of the Secretary and his staff to make sure that this is the case.'

Like a latter-day Svengali, McNamara surrounded himself with a group of 'experts' from the RAND Corporation who inherited the somewhat disparaging nickname of 'Whiz Kids' that travelled over with McNamara from the Ford Motor Company to turn around the management of the DoD. The purpose was to shape a modern defence strategy in the nuclear age by bringing in economic analysis, operations research, game theory and computing, as well as implementing modern management systems to co-ordinate the huge dimension of operations of the DoD with methods such as the Planning, Programming and Budgeting System (PPBS). The group included (among others) Harold Brown, Alain Enthoven, Patrick Gross, William Kaufmann, Jan Lodal, Frank Nicolai, Merton Joseph Peck, Charles O. Rossotti, Henry Rowen, Ivan Selin, Pierre Sprey and Adam Yarmolinsky.

The Whiz Kids invented a world where all decisions could be made based on numbers – an ideal that is still skirted on by many Masters of Business Administration (MBA) programmes and consulting firms today. They found power and comfort in assigning values to what could be quantified, and deliberately ignored everything else.

Above: William Weed Kaufmann (b. 10 November 1918, d. 14 December 2008), nuclear strategist and adviser to seven secretaries of defense.

It is fair to say that they saved and then almost destroyed the USA. However, their approach would ultimately cause a drop in quality and innovation of American cars, opening the door to the Japanese invasion from which the American automobile industry has yet to recover. The Whiz Kids' doctrine is also arguably responsible for America's continued involvement in the Vietnam War after 1965, which led to the majority of the war's 58,209 US casualties and the millions of Vietnamese military and civilian deaths. They had many of the right ideas: they brought analytical discipline to the military and American business that desperately needed it, but they inadvertently swung the pendulum too far.

Below: Henry S. Rowen (b. 11 October 1925), politician, economist and academic.

The 1964 Democratic Party Platform stated: 'The far-reaching decision has been made that the United States will design and build a supersonic air transport plane – and thereby maintain our leadership position in international aviation. Congress has provided $60 million for the development of detailed designs. Twenty airlines already have placed orders.'

Nevertheless, as chairman of the PAC-SST, McNamara was in a position to exert increasing sceptical influence over America's SST programme. As he was to say afterwards:

> Right at the beginning I thought the project was not justified, because you couldn't fly a large enough payload over a long enough nonstop distance at a low enough cost to make it pay. I'm not an aeronautical engineer or a technical expert or an airline specialist or an aircraft manufacturer but I knew that I could make the calculation on the back of an envelope.
>
> So I approached the SST with that bias. President Johnson was in favor of it. As chairman of the committee I was very skeptical from the beginning. The question, in a sense, was how to kill it. I conceived an approach that said: maybe you're right, maybe there is a commercial market, maybe what we should do is to take it with government funds up to the point where the manufacturers and the airlines can determine the economic viability of the aircraft. We'll draw up a program on that basis.

It was from this sceptical viewpoint that McNamara's team of systems analysts fed the committee a regular diet of negative reports in which the economic viability of the SST was continually questioned. Concorde thus became an important element in the economic assessments of the US SST considered by the committee.

Testing the Booms

As we have already seen, the Americans, the British and the French were very aware of the problems of 'sonic booms' from the moment the so-called 'sound barrier' was broken. They were also very aware that the general public could react badly to it. In his book *S/S/T and Sonic Boom Handbook*, published in 1970, William A. Shurcliff described the phenomena in simple, yet highly emotive, terms:

> One reason people find the sonic boom annoying is because it is very loud – a sudden loud 'bang!' (or sometimes a double bang). Loud noises are distracting and may drown out conversation or music. People dislike loud noises, ordinarily – but may accept very loud music, fire crackers, or such, on appropriate occasions.
>
> The main reason people hate sonic booms is because of startle effect. It has been known for decades that a very sudden, loud, unexpected noise produces a set of symptoms, or behaviors, called the startle syndrome. Typically, the syndrome includes hunching the shoulders, pulling the head forward and downward, crouching slightly, releasing adrenaline and increasing the rate of heartbeat. In addition the person may blink, jump, or cry out. Various stomach symptoms may result also, and there may be accompanying feelings of fear, surprise, terror.
>
> The sonic boom is particularly harassing because it has hallmarks of disasters: it is reminiscent of a violent collision of two cars, the detonation of a bomb, or an explosion in a chemical plant a mile or two away. Reacting to a sonic boom with startle, fear, and dread is not merely instinctive but, to some degree, logical and desirable. In these precarious times citizens should be wary of sudden noises suggestive of threat to life.

The British and French ran a whole range of evaluations of their own, but the Americans felt the need to evaluate the effects on sonic booms on the general population. This led to the running of a series of 1,253 sonic booms being 'dropped' over Oklahoma City over a period of six months. The experiment ran from 3 February until 29 July 1964 and was to quantify the effects of transcontinental SSTs on a city. The programme was managed by the FAA, who enlisted the aid of NASA and the USAF. Public opinion measurement was subcontracted to the National Opinion Research Center (NORC) of the University of Chicago.

This was not the first experiment, as tests had been done at Wallops Island, Virginia, in 1958 and 1960; at Nellis AFB, Nevada, in 1960 and 1961; and in St Louis, Missouri, in 1961 and 1962. However, none of these tests examined sociological and economic factors in any detail. The Oklahoma City experiments were much larger, seeking to measure the boom's effect on structures and public attitude, and to develop standards for boom prediction and insurance data. Oklahoma City was chosen as the region's population was perceived to be relatively tolerant towards such an experiment. The city had an economic dependency on the nearby FAA's Mike Monroney Aeronautical Center and Tinker AFB.

Starting on 3 February 1964, the first sonic booms began, eight booms per day which began at 7 a.m. and ended in the afternoon. The noise was limited to

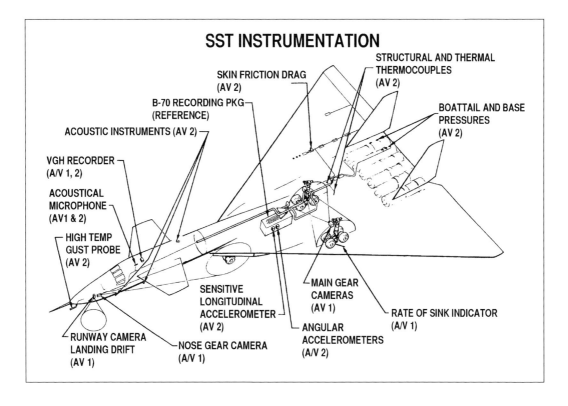

SST INSTRUMENTATION

SKIN FRICTION DRAG
(AV 2)

STRUCTURAL AND THERMAL
THERMOCOUPLES
(AV 2)

B-70 RECORDING PKG
(REFERENCE)

BOATTAIL AND BASE
PRESSURES
(AV 2)

ACOUSTIC INSTRUMENTS (AV 2)

VGH RECORDER
(A/V 1, 2)

ACOUSTICAL
MICROPHONE
(AV1 & 2)

HIGH TEMP
GUST PROBE
(AV 2)

SENSITIVE
LONGITUDINAL
ACCELEROMETER
(AV 2)

MAIN GEAR
CAMERAS
(AV 1)

RATE OF SINK INDICATOR
(A/V 1)

ANGULAR
ACCELEROMETERS
(A/V 2)

RUNWAY CAMERA
LANDING DRIFT
(AV 1)

NOSE GEAR CAMERA
(A/V 1)

1.0 to 1.5 pound-force per square foot (psf) for the first twelve weeks, then increased to 1.5 to 2.0psf for the final fourteen weeks. This range was about equal to that expected from an SST. Though eight booms per day was harsh, the peak overpressures of 2.0psf were an order of magnitude lower than that needed to shatter glass, and are considered marginally irritating according to published standards. The air force used F-104 and B-58 aircraft, with the occasional F-101 and F-106.

Oklahomans initially took the tests in their stride, as the booms were predictable and came at specific times. An FAA-hired camera crew filming a group of construction workers were surprised to find that one of the booms signalled their lunch break.

In the first fourteen weeks, 147 windows in the city's two tallest buildings, the First National Bank and Liberty National Bank, were broken. By late spring, organised civic groups were complaining, but were rebuffed by city politicians, who asked them to show legislators their support. An attempt to lodge an injunction against the tests was denied by district court judge Stephen Chandler, who said that the plaintiffs could not establish that they suffered any mental or physical harm and that the tests were a vital national need. A restraining order was then sought, which brought a pause to the tests on 13 May, until it was decided that the court had exceeded its authority.

Pressure mounted from within. The Federal Bureau of the Budget lambasted the FAA about poor experiment design, while complaints flooded into Oklahoma Senator A.S. Mike Monroney's office. Finally, East Coast newspapers began to pick up the issue, turning on the national spotlight. On 6 June, the *Saturday Review* published an article entitled 'The Era of Supersonic Morality', which criticised the manner in which the FAA had targeted a city without consulting local government. By July, the *Washington Post* reported on the turmoil at the local and state level in

For later SST sonic-boom tests, North American outfitted the XB-70 with much specialist equipment as seen in this diagram, showing where the dedicated instrumentation was installed in the XB-70A airframe. *(NAA)*

Oklahoma. Oklahoma City council members were finally beginning to respond to citizen complaints and put pressure on Washington.

This put a premature end to the tests. The results of the experiment, reported by NORC, were released beginning in February 1965. The FAA, not unsurprisingly, was displeased by the overly academic style of the report, but stressed the positive findings, saying, 'the overwhelming majority felt they could learn to live with the numbers and kinds of booms experienced'. Indeed, NORC reported that 73 per cent of subjects in the study said that they could live indefinitely with eight sonic booms per day, while 25 per cent said that they could not. About 3 per cent of the population telephoned, sued or wrote protest letters, but Oklahoma City surgeons and hospitals filed no complaints.

However, with the city population at 500,000, that 3 per cent figure represented 15,000 upset individuals. At least 15,452 complaints and 4,901 claims were lodged against the US government, most for cracked glass and plaster. The FAA rejected 94 per cent of all the claims it received, fuelling a rising tide of anger that soared even after the conclusion of the experiments.

Four reasons why the Americans were getting protective – artist's impressions of Concorde in the markings of Braniff International, United, TWA and Eastern Airlines. *(All BAC)*

The Oklahoma City experiments were partly to blame for weakening the FAA's authority in sonic-boom issues. After the tests, Lyndon B. Johnson's presidential advisory committee transferred matters of policy from the FAA to the National Academy of Science (NAS). Secretary of the Interior Stewart Udall complained that the NAS did not include one environmental preservationist, and pointed out that although the Oklahoma City tests were stacked in favour of the SST, they were still extremely negative. Indeed by 1966, national grassroots campaigns against sonic booms were beginning to affect public policy.

The FAA's poor handling of claims and its payout of only $123,000 led to a class action lawsuit against the US government.

In his 1970 book, Shurcliff strongly objected to the validity of these tests, claiming that they did not take into account what he termed 'Vulnerable Persons':

> People differ greatly in their vulnerability to startle. At the one extreme, healthy well-adjusted adults busily engaged in pleasant occupations may experience little annoyance at a sudden loud sound. Such persons may enjoy the sound

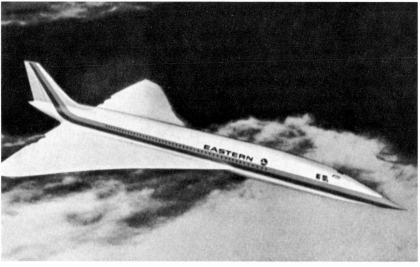

of gun-fire or a loud clap of thunder. At the other extreme are elderly persons with critical heart conditions, such that even a moderately intense 'bang!' may produce spasms/acute pain, and possibly even heart failure. Other vulnerable groups include infants and very old people, persons suffering from ulcers and insomnia, persons who are very unhappy, irritated, worried, or afraid, persons who regard the sudden loud noise as a personal affront – a betrayal of the common man in favor of big business, persons with various kinds of mental diseases, women in labor, persons in great pain, persons deadly ill.

It is ironic that pro-SST persons who call for extensive sonic boom tests to evaluate the annoyance never propose carrying out the tests on the most vulnerable groups. It would be hard to find anyone so callous as to propose booming highly vulnerable people hour after hour, day and night.

He went on to question, 'Of what value is it to find that some healthy adults can tolerate booms if the vulnerable groups obviously cannot tolerate them?'

Inter-Departmental Fighting

There was an interesting sub-plot to the main story that the sonic-boom testing brought to a head – the question of how much information should be made available to the Europeans, or as some Americans were calling them, 'the enemy'.

Whilst the Americans were quite happy to gain any information on the European project that might assist the US programme, there was the question of how much information on US work should be supplied to the British and the French. Some argued for a 'We'll tell you if you tell us' approach, while others urged a total security blackout in order not to help the enemy – and, yes, those words were used! This soon spilled over into other avenues such as whether to approve exports of US equipment for use on Concorde and whether to grant permission for the use of US wind-tunnel or other facilities by British and French engineers.

The central question had been addressed as early as February 1962 by the SST steering group chaired by Najeeb Halaby. No official position was taken at that time, but the consensus at that meeting was to withhold or delay relevant research information. 'To provide the results of Government-sponsored research to foreign manufacturers would enhance their position in developing a supersonic transport to the detriment of the economic position of the US manufacturers and the nation.' In 1964, an unusual aspect of the question was posed in connection with the series of sonic-boom tests conducted by the FAA in Oklahoma City.

A leading opponent of supersonic flight during the sixties was Bo Lundberg, the Director General of the Aeronautical Research Institute of Sweden, and in June 1964, after observing some of the Oklahoma City tests, he urged that representatives of governments of countries likely to be overflown by SSTs should come to Oklahoma City and observe for themselves. The idea was enthusiastically suggested to Halaby by Charles G. Warnick, the FAA's Director of Information Services, that the Washington-based foreign air attachés should be invited to observe the tests.

Raymond Malloy, FAA assistant administrator for international aviation affairs, warned Halaby: 'Attaches are members of the intelligence profession, and we have not yet approved a general exchange of SST data with the United Kingdom and France.'

From a relatively small disagreement on a minor point within the FAA, the issue turned into a major clash between the Department of Commerce and the Department of Defense on the central principle when it came up for scrutiny by Commerce's Advisory Committee on Export Policy Structure. In 1965 a new dimension of the problem was addressed: the supply of US technology via the Concorde programme to communist countries to which such exports were normally banned. Two questions had to be addressed. Firstly, would the US government authorise private American firms to export US-origin materials, equipment, supplies and technical data for use in the design, engineering and construction of the British-French supersonic aircraft Concorde, some of which might be exported to any country in the world? Second, would the US government authorise the export of US-origin materials, equipment, supplies and technical data for the maintenance, repair, replacement and servicing of the British-French supersonic aircraft Concorde regardless of such aircraft's location, ownership or control?

The Department of Commerce stated in both cases that it should – but that the British and French governments should be told that the US hoped they would avoid selling Concorde to Communist China, North Korea, North Vietnam and Cuba. The issue had arisen because of contract commitments demanded by British and French firms from potential US suppliers. The B.F. Goodrich company, for instance, anticipated a loss of around $9.5 million in US exports if it was unable to make those commitments.

The Department of Defense thought that the Commerce recommendation was too encompassing – it might even embrace the export of complete engines to power Concorde. Each application for export should be reviewed on its merits, with the primary decision being based on US national interest.

The topic of information release came before the PAC in 1966. McNamara was very aware of the problems encountered by American military aircraft operating at Mach 2 and above via the XB-70 research project which he had been directly involved with since 1961. Details of these problems might be given to the Concorde consortium and to the airlines, it was suggested. This would 'make the Concorde management aware of the difficulties to be faced and perhaps to induce them to proceed at a slower pace and, further, to discourage the US airlines from over-optimistic evaluation of the Concorde'. The FAA strongly advised against it; instead of deterring the consortium, such action might well encourage them to greater efforts.

NASA, the FAA and the Departments of State, Commerce and Defense all became involved in a 1966/67 inquiry by Pierre Satre, Engineering Director of Sud-Aviation, on the possibility of conducting certain Concorde wind-tunnel tests in the United States. Satre also asked for reports on the American B-70 aircraft that compared wind-tunnel test results with in-flight performance data; moreover, he offered to provide comparable Concorde data in exchange. Bernard Vierling, the Deputy Director of the FAA's Office of SST Development, was in no doubt on the wind-tunnel issue: 'I can see no reason why the US Government should subsidize the Concorde program which is in direct competition with our own supersonic transport.'

Following an inter-agency meeting, Arnold W. Frutkin, NASA assistant administrator for international affairs, noted that US wind-tunnel tests would provide useful information on Concorde performance. He suggested a low-key approach to the French that could lead to Concorde model testing at NASA's Ames and Langley research centres and the exchange of B-70 and Concorde data. Vierling was not convinced, however, warning that the Concorde delivery date represented an important competitive factor; the US should think carefully before assisting the Anglo-French project to meet its schedule.

From the other side of the Atlantic, David Bruce, American Ambassador to Britain, recommended co-operation for wider reasons. The issues involved were broader than those of the commercial race between Concorde and the US SST.

A European self-sufficiency in aerospace was in no one's interest, and US co-operation should be limited only by considerations of national security.

Considerations of diplomacy were also addressed by the Ambassador: 'If discussions with the French on wind tunnel testing proceed further, I believe it would be desirable at some point to inform the British informally what is going on so that they don't get the impression we are dealing behind their backs with the French.'

Though the use of NASA wind tunnels was not pursued, another NASA resource, an advanced flight simulator at Ames Research Center in northern California, proved invaluable in the Concorde airworthiness programme.

By February 1967, the release issue was still on the minds of the FAA, which had received requests for release of US technology not only for Concorde but also, via the British, for the Soviet Tu-144. Release would maximise the exploitation of US technology, and airlines, along with US suppliers, would welcome the maximum amount of equipment that was common to Concorde and the US SST. However, many of the requested items had potential military uses, and if Britain, France and the Soviet Union were forced to develop their own alternative technology their lead over the US SST would be narrowed. The FAA came to the conclusion that the best policy would be to exercise leniency in the export of US hardware but to be much stricter in the export of technology.

Eventually a number of US companies contributed to the Concorde programme – a list of forty-one American organisations was in the press release announcing the roll-out of the first prototype in December 1967, and by 1973 the number had risen to over seventy-five.

One of the large-scale Boeing SST models on test in the NASA wind tunnel at Langley. The model sits on hydraulic jacks that can be adjusted to put it into different attitude positions. *(NASA)*

Ideas Come Together

On 13 February 1964, the UK aerospace magazine *Flight International* reported on three designs submitted to the FAA's supersonic airliner evaluation team on 15 January 1964. Boeing's entry was essentially identical to the swing-wing Model 733 studied in 1960; it was known officially as the Model 733-197, but also referred to both as the 1966 Model and the Model 2707. The latter name became the best known in public, while Boeing continued to use 733 model numbers.

North American submitted the NAC-60 design, essentially a scaled-up B-70 with a less tapered fuselage and new compound-delta wing. The design retained the high-mounted canard and box-like engine area under the fuselage. The Lockheed CL-823 was essentially a scaled-up Concorde with a compound-delta wing (as opposed to the smoothed ogee of Concorde), with individually podded engines.

The American designs, the Boeing 2707 and the Lockheed L-2000, were to have been larger, with seating for up to 300 people. Running a few years behind Concorde, the winning Boeing 2707 machine was later redesigned to a fixed, cropped delta layout.

It was obvious that supersonic flight had to provide a shirtsleeve environment for passengers – it would be totally impracticable to fit hundreds of people with temperature-resistant pressure suits before launching them across the sky at speeds in excess of Mach 2. Many designers had lots of theories as to how this would be possible, but some realised that the XB-70 programme was attempting to supply some hard, real-time solutions. It was almost as if the aircraft had been ready made to answer some of the questions. As always, the XB-70 programme was having financial problems because of arguments between Congress and McNamara's DoD. NASA was happy to climb aboard and fund the testing with the idea that it might be a good way to bolster the SST programme, for there were many problems to be solved before an American SST could be built.

In 1965, the US had not yet come up with accurate wind-tunnel models, so it had difficulty estimating the base drag of a multi-engine aircraft. The XB-70 was able to run these tests live, during regular flight. Tests called for cameras to be placed on the fuselage so in-flight photographs could be taken to resolve boundary layer transition pattern issues. Later on, a wing glove would be installed, permitting the study of the effects of roughness on airflow, especially during the subsonic-transonic-supersonic transition.

The instrumentation was designed, manufactured and installed – mainly on air vehicle number two (A/V-2) – with data gathering, reduction and analysis performed on a non-interference basis during the XB-70 development programme. As North American Aviation stated in its final report: 'The SST flight research data was obtained in various areas as designated by the eight tasks. All of the tasks indicated were sponsored by NASA except for acoustic loads, which was sponsored by FAA.'

Prior to the loss of A/V-2, the aircraft had become a surrogate for the proposed Boeing 733 SST. The government and private researchers embarked on a major sonic-boom test programme at Edwards AFB in an effort to forecast accurately psychological reaction and structural damage associated with overpressures from supersonic transports. The National Sonic Boom Program (NSBP) was set up by the President's Office of Science and Technology, and consisted of three principal participants: the air force, NASA and the Stanford Research Institute.

The XB-70 was used to perform the tests because it most closely resembled the size of the proposed Boeing SST. The Valkyrie was the only aircraft capable of simulating the SST, primarily because weight and size had a marked effect on

A truly stunning picture of XB-70 Valkyrie 20001, seen up close and personal from one of the chase aircraft while engaged on sonic-boom tests for NASA. The wing tips are in the fully down position. *(USAF)*

sonic boom signatures. Although overpressures of equal peak magnitudes could have been obtained by using F-104s and B-58s, the duration of the boom itself varied with each aircraft as to the shape of the shock waves themselves and the forces involved.

The NSBP began on 6 June 1966 when A/V-2 performed the initial sonic-boom test, reaching Mach 3.05 at 72,000ft. The second NSBP test was conducted two days later on 8 June – however, it was followed by a mid-air collision that destroyed the XB-70.

Both the air force and NASA were unsure that A/V-1, with its Mach 2.5 speed limitation, could continue the research since the Boeing SST was planned as a Mach 2.7 aircraft. A/V-1 had not flown since 9 May because the original test programme was scheduled to end in early June. Nevertheless, given that A/V-1 was the only large supersonic aircraft available, NASA thought that it had no choice other than to install a duplicate set of test equipment in it. During this period A/V-1 was also equipped with improved escape capsules and an automated Air Induction Control System (AICS) thereby eliminating its troublesome manual AICS.

Subsequent to the XB-70 flight-test development programme, two flight-research programmes were initiated on the remaining XB-70. The first programme was for sonic-boom measurements and was sponsored jointly by NASA and the USAF.

The first of these flights (No 1-50) was on 11 March 1966, the programme being completed on 1 January 1967 (flight No 1-60). The primary purpose of the test programme was to determine the proper method of combining the theoretical sonic-boom intensity due to lift and due to volume for the far field case. The pressure signatures of several aircraft, but principally the XB-70, were measured on the ground at various distances from the ground track of the air vehicle. The atmospheric effects on the sonic-boom intensity were also investigated.

The second follow-on programme was sponsored by NASA and was an investigation into the control of structural dynamics. The first flight (No l-61) took place on 25 April 1967, with completion of the programme on 4 February 1969 (No 1-83), when the surviving XB-70 was ferried to Wright-Patterson AFB Air Museum. To conduct the structure dynamics investigation, the air vehicle was modified for the installation of an Exciter Vane System in the nose section and an elevon control system entitled Identically Located Accelerometers and Forces (ILAF). The Exciter Vane System consisted of two small vanes protruding from both sides of the nose section, tied together through the fuselage by a 'sewer pipe' and hydraulically driven. The system was controllable from the cockpit for both frequency and amplitude, which provided controlled dynamics to the air vehicle structure. The ILAF system tied into the XB-70 Flight Augmentation Control System which provided elevon control for structural dynamic dampening. The concept was based on locating the input accelerometers near the elevons (for system stability), mixing this input signal with computer-generated signals which cancelled normal flight accelerations and provided a structural dynamics frequency spectrum.

Spooks, Spies and Intelligence Gatherers

Spying is not always the world of James Bond. Sometimes political and industrial espionage and intelligence gathering have no beautiful women, no 'shaken but not stirred martinis' or fast cars, just methodical gathering of information.

Behind the scenes, the initial concern caused by the Concorde programme had faded by 1964, and Concorde was not the centre of American SST policy-making attention. As in the past, almost all significant American-European SST exchanges were limited purely to technical information. In fact, from the American perception, Concorde seemed to be in deep political and technical trouble. By now the American SST programme had evolved into something that was a national response to a foreign project. For any response to be effective it had to be based on the largest amount of information about the activities and progress of the competition. Information was to come from a number of sources, ranging from reports from individuals to considered judgements handed down to the PAC-SST from the CIA. To develop an evaluation of the Anglo-French project seemed an eminently suitable idea. As Walter Heller, the chairman of the Council of Economic Advisors told Vice-President Johnson in March 1963: 'We understand the great difficulties in obtaining "hard" intelligence on this program and of making authoritative economic analysis of its prospects, but we endorse any efforts to improve and expand our information on this venture.'

Joseph Anthony Califano Jr, who, as a young man, acted as Executive Secretary of the President's Advisory Committee on Supersonic Transport.

With hindsight, much of this 'information' as presented to the PAC-SST appears to be suspect. It seems that whoever was compiling reports and deciding upon the data for inclusion in the agendas was being highly selective in their choice of material – almost to the point where the committee was being manipulated by a biased mind; only being told what the presenter wanted them to know.

Within the FAA, Gordon M. Bain, the SST programme director, provided Halaby with an 'Intelligence Estimate of Concorde' based on screened information from the CIA, the Department of Defense Intelligence, the Department of State and limited publicly available press reports. Bain's report listed a number of problem areas, including placing great negative emphasis on the fact that 'each airplane will be

partly metric (French portion) and partly in inches (British portion)', implying that this was an inherently bad – even dangerous – aspect to the design.

While this may seem strange and somewhat problematic to the layman, to work in both metric and imperial dimensions was at the time quite a common occurrence for engineers, and is not difficult as long as systems and assemblies are kept separate. In reality, what was eventually decided upon was the simple solution of allowing both sides to work in the dimensional scales to which they were accustomed. A common system of numbering engineering drawings was established before manufacture of the prototype aircraft began. French drawings were dimensioned in metric measurements, and British drawings in feet and inches. At interface points in the structure, the relevant drawings were dimensioned in both scales.

It was also a very simplistic way of describing how the British and the French were going about building the aircraft. Even with the potential restrictions on American parts being used, a number of other manufacturers were supplying parts and sub-assemblies.

In late 1964, the newly elected Labour government called for a thorough review of British participation in the programme. The CIA reported in October that the Labour Party's stance would have serious repercussions for Concorde, and McNamara was even warned in November 1964 that Britain might withdraw completely. However, McNamara's key SST aide, Joseph Califano, believed that the British would probably continue to participate, though in his view the British reappraisal had clearly weakened Concorde. 'Whatever the outcome,' Califano told McNamara, 'the introduction of so much strain and uncertainty into the Concorde program because of the political factors makes it doubtful whether the degree of cooperation that has thus prevailed between the British and French can be maintained.'

Califano was appointed Special Assistant to the Secretary and Deputy Secretary of Defense on 1 April 1964. He had special responsibilities for Department of Defense liaison with the Office of the President of the United States. He also acted as Executive Secretary of the President's Advisory Committee on Supersonic Transport, as the Department of Defense representative on the President's Committee on the Economic Impact of Defense and Disarmament, and as a member of the Federal Radiation Council.

On 26 July 1965, Califano was appointed Special Assistant to Lyndon B. Johnson. In this position, he served as Johnson's top domestic aide, developing the president's legislative programme as well as helping to co-ordinate economic policies and handling domestic crises. He served in this position until 20 January 1969. While in this post *The New York Times* called him the 'Deputy President for Domestic Affairs'.

John Alexander McCone (b. 4 January 1902, d. 14 February 1991), who was CIA Director from 1961 to 1965.

In the second half of 1964, CIA Director John McCone promised Califano a report 'on the progress of the Concorde and the estimated operational date; also the British engineer's opinion of a few of the problems and questions raised in the committee's memorandum to the President'. Despite extensive searches, the identity of 'the British engineer' remains a mystery.

Other items of published information were scrutinised, along with a detailed assessment of two documents presented by Lieutenant Colonel Robert E. Pursley, a DoD analyst. These documents were a BAC-Sud report on 'the revised long-range aircraft' published in April 1964 and Sir George Edwards' Concorde lecture to the Institute of Transport in London in February that year.

From the views of secret CIA informants to public calls to the faithful, all came under scrutiny of the American SST analysts. In the summer of 1964, great importance was attached to a report on the 'mission performance potential' of Concorde compiled by staff at the NASA Langley Research Center in Virginia. This report focused on the reliability of the fuel-transfer system needed to adjust Concorde's centre of gravity; another question was whether the Bristol/Rolls-Royce Olympus engine could be developed on schedule.

Based on information supplied to the President's Advisory Committee and other data obtained by NASA, augmented by wind-tunnel tests, the Langley analysis was regarded by the Americans as the best Concorde information available outside the Anglo-French design team. The Director of Aeronautics Research and Engineering at the Pentagon went so far as to claim that it was 'maybe better than theirs'.

Design revisions had also set the Concorde programme back as much as two years and development costs were spiralling (estimated at $400 million for the British share in November 1964). A NASA analysis of the Concorde 'optimistically' estimated that Concorde direct operating costs would be 1.4 cents per seat-mile – compared with 1.0 to 1.1 cents per seat-mile for the subsonic Boeing 707. Califano also indicated that Concorde's performance would probably further deteriorate.

Airline assessments of Concorde were also were fed into the deliberations of the US federal agencies and the President's Advisory Committee. At a meeting of the committee in May 1965, members discussed how information on Concorde

One of the wooden Concorde mock-ups built was placed on display at the 27th Paris Air Show. The relationships between the individual component parts of an assembly could often be better understood by seeing the items 'in the flesh' rather than on a drawing or sketch. An overall impression of the finished article can also be gained from observation and comparison with a scale replica. In the days before computer-aided design and 3D graphics, the construction of engineering models and mock-ups was commonplace. *(Simon Peters Collection)*

should be obtained. 'We have talked many times about gathering information on the Concorde,' McNamara complained to the meeting, 'but we have not evolved any systematic way of doing it.' He promptly laid down the procedure: the FAA administrator would submit regular status reports on both the American and foreign SST programmes, drawing on information from the CIA, the Defense Intelligence Agency and NASA, as appropriate.

At the end of 1964 only the strongest SST proponents, including Halaby and potential SST contractors like Lockheed, even bothered stressing the danger of Concorde success. Both SST proponents and sceptics in the US also continued their long-standing aversion to joint SST development with the Europeans. In 1965, the Americans squashed a new feeler by the British and French for co-operation and, according to the French, for 'dividing the world SST market' between the US and the Europeans.

On 3 December 1964, the White House daily diary of President Johnson recorded:

Announced today on the recommendation of the President's Advisory Committee on Supersonic Transport he has directed the Administrator of the Federal Aviation Agency to extend the current contracts of the engine and airframe manufacturers so that they can continue to study the problems associated with airframe and engine on a commercial supersonic transport.

American Disdain for the Europeans

The generally disdainful American view of Concorde and the European effort was expressed at the PAC meeting on 30 March 1965, when CIA Director John McCone, in presenting the current intelligence on Concorde – paying careful attention to noting that the CIA had not used 'clandestine sources' because of the 'risk of offending one of the host countries' – minimised Concorde's accomplishments. He reported that little European work seemed to have been done on the sonic-boom problem and that extensive design modifications and economic uncertainties would surely cause further delays. This is particularly surprising considering the myriad of papers presented in the late 1950s and early 1960s originating from Europe that particularly highlighted the sonic-boom concerns.

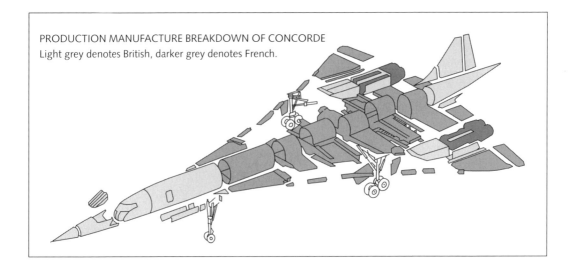

PRODUCTION MANUFACTURE BREAKDOWN OF CONCORDE
Light grey denotes British, darker grey denotes French.

McCone went on to remind the PAC-SST members that as one moved gradually upward from the Mach 1.5 to the Mach 2 range unexpected technical problems were bound to arise, and these would take time to correct. He was not at all worried about Concorde's alleged two-to-three-year lead, and suggested at any rate that Anglo-French forecasts be taken 'with a grain of salt … quite a large one'. Halaby, of course, disagreed. He noted that Concorde had already won significant airline commitment (in addition to BOAC and Air France, a total of forty-eight delivery positions had been reserved by other airlines), that the Concorde managers 'think they will muddle through' and that, in any case, Concorde 'was not another Comet'.

John Alexander McCone was an American businessman and politician, born in San Francisco, California, in 1902, who served as Director of Central Intelligence during the height of the Cold War. He graduated from the University of California, Berkeley in 1922 with a BSc in Mechanical Engineering, beginning his career in Los Angeles' Llewellyn Iron Works. He rose swiftly and in 1929, when several works merged to become the Consolidated Steel Corporation, he became executive vice-president. Most importantly, he was chairman of the US Atomic Energy Commission from 1958 to 1961, and then was the Director of the CIA until 1965.

According to journalist Seymour Hersh, in December 1960, while still Atomic Energy Commission chairman, McCone revealed CIA information about Israel's Dimona nuclear weapons plant to *The New York Times*. Hersh writes that John F. Kennedy was 'fixated' on the Israeli nuclear weapons programme and appointed McCone CIA Director in part because of his willingness to deal with this and other nuclear weapons issues – and despite the fact that McCone was a Republican.

He was a key figure in the Executive Committee of the National Security Council (EXCOMM) during the October 1962 Cuban Missile Crisis. In the famous 'Honeymoon' telegram of 20 September 1962, he insisted that the CIA remain imaginative when it came to Soviet weapons policy towards Cuba, as a 19 September National Intelligence Estimate had concluded it was unlikely that nuclear missiles would be placed on the island. The telegram was so named because McCone sent it while on his honeymoon in Paris, accompanied not only by his bride but by a CIA cipher team as well!

McCone's suspicions of the inaccuracy of this assessment proved to be correct, as it was later found the Soviet Union had followed up its conventional military build-up with the installation of Medium Range Ballistic Missiles (MRBM) and Intermediate Range Ballistic Missiles (IRBM), sparking off the crisis in October when they were later spotted by the CIA's Lockheed U-2 surveillance flights.

McNamara strongly backed McCone, calling his review 'a very interesting report, the best we have had so far'. McNamara argued that the American SST should be a profitable commercial venture and that the pace of Concorde work should not dictate American SST development. Again, this was a classic case of McNamara at work – reducing everything to numbers at the expense of everything else. He suggested that the US would ultimately build a better SST; there was therefore no need to worry about Concorde's lead.

McNamara was also receiving economic evaluations that supported his scepticism about Concorde from an SST economics task force that he, as Secretary of Defense, had recently established in the Pentagon in early 1965. This group was headed by Stephen Enke, a respected economist and another Concorde sceptic. The estimates of the task force gave Concorde only a minor market niche, and Enke was convinced that it would have a hard time keeping up with the American competition. Anglo-French dates for commercial Concorde operation were termed as being 'patently unrealistic'. The British and French were inexperienced at sustaining Mach 2.0 speeds. One task force member noted, 'The American SST has great growth potential, the Concorde almost none.' According to Enke's group, there was still no need for an accelerated American SST programme.

Enke widened his intelligence network by enlisting the help of John S. Meadows, a civil air attaché in the American Embassy in London, sending him a long list of questions. Enke went on to suggest that Meadows and his opposite number in Paris might get together in order to 'piece together a reasonable facsimile of the truth'. Enke also made reference to David Henderson, the chief economist at the British Ministry of Aviation and noted Concorde critic.

Henderson was to visit Enke and his Pentagon colleagues in Washington to evaluate both Concorde and the American SST. This visit seemed a godsend to McNamara – here was an opportunity to 'stretch out' the Concorde programme so that the USA could continue its own aims in a more orderly and economical manner. Perhaps Henderson could be 'fed' selected information that would prove disquieting and therefore slow the European programme down.

4

Pressure to Cancel – and a Pause?

Over the years there have been conflicting accounts of American pressure being placed in particular on British politicians to cancel Concorde. It seems that the first event involved Julian Amery, who signed the original Anglo-French agreement. As he recalled in 1976:

> Before we took the decision in cabinet, the former president of the World Bank, Mr Eugene Black, asked to see me in London – we had a bit of a talk about international monetary problems and then he went straight into an effort, a very gifted effort, to try and persuade me not to go ahead with the supersonic transport. That was in 1962. This in fact encouraged me to think if the Americans were so much against it, we'd be wise to try. We'd probably get a lead on them.
>
> Even after the Concorde agreement had been signed, we were subjected to a ceaseless barrage of advice from Washington to stop the project. Senior American ministers and officials visiting London to see the Chancellor of the Exchequer or Foreign Secretary or the Minister of Defence or the Prime Minister would, at the end of their conversations on other and larger issues, raise the question of Concorde. Without producing particular arguments, they would make the concerted point that there were very strong feelings in Washington that Britain ought to cancel it.

Whether this pressure to cancel was instigated to leave the field clear for the Americans to succeed at their own pace, or whether it was done because the removal of Concorde meant that there was no race, and therefore no need for the Americans to compete, was open to question.

However, in at least one case, according to a former British Labour minister, this was made quite explicit. Denis Healey, Minister of Defence from 1964 to 1970, recalls:

> In Washington, McNamara was equally hostile to the supersonic transport aircraft that Boeing and the Congress were pressing on him. At one point he offered me an SST disarmament pact – Washington would not support the Boeing SST if we cancelled Concorde. I told him that such a pact would be meaningless; Britain could not get out of its agreement with France, and if Congress wanted an SST the United States would build one, whatever McNamara promised.

Labour politician Denis Winston Healey, Baron Healey CH, MBE, PC (b. 30 August 1917) who served as Secretary of State for Defence from 1964 to 1970 and Chancellor of the Exchequer from 1974 to 1979.

James Harold Wilson, Baron Wilson of Rievaulx KG, OBE, FRS, PC (b. 11 March 1916, d. 24 May 1995), who was Labour Prime Minister first from 1964 to 1970, and again from 1974 to 1976.

With all this pressure being applied to them, the British took great care in keeping the French informed of these developments. Sir Pierson Dixon, British Ambassador in Paris, was told, 'It is important that the French should not hear of this conversation from some other source, and suspect that the Anglo-Saxons have been ganging-up on them.'

By their 5 May 1965 meeting, the PAC members, including a defeated Halaby, appeared even less troubled than before by Concorde and were more confident of the American SST's ultimate success. McNamara, in his usual two-faced way of appearing to support the programme but at the same time sabotaging it at every stage, predicted that the American SST would be 'far more successful commercially than the Concorde' but stated at the same time that the US need not feel the pressure of a 'crash' Concorde effort. The FAA therefore failed to use the spectre of Concorde competition to speed up the American programme.

A Pause?

With the new Labour government in the UK under Prime Minister Harold Wilson, the whole Concorde project came under review – along with the distinct possibility that Britain would pull out. However, the Anglo-French agreement contained no cancellation clause, and the fear of being sued for heavy damages by the French in the International Court of Justice at The Hague was to lead to Britain's reluctant continuation of the programme.

There was also the possibility that transatlantic collaboration might be on the cards again – Marc Jacquet, the French Minister of Transport, floated the idea of an Anglo-French approach to the US in an off-the-record manner during conversation with Roy Jenkins, Harold Wilson's new Minister of Aviation. At a meeting of the Cabinet's Economic Development Committee on 16 November 1964, Jenkins presented a discussion paper offering five options: unilaterally break the treaty; propose an alternative £3 million research programme; renegotiate the agreement to cover only the development of two prototype aircraft; suggest bringing West Germany and Italy into the Concorde programme; and propose a joint approach to the US for a tripartite project, as suggested by Jacquet.

In a Foreign Office telegram of background instructions to Sir Pierson Dixon accompanying a formal aide-memoire intended for the French foreign minister, the Ambassador was told that ministers were attracted by Jacquet's idea of an approach to the US but, as usual in the strange world of international politics where you never trusted anyone – especially the French – he was warned of a possible ulterior motive:

There is, of course, a danger that in dropping hints about a joint Anglo-French approach to the Americans, the French are baiting a trap for us. If we propose such a move formally they may take it (quite wrongly) as confirmation of their suspicions that we and the Americans have been up to something. Nevertheless, the risk must be accepted.

The telegram continued that the advantages of reaching an understanding with the US on a more sensible approach to the supersonic era were obvious.

Accordingly, Britain suggested that if the French government agreed on a joint approach to the US, possible proposals could include American participation in the construction of two Concorde prototypes and further development and production, a US agreement to slow up the development of a Mach 3 SST, and a British and French share in development of the American SST.

Whatever Jacquet may have indicated off the record, the official on-the-record response from Paris was muted. The French government did not reject the idea of a joint approach to the Americans but insisted that Britain and France should make it clear that the Concorde programme would continue whether or not any joint approach bore fruit. Despite considerable doubts on Concorde economics, Britain concurred, and in January 1965 Prime Minister Wilson and President Georges Pompidou confirmed the continuation of the programme. It was left to Jenkins and Jacquet to pursue the attempt to forge an agreement with the USA.

Halaby was closely following the Anglo-French discussions on Concorde after the Labour government's election and, towards the end of November 1964, had received a report from Raymond B. Malloy, his assistant administrator for international aviation affairs. Malloy wrote that the French would prefer to go it alone – if they had an engine and the necessary capital. A suitable non-British engine could be obtained only from the US, while capital might come from West Germany or other European countries. The French industry could be more severely hurt than the British by cancellation. He recommended that the US government should as a matter of priority explore the degree to which it would be prepared to offer assistance to the French if the British withdrew.

Prime Minister Wilson paid his first official visit to President Johnson in Washington on 16–18 December 1965. Defence, foreign policy and economic policy were the main items on the agenda, but as Najeeb Halaby pointed out in a prior memo to the president, the British might well suggest an Anglo-American or tripartite review of the need for and timing of an SST. Halaby strongly advised the president not to become involved in Concorde discussions: 'There is now no basis for our agreement to collaborate on the construction of any supersonic transport.'

Neither side raised the SST issue at the Wilson-Johnson talks, but Halaby informed the White House in January that it was to be raised the following month at a tripartite ministerial meeting in London. Roy Jenkins had proposed that he, Halaby and Marc Jacquet should 'discuss the possibility of an agreement on rate of progress on the US SST and the Concorde' and Jenkins had stated that he felt agreements to delay volume production until more experience was available would benefit both aircraft.

This tentative suggestion by Roy Jenkins of what was termed 'time-phasing' – that the Americans and Europeans might agree on schedules for the two machines in the interests of avoiding a race – was to be picked up and looked at throughout the second half of the 1960s.

In November 1964, in a follow-up letter to their 1963 report, Black and Osborne came up with a more drastic suggestion: a development moratorium. They suggested that both sides should pause their SST programmes so as to refine their studies and obtain better information on costs and environmental effects. In the US, studies had shown widely differing cost estimates, while Concorde cost estimates had risen substantially. Nobody thought that a supersonic race was a good idea, but there were the problems of national pride and of the special interests of the national aircraft and engine industries. Hence a revised version of the Black-Osborne proposals:

a. That the United States, Great Britain and France reach an inter-governmental agreement to stretch out the SST development and construction period for an agreed period and consequently not now to fund the heavy costs of pre-production and prototype construction which now faces the Concorde nations, as well as the United States.

b. A technological undertaking with Britain and France devoted to the problems of the sonic boom, airport and community noise levels and all the other new phenomena which will be met with supersonic flight at altitudes never before used by commercial aircraft.

c. A further period wherein our government will underwrite a series of improvement studies in the aircraft and engine industries designed to lower still further the direct operating costs, further improve flight characteristics, and more nearly reach a period when there will be more protracted and definite flight experience with the variable geometry wing and the double delta configurations.

Parts of the first Concorde – designated 001 – seen under construction at the Sud-Aviation factory at St Martin-Tolouse in March 1966. *(Simon Peters Collection)*

Black and Osborne emphasised that they were not recommending that the SST programmes should be abandoned, but the heavy additional costs faced by the Concorde project and the lack of knowledge in important areas within the whole SST field pointed to a temporary slowdown:

It also seems to us that our own current budgetary requirements and Britain's economic situation may well coincide with the need to slow down what has tended to become an uneconomic pressure to the SST program. To have a billion-dollar failure in Europe or the United States would serve nobody; a sensible delay appeared to be in order.

After such a hiatus, we can both proceed to the construction of prototypes and production aircraft if we will, and compete for the markets of the world on the basis of the excellence of our respective aircraft.

PREMIER VOL : 28 FEVRIER 1968
RESTE ■ MOIS POUR SA REALISATION
CONCORDE Prototype 001

In a wide-ranging report published in April 1965, Enke posted the question: 'How can the US best counter Concorde?' He answered his own question by suggesting that it could be done by not engaging in a race. The DoD consultant went on to say that crash-development programmes would be costly, and that the airlines were in no hurry to operate SSTs. Psychologically, the US appeared to be responding to foreign programmes; he thought it would be far better first to determine what was in America's own best interests and then influence foreign competition. Enke went on to consider three possible countermoves the United States could make. First, a 'gentlemen's agreement' with France and Britain on deferred dates for first flights of airline prototypes – as already suggested by Roy Jenkins – and possibly on dates of first deliveries to airlines. Second, the US government could prevent US airlines from purchasing Concorde – or any airline from operating it into and out of the USA.

Enke cold-bloodedly suggested that the use of US airports by Concorde might even be delayed pending further sonic-boom tests 'with these being completed "satisfactorily" shortly before airline operation of the US SST commences'. It was also quite possible that US import duties might be imposed if the Concorde sales price reflected British and French subsidies. Third, but something that was an extreme measure that could well involve major international reactions, Enke admitted that the USA might aim to detach Britain from its agreement with France.

The President Explains ...

President Johnson was fielding questions from the press at a somewhat rambling and very idiosyncratic news conference on 17 June 1965:

> The Russians have made considerable advances in that field. We watched them with interest and we are glad they have been successful.
>
> The French and the British have made rapid strides in that field and as you know it won't be long before they have their plane ready. We have carefully studied it and tested the sonic boom and other things necessary. I told the committee of the Vice President, the Secretary of the Treasury, Mr Webb, Mr McNamara, Mr Halaby and others – we are going to build it if the Congress gives us some money. We want the best plane and we want one the airlines will buy, so, therefore, it must be a sizeable undertaking involving hundreds of millions – over a billion dollars for the first plane – and it has got to be at a price they will buy and can use to haul people 2,000 miles an hour, or however fast it goes – 2,200 some of them. The Russian, I think, is 1,600.
>
> To do that we have got to get the best brains in this country who know how to build a plane, and that is not a civil service worker or ex-governor or even manager of an airport.
>
> So, Mr McNamara and the Secretary of the Treasury – because of the balance of payments we want these people to buy our planes instead of buying abroad – Mr McCone worked with us because of his experience in business before he left; Mr Webb because of the NASA interest. And we looked to try to get the best man in the United States without regard to politics, without regard to anything, and we think we got the best man in the United States. His name is 'Bozo' McKee.
>
> He was the head of Wright Field, he was a procurement expert, and Mr McNamara said he has been on a good many different sides with him and against him, but he considered him the best man. Mr Webb grabbed him up for the space program – he is 50 and some odd years and he has an $8,000 retirement – and so he got him and sent him to some of his NASA centers to give

expert advice on procurement and building and construction, because that is his business. He built a lot of airplanes. He was in charge of Wright Field.

I called him one morning at 7.30 – they agreed he was best and I said, 'What are you doing?' And he said he didn't have his britches on. And I said, 'Get them on and come on up.' I asked him to take this job and he said he didn't like the idea of being tied down and looked forward to a vacation. I said he could have it after he gave us air supremacy, and if he could do it after 2 or 3 years he could go back to Palm Springs or Nassau. And like most men trained by West Point and Annapolis, or whatever, he said, 'If that is what the Commander in Chief wants me to do I will do it.' ('I have been separated from my wife in three wars' – that was Maxwell Taylor who was separated from his wife.) I asked Mr McKee to do the job. But they had gotten into an argument with General Quesada – former Administrator, Federal Aviation Agency – and they had put a provision in the act that the head must be a civilian. The head or deputy is a general but he is not going to build a transport. We want the man to head it and be responsible for it, and we asked the Congress – as you do in extreme cases – to permit this man to move over from NASA, where he didn't have to be confirmed, to FAA at the same salary.

He kept his $8,000 retirement and got the job, whatever it pays – 28 or 30. So, we sent the bill up there and Congressman Harris had been against the General because of the problem with General Quesada. But he thought it was merited, and I called him down in Arkansas and he said we ought to get the best man.

But he is the most experienced and he is the best now. The bill has passed the House overwhelmingly. Only one Democrat voted against it. It is in the Senate. It is up today and I hope, as I speak, the roll is called on it and I hope McKee will take that job. And I told him we want him to go full steam ahead, around the clock, until we obtain the best plane at the best price that was achievable.

In Bristol, part of the centre fuselage is wheeled out for testing. *(BAC)*

At the swearing-in ceremony for General McKee held at 11.27 a.m. in the Cabinet Room at the White House on 1 July 1965, Lyndon Johnson shed more light on the proceedings:

> This is a ceremony of more than usual significance. It is one of the relatively rare occasions when a native of the State of Texas is leaving the Government voluntarily. I hope that none will regard that as an ominous link in an ominous chain.
>
> Jeeb Halaby gave up the quiet, everyday pleasures of being a test pilot to face the perils and the dangers of bureaucratic life in Washington. But every passenger who flies across this country in a plane owes him a deep debt of personal gratitude. In 4 years of dedicated, tireless service he has done much to assure public confidence in the safety of air travel.
>
> By the inspiration of his vigorous leadership, he has greatly advanced the performance of the fine agency that he has headed. And certainly Mr Halaby has won a place in history as the first regulator – in my memory – to fine himself for violating one of his own regulations. I am grateful to him for his willingness to serve his country by remaining in his post at great personal sacrifice for many months, and I wish him every success ahead.
>
> Now the man who takes the direction of the FAA today leaves the perils and the dangers of retirement to resume the quiet, everyday pleasures of an 18-hour workload. Don't know whether it is more politic to call him 'General', or 'Mister', or 'Bill', but whatever the title of the man, I know that every knowledgeable person in this Government and out of it calls 'Bozo' McKee the best man for the important job that I am assigning him this morning.
>
> You know without my repeating it what that assignment is. It is to develop a supersonic transport which is, first, safe for the passenger, second, superior to any other commercial aircraft, and third, economically profitable to build and operate.
>
> All about the man and about his record, I think, is conclusive evidence that he is the man to direct this effort. I am very proud to have him aboard. And in that connection, I have this announcement to make.
>
> I have received the second interim report of the President's Advisory Committee on Supersonic Transport. This Committee has conducted an intensive appraisal of the status of our supersonic transport program. Based on this review, the Committee members have recommended a plan of action to move the program forward at the fastest possible rate consistent with the attainment of those goals that I have outlined – that is, to develop a supersonic transport, safe for the passenger, superior to any commercial aircraft, and economically profitable to build and to operate.
>
> The Committee advises me that substantial program progress has been made within the last several months. The Committee believes there is a high degree of probability that with future work on the basic technological problems, a commercially profitable supersonic transport can be developed. It has also stated, however, that much work must be done before construction of a prototype aircraft is initiated – if the large financial and developmental risks underlying the program are to be minimized.
>
> On this basis, the Committee has recommended a substantial increase in the tempo of the program.

William Fulton 'Bozo' McKee (b. 17 October 1906, d. 28 February 1987) was appointed by President Johnson to head up the FAA, replacing Najeeb Halaby.

I have approved the Committee's five recommendations. I have directed their implementation as soon as possible. Those five recommendations might well be mentioned here and they are that:

1. The next phase of design cover an 18-month period beginning about 1 August 1965.
2. The four manufacturers – Boeing Company, Lockheed Aircraft Company, General Electric Company, Pratt & Whitney Division of United Aircraft Corporation – be invited to continue in this phase of the program.
3. The FAA Administrator be authorized to enter into contracts with the airframe manufacturers to undertake detailed airframe design work and tests over the next 18 months.
4. The FAA Administrator be authorized to enter into contracts with the engine manufacturers to construct and to test over the next 18 months demonstrator engines to prove the basic features of the engines.
5. And finally – and very importantly, Mr Magnuson – that the Congress be requested to appropriate – Mr. Mahon – the necessary funds to initiate the next phase of the program. And for this purpose I shall request an appropriation of $140 million.

The objectives of this 18-month design phase are as follows:

First, to provide a sound foundation upon which realistic estimates of operating performance and development and production costs can be based.

Second, to take advantage of the flight experience of the SR-71, the XB-70, and the variable swept wing F-111 – all of which will be extensively flown at supersonic speeds over the next 18 months.

Third, to reduce developmental risks and developmental costs while retaining the capability to accelerate the program in its later phases, depending upon the technological progress of the manufacturers.

And, fourth, to provide a basis for judgment as to the manner in which the program should proceed after the 18-month period, and to determine with much greater precision and knowledge the work that should be done in the succeeding phases of the program.

I might add here that all of the talent in the Federal Government is going to be available to the FAA Administrator in cooperating and in coordinating with him in this great job. The distinguished Secretary of Defense is going to offer counsel and assistance and facilities and resources of his Department. The distinguished Secretary of Commerce, the Secretary of the Treasury, the Space Administrator, and others, are all involved in this effort, and it is going to succeed.

The program that I have just approved represents a very significant increase in the level of our effort – and a threefold increase in the amount of funds that we are spending. We believe that the increase is clearly justified by the progress that has been made over the last 4 years and particularly by that made over the last several months under the plan of action approved last May.

The program demands much hard work and much hard thinking. As I have been since President Kennedy first asked me to chair this Committee, I am confident that this country can achieve the level of technological advance that is required to develop and produce a supersonic transport.

So, given the ability of industry and the Government and the people all working together, I have not the slightest doubt that under the predicate laid and the preliminary work done through the years by men like Jeeb Halaby, and carried through under the direction of Bozo McKee, America will proudly reach her goal in due time and on time.

Almost all the photographs from BAC and Sud-Aviation were captioned in English and French:
The Concorde static test aircraft under construction at the Hers Laboratory, Toulouse. When structural work is completed, the aircraft will be transferred to the CEAT test centre.
L'avion d'essais statiques Concorde en construction au laboratoire de l'Hers à Toulouse. Lorsque les travaux de structure seront terminés, l'avion sera transféré au centre d'essais du CEAT.

This rear fuselage section, under construction at BAC Weybridge, is part of the airframe destined for fatigue research at the Royal Aircraft Establishment, Farnborough.
Cette partie arrière de fuselage, en cours de construction à BAC Weybridge est un composant de la cellule destinée aux essais de fatigue qui seront effectués au RAE à Farnborough. (BAC)

Halaby Leaves Office – and Makes a Point

The outgoing Halaby was not leaving without one final try at urging a faster pace of development. In a memo to Johnson he argued that the selection of companies to build prototypes should begin 'much sooner than the first part of 1967'. The US could not afford further delay, he insisted; that would play 'psychologically and commercially' into the hands of the French, British and Russian governments and industries. Halaby urged the president to give General McKee the authority to 'carry out an expedited program to achieve the objectives you have so wisely set'. He also pointedly urged the president to abolish the PAC by the end of the year – it seems he must have realised who the real enemy was.

The Concorde fatigue test specimen in the structures laboratory at the Royal Aircraft Establishment, Farnborough, being raised to enable a dummy undercarriage to be installed and the temporary assembly jigs to be removed. *(BAC)*

Najeeb Halaby had placed his dissent on record; he could not agree that a delay of three years could be tolerated without jeopardising the market for the US SST, and the United States could not safely assume that France and the United Kingdom would fail in their challenge to US leadership. Throughout 1966 the PAC was faced with a basic dilemma: to what extent should the timing of the American SST programme reflect the development pace of Concorde? And if the Concorde timing was relevant – despite the no-race arguments, it clearly was highly relevant in market terms – how credible were the announced Concorde target dates? Conflicting intelligence and conflicting opinions somehow had to be accommodated, against a background of a widening gap between the FAA, who favoured a 'fastest, soonest' programme, and the Department of Defense, who cautioned that all options should be checked and double-checked before proceeding.

Somewhat surprisingly, no one really questioned why Defense – a department of the US government with no direct interest in operating a supersonic transport – had emerged as the most influential agency in shaping the US effort. The basic

reason for this was President Johnson's unswerving trust in and high opinion of Robert McNamara. For whatever reason, Johnson does not appear to have been aware of what was going on behind the scenes with McNamara attempting to kill the entire project off. Najeeb Halaby was later to refer to the 'paralysis by analysis' of the SST programme that occurred in the later days of the Johnson administration. 'As inspiration yielded to calculation, the greatest calculator of them all was Bob McNamara, and with a very bright, aggressively analytical Joe Califano at his side, he had maximum authority and minimum responsibility for diagnosis and dissection of the SST program.'

Despite all that Halaby said, the PAC-SST committee, under the chairmanship of Robert McNamara, was to stay in business, and in control, until September 1968.

Indeed, in March 1966, McNamara asserted his authority by advising General McKee of the view of a group of PAC-SST members, including those of the chairman. The US SST programme should be scheduled at an optimal rate to provide a safe aircraft as soon as possible that would be profitable to its developers, manufacturers and operators. The pace of the programme should not depend on an uneconomic desire to race Concorde into commercial service.

Enke Fact-Finds

In 1965 and 1966 Stephen Enke made two fact-finding visits to Europe in order to decide for himself the status and prospects of Concorde. In May 1965 he had suggested to the McNamara committee that both the US and the Concorde partnership had much to gain from slowing the SST race.

Several kinds of mutually advantageous arrangements were conceivable, 'or the US might detach the UK from the consortium by offers of subcontracting work on the US SST'.

The following month he flew to Britain for talks with BAC at Bristol and the Ministry of Aviation in London, gaining the impression that the British officials were very worried about the expected US competition. 'Although never openly suggested, a possible deal was in the air ... At present the two countries may unknowingly and unnecessarily be on a collision course.'

A few months later, Enke was again telling that message and also seeking wider backing within the executive branch. There was an urgent need to limit wasteful SST competition through formal agreements with Britain and France, he told the Bureau of the Budget and the State Department Policy Planning Council, but admitted that there was hardly any support within the McNamara committee for a Concorde deal.

In January 1966, Enke, by then a deputy assistant secretary of defense, flew over to Europe for further talks in Paris and London. 'Some French and British officials want a deal on the Concorde,' he told McNamara. The core of his message was:

1. A significant number of influential government officials in France and especially in Britain appeared anxious to reach some agreement with the US to rationalise competition in commercial supersonics.
2. The keenest interest was in 'time phasing'.
3. Robert Vergnaud, the principal French official on Concorde, still appeared interested in a division of the market, with the Anglo-French team concentrating on a medium-range machine and the US on long-range SSTs.
4. Any negotiations by the Americans would have to be conducted jointly with France and Britain. Britain was a reluctant partner in the Concorde

enterprise, and 'a weak flank that can be exploited indirectly', but any
attempt to detach the UK from the Concorde venture was now unrealistic.
5. A pretext existed for continuing the dialogue at the ministerial level, but it
   was questionable whether the FAA could best represent the total interests of
   the US.

In his detailed account of his talks in Paris and London, Enke was blunt in
reporting his impressions. In Paris, at a dinner hosted by Stanley M. Cleveland,
Minister for Economic Affairs, at the American Embassy, General R. Le Camus
of the French Ministry of Defence accused the Americans of trying to destroy the
French and European aircraft industries. Enke retorted that it was true only that
the Anglo-French and US SST programmes seemed to be on a collision course and
increasing speed; was it really necessary that someone be hurt?

Though the time-phasing issue continued to be examined, the discussions
proved inconclusive. Eugene Black raised the topic in London with James
Callaghan, the British Chancellor of the Exchequer; and both Black and Osborne
continued to provide useful informal channels for the exchange of SST ideas
between Washington and London. Robert McNamara's view, however, remained
unchanged: America should make no move to propose a transatlantic agreement
to rationalise SST competition, for it would probably be impossible to reach any
such agreement that would benefit the USA.

American unease over the European SST refused to go away, and renewed
concern began to grow during the latter half of 1965. This development was due to
a genuine worry about Concorde as a threat to American aviation interests and to
a reinvigorated FAA lobbying effort to influence PAC members that was directed
by two air force generals: William McKee, the new FAA administrator, and Jewell
Maxwell, the new director of the SST programme.

Regular reports continued to chronicle Concorde and Tu-144 progress over the
next few years. In October 1965, a Concorde intelligence summary reported that
management of the programme was 'operating smoothly', which doubtless would
have surprised the British and French programme managers at the time.

The techniques used for acquiring useful intelligence ranged from sophisticated,
covert means of dark-art spying by the CIA to reading public material that
appeared in the aviation press, and simple observation – an example of that
coming from Bernard J. Vierling, Maxwell's deputy in the FAA SST office. Vierling
provided a list of questions prior to a visit to the BAC plant at Bristol. One of these
was: 'Request to look at a representative part such as a bulkhead on premise of
looking at type and thickness of structure. Count number of same bulkheads that
are available. This may show us how many airplanes are committed.'

In March 1967, the CIA Directorate of Intelligence produced a special twelve-
page report on the European SST called 'The Supersonic Transport Race: The
European Side' as part of its weekly reviews. This was followed in May of the same
year by a top-secret intelligence memorandum entitled 'New Evidence on the
Soviet Supersonic Transport'.

What Were the Soviets Doing?

Whilst it is understandable how the CIA could gain access to information in the
west, the level of detail contained in the report on Soviet activities is impressive.
Although to this day both reports are still heavily 'sanitized', as the CIA Historical
Review Program calls it, the document on the Tu-144, complete with 'sanitized
areas' reads thus:

Recent information indicates that the USSR is pressing development of the Tu-144 supersonic transport (SST) with some urgency.

Engine tests in February suggest that a stage has been reached consistent with a first flight in late 1967 or the first half of 1968. Because prestige and propaganda are undoubtedly key elements in the Soviet SST program, the USSR can be expected to make every effort to have the first flight precede the initial flight of the Anglo-French SST (scheduled for late February 1968), thus giving the Soviet Union 'the world's first SST'. A first flight in late 1967, if it can be accomplished, would have great appeal to Soviet leaders in connection with celebration of the 50th anniversary of the Bolshevik Revolution. Even if the SST is not ready for flight, the USSR may be able to announce the completion of the first prototype by that time. It is almost certain, however, that the Tu-144 will not appear at the Paris Air Show in late May or early June.

The report went on to state:

The SST engines are being developed by the Kuznetsov Design Bureau in Kuybyshev, and it is likely that the prototype aircraft will be produced at Kuybyshev Airframe Plant No.18. The completed prototype should be detectable ... before it is flown in public.

The NK-144 engine for this aircraft was being tested in Kuybyshev in February 1967 and, although the exact stage of development is not entirely clear, a degree of urgency was indicated. Kuybyshev is the location of both the Kuznetsov Special Design Bureau (OKB), which is developing the NK-144 engine, and

Supposedly taken inside the Kuybyshev Airframe Plant, one of the Tu-144 fuselages comes together. The cut-out on the top of the fuselage just to the rear of the cockpit suggests this is the location of the two retractable canards fitted to production machines. *(Simon Peters Collection)*

Bench-testing
an Olympus 593
Concorde engine
and afterburner
assembly at
SNECMA at
Melun-Villaroche.
(SNECMA)

Aircraft Engine Plant ... the only known producer of the Kuznetsov engines. In
addition, Kuybyshev Airframe Plant ... is believed to be the most likely site for
the construction of the Tu-144 prototypes.

Recent unconfirmed information in a Czechoslovak aviation publication had
provided data on the size and passenger complement of the Tu-144. The length
of the aircraft reportedly is about 194ft, wingspan about 89ft and a wing area of
5,700ft. The large wing area is in sharp contrast to the figure of 3,860ft specified
for Concorde, and denotes a Soviet design concept of low wing loading, favorable
for take-off and landing and for subsonic flight in general. The passenger
complement is given as 145, an increase of 24 over the previously announced
Soviet figure of 12 ... it is possible that the larger figure may represent high-
density seating in an aircraft somewhat larger than Concorde.

In the section 'Prospects for Initial Flight', the report stated:

> Several Soviet sources have stated unofficially that the Tu-144 will be displayed for the first time during the anniversary celebration in November 1967, an appropriate occasion for the initial public display of the SST in flight, if it can be accomplished; or the announcement of completion of the first prototype, even if it was not yet ready for flight.
>
> The fact that Western electrical equipment ordered for the Tu-144 prototypes is scheduled to be delivered in July is consistent with a first flight in late 1967 or early 1968, and the urgency associated with the engine tests indicates that the program is on a tight schedule. In addition, a Western businessman remarked in a message of 19 April that Professor Tupolev is very concerned about time scale for development and delivery of prototypes. This ... cannot be firmly associated with the SST program – it could refer to another Tupolev aircraft – but it is possible that the Tu-144 is the aircraft concerned.
>
> A first flight by the Tu-144 in late 1967 or early 1968 would give the USSR a legitimate claim to 'the world's first SST' – the Anglo-French Concorde is not

Positioning a French-built wing/fuselage section on the fatigue specimen assembly jig at BAC Filton, near Bristol. *(BAC)*

scheduled to fly until late February 1968 – and this is believed to be a major goal of the Soviet SST program. Officials of Aeroflot, the Soviet state airline, have indicated a requirement for only 10 or 20 of these aircraft, and the USSR has not made significant efforts to promote the sale of the Tu-144 in the West. Because the production of such a small number of these aircraft cannot be justified solely on commercial grounds, it seems clear that prestige and propaganda are key elements in the Soviet SST program.

Although the Tu-144 is being widely publicized – the Soviet display at Expo 67, for example, includes a 12-meter model of the aircraft – Soviet officials have stated that the Tu-144 will not be shown at the Paris Air Show this spring (26 May–4 June). In addition, the evidence indicating that tests of the thrust reverser were just beginning in late February virtually excludes the possibility that the Tu-144 would be ready for even a last-minute appearance at Paris. This aircraft will require at least two or three months of preflight preparation, including checkouts of the numerous and complex aircraft subsystems, final engine tests, and taxi trials. Even if the engines were ready for installation by the end of March and the final assembly of the first prototype was completed in April, for example, it would be at least June or July before the aircraft was ready for its first flight, thus excluding the possibility of an appearance in Paris.

It is probable that the existence of a completed prototype will be detected before the aircraft is flown in public ... In addition, much of the extensive preflight work must be carried out in the open, and the aircraft might be sighted even before it was ready for flight.

Kuybyshev Airframe Plant ... which has been a major producer of Tupolev aircraft, is believed to be the most likely site for the construction of Tu-144 prototypes. Prototype aircraft usually are produced at a plant closely associated with the designer's OKB, and the other plants with recent Tupolev associations are involved in programs that make the concurrent production of Tu-144 prototypes unlikely. Plant No.18 is one of the largest airframe plants in the USSR and would have adequate facilities for the construction of Tu-144 prototypes in addition to the limited production and modification programs for other aircraft now in progress. The location in Kuybyshev of the Kuznetsov OKB and Aircraft Engine Plant No.Z4 also favors the selection of Plant No.18 for the production of the Tu-144 prototypes.

The report closed with an aerial photograph of the Kuybyshev Airframe Plant 18, dated December 1959, almost certainly taken during one of the U-2 overflights that peaked with the shooting down of Francis Gary Powers.

More CIA Reports

The earlier 17 March 1967 report, 'The Supersonic Transport Race: The European Side', was marked 'Secret: No Foreign Dissem', meaning that is was not to be released to foreign governments. It also explained about special reports and supplements to the Current Intelligence Weeklies issued by the Office of Current Intelligence:

The Special Reports are published separately to permit more comprehensive treatment of a subject. They are prepared by the Office of Current Intelligence, the Office of Research and Reports, or the Directorate of Science and Technology. Special Reports are coordinated as appropriate among the Directorates of CIA but, except for the normal substantive exchange with other agencies at the working level, have not been coordinated outside CIA unless specifically indicated.

The body of the report first laid out the background and then told the current status:

The Anglo-French developers of supersonic transport aircraft (SST) are in a close race with the USSR to be the first to fly a prototype. At this point it appears the Soviets could be the first to attain that goal, possibly even by the end of this year – although they apparently will not be a major competitor in the world aircraft market.

The British and French have settled some of their technical and economic differences about the joint Concorde project which had caused delays and at one time threatened to end British participation. They are now well on the way toward meeting their February 1968 target date for the initial flight of a Concorde prototype.

After the first test flights technical considerations will determine how soon the SSTs will be ready for commercial use. Both the Soviets and the British and French plan to have their respective aircraft in limited service by 1971. In the case of the Concorde, technical problems are likely to delay full service use perhaps by as much as two years or more beyond 1971.

The full scope of the technical problems likely to be encountered by a commercial airliner flying at twice the speed of sound will not be known until the SSTs are test flown. There are preliminary indications, however, that troublesome problems will be found in the operation and maintenance of the engine and the fuel system. There are also problems attendant on supersonic flight over populated areas, such as the effects of sonic boom, that have yet to be solved.

The Anglo-French Concorde – Political, as well as economic and technical, considerations have weighed heavily in decisions about the Concorde project. At the time of the program initiation in November 1962, Britain was seeking entry into the European Economic Community, and sought to demonstrate its interest by establishing other ties with the continental Europeans. The project was also expected to help upgrade the UK's slumping, state-supported aircraft industry. In late 1964 the newly installed Labor [sic] government in Britain had serious reservations about the costs of the project and seriously considered withdrawing. London still harbors doubts about the Concorde's economic viability but seems committed to seeing it through.

The French, unlike the British, have never shown any doubts. President de Gaulle views the Concorde as an important step in demonstrating the technical competence required of a major power. He sees the project as a means to enhance French prestige by proving that a European aircraft industry strong enough to survive US competition can be created.

Points of Difference – The British and French still differ considerably on important technical and economic aspects of the Concorde project. Paris advocates an all-out effort to sell as many Concordes as possible before US competition comes to bear. London, on the other hand, continues to believe that development of an expanded version of the present Concorde will be necessary to compete effectively with the larger Boeing 2707 SST.

The French believe the Concorde must be in service two and a half or three years before the US plane if it is to capture a reasonable share of the market. At French insistence, the first prototypes will be a 126-passenger version and the preproduction aircraft a lengthened 138-passenger version. The French have

Another view inside the Kuybyshev Airframe Plant, showing what is believed to be the prototype Tu-144 under construction. The open hatch in the roof of the cockpit suggests that this machine was fitted with ejector seats. *(Simon Peters Collection)*

flatly rejected any further increases in size or capacity, even though this seating capacity will be only half that of the Boeing 2707.

UK thinking follows a much more different pattern ... They want a vehicle with greater passenger capacity and more powerful engines, and believe that these technical adjustments should be made during the development and testing of the first prototypes.

The rising costs of the Concorde have also impaired cooperation between the two countries on the project. When the program was launched in 1962, its projected cost was $450 million to be shared equally between the two governments. By late 1964 when Prime Minister Wilson took office the project's anticipated costs had risen to almost $800 million. At that time London somewhat hastily informed the French it wanted to reappraise the program because of the rising costs and Britain's balance-of-payments problems, and implied it might withdraw. After a more considered review, the Labor [sic] government decided to continue to participate ... The estimated cost is now up to $1.4 billion, however, and it is clear that in any event London will continue to have doubts about the project on economic grounds.

In late 1966 the UK Treasury and the Ministry of Aviation for the second time in two years refused an inquiry into the cost-sharing arrangement between Paris and London, despite pressure from Parliament ...

If the French are concerned about the soaring costs, they have not shown it ... There has been virtually no public debate in France about pouring money into the Concorde, even thought the French Government, like the British will probably recover only a fraction of its expenditures for research and development.

The Orders Game – The developers of the Concorde are, of course, very interested in the potential market for their plane. To amortize the tooling costs alone, for example, will require sales of more than 130 aircraft. As for research and development costs, a portion of these is expected to be realized from a special levy on each plane sold. It is not known how much this levy will be, or how many planes would have to be sold before all costs could be written off.

Tu-144 CCCP-68001 – the prototype in flight being accompanied by analog-aircraft '21-11' performing the first flight. It is alleged that on the last day of 1968, 'with pilot E.V. Elyan in the cockpit and without international observers, the prototype aircraft performed the first ever flight with a duration of 37 minutes. The crew reported that the aircraft proved to be flexible and easily piloted.' (PSC Tupolev)

As of 10 March 1967, sixteen major airlines had taken options for 72 Concordes (there are at least 115 options for the Boeing 2707). The options do not commit purchasers to buy the aircraft, even after it is certified for commercial service. The most recent options, for three Concordes, were taken on 9 March by the German airline, Lufthansa. There may be other orders shortly ...

These estimates of potential sales appear overly optimistic, particularly that for 1980, especially if SST flights are restricted to over-water routes. The operation of the SSTs could be very profitable for the airlines, but this will depend on a high level of aircraft performance, and the Concorde has technical deficiencies which will have to be corrected. Many airlines have taken options on both the Anglo-French and the American SSTs, so that the comparative quality of the performance of the two planes will have a decisive impact on future sales. The Concorde project will almost certainly have to adjust its timetable if the plane is to be brought up to its optimum technical efficiency before it is turned over to the airlines.

Production Progress – Cooperation between the British and the French at the production level has gone well. The British Aircraft Corporation and France's government-controlled Sud-Aviation have formed a company to produce and market the Concorde. Britain's Bristol Siddeley, and Société Nationale d'Etude et Construction de Moteurs de Aviation (SNECMA) will produce the engine. The first prototype is being constructed in France with engines made in Britain. The first exchange of major components for the airframe was made in mid-1966 on schedule. Equally good progress is being made with the Olympus 593 engine, about a dozen of which were built last year. The French-built prototype is scheduled to be test-flown in February 1968 and to be certified for commercial service by mid-1971. At present the developers are slightly ahead of schedule. Work on the second prototype, which is being built in Britain, is about six months behind that of its French counterpart.

The projected cost of $1.4 billion is understood to cover the construction of the two prototypes, two preproduction aircraft, and two airframes for static tests, the tooling costs for these six planes, test flights up to the receipt of a certificate of air worthiness in 1971, and the construction of 80 Olympus engines. This figure also includes a contingency fund of $225 million to finance two years of further development after certification to bring the aircraft up to its full planned performance and another of $140 million to cover higher wages and other likely expenses.

Technical Problems – Technical deficiencies in the Concorde could delay completion of the project two years or more. All of the anticipated problems can probably be solved through normal engineering approaches, but the British and French have only lately begun serious study of some of these problems. If some of the deficiencies are not adequately corrected in the rush to get the plane into service, the Concorde could be an aircraft of very marginal performance requiring extensive ground maintenance time.

The initial service design is expected to contain shortcomings in range performance, in the operation of equipment, and in maintenance. The most serious of these problems are likely to involve the engine. The design changes made to date have required significantly more engine development than originally planned. The changes made to increase the thrust of the engines may mean that either the load (138 passengers) or the range (3,500 nautical miles) of the vehicle will have to be reduced. Moreover, the development of new engines with even greater thrust must be started soon, if growth versions of the presently projected aircraft are to be ready in time to meet the demand.

There is also concern that the time between overhauls of the engine will be too short. Neither France nor the UK has a lubricant that is satisfactory for more than 100 hours of operations. The Concorde is programed initially for a minimum of 500 hours between overhauls.

Another potential hazard relates to the fuel system. The French plan to use a sealant in the fuel system, which US experience shows is not satisfactory in an SST. If this sealant is used, frequent draining, cleaning, and reseating of the fuel tanks would be required to prevent serious corrosion. This type of maintenance involves difficult procedures which necessitate a great deal of ground time. This would be unacceptable to the airlines, because a high rate of utilization is necessary to make operation of the Concorde profitable.

The airframe of the Concorde will be constructed of an aluminum alloy. The French have developed a new spot welding technique that will be used along with conventional riveted and bolted construction. The aim is to develop a structure with a flying life of 45,000 hours. The partners appear to have exercised very thorough quality control in the development of the airframe. Aluminum has basic limitations, however, and in order to fly faster than the Concorde's planned speed of 1,450 miles per hour, the airframe, or at least the most vulnerable parts of it, must be constructed of a stronger metal, like titanium.

There are other potential troubles for the Concorde, as well as for the US and Soviet SSTs, the seriousness of which will not be fully determined until the prototypes are test-flown. For example, there are uncertainties about the effect of drag – the resistance to movement brought to bear on a plane by the air through which it passes; the turbulence at the altitude the SSTs are to fly will be severe. One US Air Force test pilot compared supersonic flight at 70,000ft with travel in a Greyhound bus going over a washboard road at 200 miles an hour ...

Two further problems not directly related to technical performance are sonic boom and the limitations imposed by today's airport facilities. The sonic boom caused by an SST can shatter windows and do other physical damage that go beyond mere annoyance for people on the ground. Neither Concorde partner apparently gave this problem much consideration. Each simply took eventual public acceptance for granted, until tests conducted by the US Government demonstrated the seriousness of the problems of supersonic flight over populated areas. The British are now studying the problem, but what recommendations, if any, they have come up with are not known. The British say they would be satisfied to concentrate on putting the Concorde into use exclusively on over-water routes, but the French expect the plane to be used on routes over continental Europe.

Most airports do not have all the facilities necessary to handle SSTs. The necessary landing strips, maintenance facilities, guidance systems and the like will be installed in time, but for at least a decade or so the lack of proper facilities will probably limit use of the SSTs. Airport noise will be another problem. The noise level of a supersonic plane flying at subsonic speeds is somewhat higher than that of today's largest subsonic jet airliners. The Concorde's developers believe the difference is not great enough, however, to preclude eventual public acceptance of the nuisance.

This last paragraph is somewhat puzzling. What special facilities would be needed to allow an SST to be used at an airport? Concorde was expected to fit into any normal airport landing and take-off pattern that included standard runway lengths, and it required no different 'guidance systems' to any other jet airliner. Likewise, additional maintenance facilities would be no different to that required for the introduction into service for any new machine. It is almost as if the compilers of the report were desperate to find a reason, any reason, to place obstacles in Concorde's path. The report continued:

The Soviet Tu-144 – The Soviet Union may be the first nation to fly an SST, but apparently will not be a major competitor in the world aircraft market. The Soviets have not seriously competed for options on their Tu-144. The Soviet statement that only 10 or 20 SSTs will be needed by Aeroflot, the Soviet civil airline, also suggests that the USSR does not plan to manufacture the TU-144 on a large scale.

The TU-144 prototypes will probably be unable to achieve the flight performance presently being advertised by the Soviet Union. Although the Soviets have announced that the TU-144 would have a range of 3,500 miles and a passenger capacity of 121, Western estimates indicate that the aircraft will not attain that capability. Its range may be as low as only 2,500 miles with 80 passengers, or 1,800 miles with a full load of 121 passengers.

The USSR first displayed a model of the Tu-144 in June 1965 at an international air show in Paris. This showing was followed by a propaganda campaign indicating that the USSR intends to be the first country to fly an SST. To achieve this end the Soviet aircraft industry is believed to be working to complete a prototype late this year, perhaps on the occasion of the 50th anniversary of the Bolshevik Revolution, or early in 1968. Even if the test flight is delayed until early 1968, Soviet SSTs could enter limited Aeroflot service by late 1970 or early 1971 provided the Soviets overcome the same problems that threaten to delay the Concorde's timetable. Like the developers of the Concorde,

Tu-144 with nose down, canards out, roars down the runway. The similarity to Concorde is striking. *(PSC Tupolev)*

the Soviets will not be aware of the full extent of some of these problems until their SST is test-flown.

Future Developments – The developers of both the Concorde and the TU-144 will continue to work toward getting a prototype into the air within a year. Their progress beyond that point will depend a great deal on the seriousness of the technical problems they encounter in test flights, on the extent to which corrective measures have been tentatively developed, and on the level of performance each developer will deem satisfactory for his aircraft.

The technical deficiencies will almost certainly prove formidable enough to delay certification of the Concorde beyond the target date of mid-1971. Whether the development of the TU-144 is also held up probably hinges on how well the Soviets have anticipated the expected technical deficiencies and developed possible remedies for them, a question about which very little information is available.

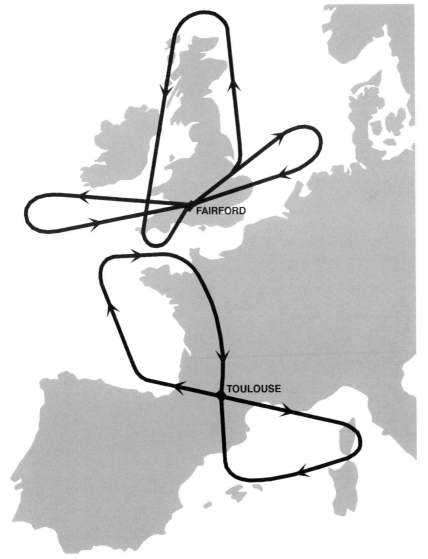

The British and the French announced their planned test routes well in advance: 001 would fly two routes out of Toulouse, while 002 had the option of flying three routes out of Fairford.

The Concorde fuselage specimen undergoing pressure tests in the big water tank at Filton. The 60ft-long specimen was submerged in 200,000 gallons of water while over 450 strain gauges measured fuselage stresses at pressures ranging from 0 to 16lb per sq. in. (BAC)

In August 1965, Enke's task force produced an important study which concluded that Concorde would displace approximately 23 per cent of the 100-odd American SSTs expected to be sold by 1985 under a sonic-boom-induced restricted route condition. The study concluded that Concorde's lower plane-mile costs – in contrast to its higher seat-mile costs – would make it more suitable for low-density routes and hours. Cheaper subsonic airfares would hurt the larger capacity American SST more than Concorde, as would route restrictions, given the resulting limited demand for SST air travel. British and French production techniques tended to be less capital intensive than American ones. It went on to say: 'The US SST needs a relatively large supersonic market – which probably means only moderately restricted routes for Concorde competition to be unimportant.'

5

A Change of Tactics

Slowly a new tactic was starting to emerge. It was beginning to look like the unthinkable may happen – that America could not or would not be able to compete with Concorde in a commercial time frame that would minimise the damage to American interests.

There were thoughts that perhaps the French – or more likely the British – could be pressured into throwing in the towel, and that would have a tremendous impact on the Concorde programme. Enke, McNamara, the Department of Defense and the FAA were not the only ones considering how the US might inhibit, damage or even stop the Concorde programme.

Disinformation

In another SST paper, Daniel J. Edwards, a US Treasury analyst, presented a plan for deliberate misinformation, which was endorsed by Dr J. Stockfisch, Deputy Assistant Secretary of the Treasury. Concorde, they reasoned, was probably more a psychological threat than an economic one, and it was time to consider making use of counter-psychological warfare on the Concorde developers:

> Public relations people might devote some of our resources to 'saying' that the United States is giving serious consideration to meeting the Concorde on entry date. This tactic could be done either without specifying the date, in which case it may actually turn out to be the truth, or, alternatively, we could state that the United States will try to make the 1970 entry date because of some unspecified technological breakthrough. Resources devoted in this manner could buy us a great deal of really precious research and development time. An announcement of a 1970 target date might be the straw that broke the Concorde 'back'. Under this pressure the Concorde people might crash their program so drastically that they would produce a very uneconomical aircraft. The Concorde people might even come running to the United States to negotiate earliest entry dates for each. If we could negotiate for earliest entry of Concorde in mid-1973 and earliest entry of the American SST for the beginning of 1975 we would gain worthwhile advantages over the Concorde, although this alternative would be a second-best. The American SST has great growth potential, the Concorde almost none. We need to consider buying R&D time in many different ways.

The Department of Defense came up with another 'avenue of attack'. In a paper called 'Overall Strategic Issues Affecting the SST Program' presented to the PAC-SST on 5 May 1965, they called for the SST 'mission' to be specified, as was the custom in military projects, before deciding whether or not to build an SST. The paper went on:

It is not clear how the US ought to respond to the Concorde; what is appropriate depends on what we are trying to do and this is not yet clearly defined. There are numerous possible responses which include use of diplomatic and economic resources to delay the Concorde to make it look less promising to the consortium, and to detach Britain from the effort. The current response resembles 'war' more than 'economics'. There has been little explicit analysis of how much the US would be willing to 'pay' for a delay or cessation of competition. Similarly, no one has analyzed what the consortium would 'pay' for a delay in US competition. An agreement might take the form of a guaranteed low Concorde price and early delivery to US airlines combined with British and French support for lower IATA [International Air Transport Association] subsonic fares and purchase of some US subsonics in return for a stretch-out or abandonment of the current US SST effort. Such agreements ought to be considered in some detail to see if there are not some which would serve the goals of the US even better than the present SST program.

The FAA was employing a well-planned and effective lobbying campaign that emphasised the Concorde threat. The agency told the PAC-SST in early October 1965 that the gap between the time of the announced Concorde commercial introduction (1971–72) and estimated American SST commercial availability

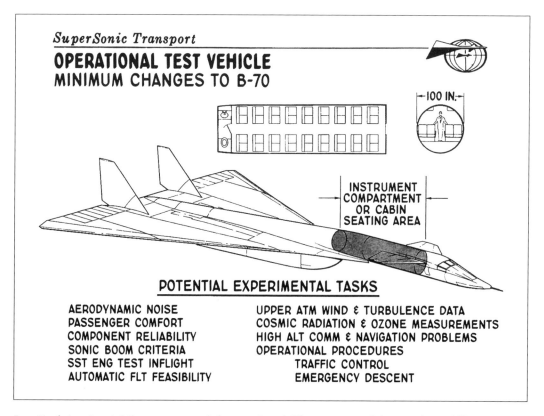

From North American Aviation came proposals for a number of different versions of the B-70 that could be used as an SST. The first was this operational test vehicle that had the compartment aft of the cockpit converted into a 100in-wide four-abreast seating area. While it was not cleared for commercial airline use, this B-70 could be involved in a number of tasks ahead of a commercial SST design. North American also proposed a number of other modifications that would allow up to seventy-six passengers to be carried by 'stretching' the fuselage somewhat. *(NAA)*

(mid-1975) was sufficient to assure an adequate market for Concorde given a reasonably economic design.

The US 'must assume that the Concorde will be a successful program', declared the FAA. The notion that Concorde might be a real future competitor assumed new credence at the 9 October PAC meeting where Osborne and Boeing (via Secretary of Commerce John Connor) reported that Concorde would actually meet its announced schedule. Media reports helped the FAA case.

Although mentioning Concorde cost increases, the aviation press also reported that the technical feasibility of every Concorde system had been

SST

Approved For Release 2000/08/16 : NLJ-007-045-3-1-~~Secret~~ 6

No Foreign Dissem

**DIRECTORATE OF
INTELLIGENCE**

The Supersonic Transport Race: The European Side

Special Report
WEEKLY REVIEW

~~Secret~~

№ 1

17 March 1967
SC No. 00761/67A

Approved For Release 2000/08/16 : NLJ-007-045-3-1-4

The cover of the CIA Directorate of Intelligence special report 'The Supersonic Transport Race: the European Side'.

'determined' and that Concorde would fly in March 1968, allegedly giving it at least a two-year edge over any competitor. Similarly, an FAA 'intelligence summary' for PAC members found the aircraft's advertised performance data was 'reasonably valid', and the development was on schedule; the Concorde's technical systems and design generally possessed 'no problems'; the aircraft's range had been extended to 4,150 statute miles with what was determined as 'adequate' fuel reserves; and, with the holding fifty total orders, airline confidence was 'rapidly increasing'.

Finally, McKee and Maxwell pressed their campaign by asking the key FAA official for Concorde matters, Raymond B. Malloy, assistant FAA administrator for Europe, Africa and the Middle East, to prepare an 'authoritative view' on Concorde's competitive position for use at the PAC meeting on 6 November 1965. Although acknowledging major problems with Concorde in several technical areas, Malloy stressed in his resulting brief the aircraft's 'high political significance as representative of the new commitment of Europe to collaborate and cooperate in order to meet the US challenge to the European aircraft industry'. According to Malloy, neither the British nor the French, especially Charles de Gaulle, would abandon Concorde, at least through the construction of two prototypes.

At the 6 November PAC meeting McKee read verbatim from Malloy's report. This FAA counter-attack, based largely on portraying Concorde as an effective rival, achieved some success. Black then spoke up in favour of establishing an earlier delivery date for the American SST. The PAC concluded in the annex to its third interim report to the president, transmitted on 15 November, that Concorde could 'prove to be a serious competitive threat', especially on low-density routes. Still, certain technical difficulties and Concorde's high operating costs per seat-mile (compared to the American SST) were also mentioned; weight increases in Concorde's configuration, from 326,000lb to about 360,000lb, indicated that the aircraft was approaching or had reached 'its limit of growth without requiring major redesign'.

Enke immediately attempted to block the FAA resurgence. In January 1966, he flew to Paris and London to meet with high-level French and British officials, ostensibly to deal with various economic and sonic-boom research problems, but really to discuss 'time phasing' – proportionately slowing down both the Anglo-French and American programmes.

He sent back less than favourable assessments of the Concorde: economic prospects were pessimistic and the airlines were not enthusiastic about the aircraft. Significantly, Enke reported that the British and French had different performance and political goals; Concorde was a matter of pride and national prestige to the French, while the British tended to view it as a price they had to pay to avoid a French veto of British membership of the Common Market. 'Great Britain,' Enke wrote, 'was the reluctant partner', with the British mood being one of 'fatalistic hopelessness that combined an awareness of financial losses ahead with a belief that little could be done about it'. He concluded that the time was ripe to explore time phasing and design differentiation with the British and French. Then, to the FAA's great dismay, his discussions and views were leaked to the British press.

The FAA quickly counter-attacked, emphasising the positive aspects of Concorde's development. It received additional favourable Concorde reviews from TWA, Lockheed and Boeing, and so began to organise and assess Concorde information systematically.

On 2 March 1966, President Johnson presented a special message to the Congress on transportation. Part of this message read:

The United States is pre-eminent in the field of aircraft design and manufacture. We intend to maintain that leadership. As I said in my State of the Union Message, I am proposing a program to construct and flight test a new 2000-mile-per-hour supersonic aircraft.

Our supersonic transport must be reliable and safe for the passenger.

It must be profitable for both the airlines and the manufacturers.

Its operating performance must be superior to any comparable aircraft.

It must be introduced into the market in a timely manner.

We have underway an intensive research and design program on the supersonic transport, supported by appropriations of $231 million.

The design competition for this aircraft and its engines is intense and resourceful.

I am requesting $200 million in Fiscal Year 1967 appropriations to initiate the prototype phase of the supersonic transport. My request includes funds for the completion of design competition, expanded economic and sonic boom studies, and the start of prototype construction.

We hope to conduct first flight tests of the supersonic transport by 1970, and to introduce it into commercial service by 1974.

It was not long before Concorde's image again began to decline in the eyes of key American decision-makers. Those that wanted to took great delight in any problem that was mentioned. The CIA reported in late March 1966 on Concorde's engine difficulties. At the PAC meeting on 6 May 1966, McNamara stated that this negative information demonstrated that although 'not a failure, the Concorde did have a few problems'. He added that lack of supersonic experience had led the British and French to underestimate the aircraft's technical difficulties. Both McCone and McNamara once more explicitly warned against letting Concorde influence American SST development.

The information on Concorde that the Americans received – from both public and private sources – was contradictory. Some of the data indicated that the aircraft was proceeding smoothly and on schedule, and the FAA particularly was more than willing to believe Concorde claims. The FAA was assisted in early July 1966 by Juan Trippe of Pan American, who told the PAC that Concorde's timetable was realistic and that its performance characteristics had improved. He pointedly added, 'Any place that we [Pan American] don't have such a ship [Concorde] covered, as more or less a loss leader for advertising purposes and so forth, we think we would be in trouble during the period after Concorde delivery.'

Again the lack of American confidence in the Concorde programme won over. The most credible US sources throughout the rest of 1966 stressed Concorde's long-term problems, such as substantial cost increases, what they saw as the Europeans' neglect of the sonic-boom issue and the likelihood of a substantial delay.

Over in Europe, progress was being made in overcoming some of the problems. The Olympus 593 had development, or 'stretch', potential, and the engine manufacturers were able to offer an increase in power sufficient to meet the first aircraft growth stage. This stage took the all-up weight from the 262,000lb of the preliminary design up to 286,000lb, and the seating capacity from 90 to 100. The first airline response to this increase was not encouraging; it was regarded as no more than a step in the right direction.

Further progress depended on greater engine power, and Bristol Siddeley and SNECMA decided on a redesign of the Olympus to provide a reserve, not only for the immediate situation but also for the future weight increases that would occur in Concorde development, as they do in every other civil aircraft programme. The new engine was given the designation 593B.

A large-scale model of Concorde undergoes testing in the low-speed wind tunnel at Filton in order to carry out research into the landing and take-off characteristics of the design. *(BAC)*

With the assurance of additional power, the redesign of Concorde could go forward. An increase was made in the wing and fin area, additional under-floor fuel tankage was provided and, to compensate for the loss of baggage space that this caused, extra space for baggage stowage was provided in the rear fuselage. This was made available by eliminating the ventral passenger door originally proposed and substituting for it a second port-side door.

These changes had the effect of increasing the maximum take-off weight to 326,000lb and passenger capacity to 118. Although development went on for much of 1964, this design was essentially the Concorde prototype design. Early in 1965 it was 'frozen' – which meant that no major changes were to be subsequently introduced – and the first metal was cut for the two prototype aircraft.

Both CIA Director McCone and McNamara once more explicitly warned against letting Concorde influence American SST development. McCone specifically did not want Concorde to force what he saw as an unhealthy telescoping of the

American effort. McNamara even went to the extreme of instructing the FAA to report any instances of where the Americans were 'doing something differently than they would do if there was no Concorde'.

Once more the basic lack of American confidence in the Concorde programme was to prevail. This was brought about not only by a US disregard of Concorde, but also because the Americans generally disparaged the entire European aviation industry. Juan Trippe spoke of the 'miserable performance in Europe compared to what we have done in this country' and admitted that Pan American's Concorde orders were nothing but 'a sort of an insurance program' to cover the airline if an American SST was delayed.

Supporting American poor opinion of European commercial aviation, CIA reports emphasised Concorde's major technical and non-technical problems, and, though acknowledging that the aircraft was currently on schedule, warned of serious future delays in its production phase. The search for solutions to technical problems, according to the CIA, could delay the programme for up to two years. In the non-technical area, the CIA dwelled on potentially fatal disagreements between the British and the French. The French, worried about the proposed American SST and unsure of their British partners, wanted to enter production quickly, and rejected a British proposal to increase Concorde passenger capacity to 167; the British, on the other hand, already doubting the aircraft's economic strength, felt that a larger machine was needed to compete with the Americans on transatlantic routes, which would require more development time. How this was to happen was never made clear by the CIA, for any size increase – let alone one that was over 50 per cent bigger – would have meant starting again with a blank sheet of paper. But then, perhaps that was the impression they were trying to create.

According to the CIA, as in Enke's earlier report, the British had 'an uneasy feeling that they were being led into a venture that could prove disastrous' and that Concorde still faced long-term difficulties, lack of good growth prospects and increasing development costs.

Enke and his group naturally continued to minimise the seriousness of the Concorde challenge, arguing that even a year's slippage in the American effort would have little impact on American SST sales. The number of 'options' held for the American SST was nearly twice the amount for Concorde, and the list included the names of several prominent operators who had not taken Concorde options.

This point did not go unnoticed. Even among those who were well disposed towards Concorde, fears were expressed that once again the pioneering would be done on one side of the Atlantic and the exploitation on the other. Those of this school of thought conceded that Concorde would be first into service, but they asked: 'Won't it soon be overtaken by the larger and faster American type? Isn't this the reasoning that has decided some very experienced operators to ignore Concorde and wait for the 2707?' There was a recent precedent – the Comet and the 707 – that gave some weight to these views, but the two situations were very different. Concorde would have a substantial lead over the American aircraft in getting into service and at the worst – from the European viewpoint – this lead would be four or five years. That was too long a time for any major airline to stay uncompetitive by keeping out of supersonic operation. Unlike the Comet 1, which was not capable of flying from London to New York nonstop, Concorde would have a nonstop transatlantic capability and would carry an economic payload. Most important of all, the productivity of the two SSTs would be so different that, when both were in service, they would each fit into a niche that the other could not fill.

Concorde would have four or five years to prove its time-saving attractions and its profitability – and to make the business traveller supersonic-minded. When the 2707 entered service on the crack routes, Concorde would be operated on the many less densely trafficked but still important routes on which the larger American aircraft would not be viable. There would be a place and a need for the two types as far ahead as one could see.

In the interval, the options arrangements had one great and lasting benefit for the Concorde manufacturers. Option-holding airlines seized the opportunity to take an active part in shaping the design. First into the field were the original three option holders: Pan American, BOAC and Air France. They set up a technical committee – speedily nicknamed the 'Troika' – to maintain liaison with the builders. All of the sixteen American option holders also formed a committee under the chairmanship of William Mentzer, President of United Airlines.

This was something without precedent in the civil aircraft business. Previously it had not been unusual for one or two major airlines to be associated with the

The cover of the CIA Directorate of Intelligence Memorandum 'New Evidence on the Soviet Supersonic Transport'. As can be seen, it was once 'Top Secret'.

development of an air-transport design, and indeed the sales of some new types had been hampered by being too closely tailored to the specific needs of a single operator. BAC and Aérospatiale could, and did, count themselves fortunate to have the advice and the constructive criticism of major airlines, making up between them a good cross-section of the international air transport market. Their co-operation was invaluable in such areas as performance and economics, noise, interior layout, product support, ground handling and servicing, maintainability and reliability.

In parallel with design work for the pre-production aircraft, building of the two prototypes – 001 at Toulouse and 002 at Filton – was going forward, although not as rapidly as had been hoped when the programme began in 1965. Some of the problems arose from the fact that this kind of Anglo-French manufacturing collaboration was something new and needed a period for bedding down. In a sense, the programme was a prototype and a forerunner of better things to come, just as the aircraft was. A great part of the delay was also caused by difficulties in getting on-time delivery of equipment and components from outside suppliers, although this was only to be expected, for many suppliers had to mount their own extensive research programmes to develop their products up to the higher standards demanded by Concorde operational requirements.

At the PAC meeting on 9 October 1966 presidential science adviser Donald Hornig added that the Concorde developers had 'sort of shut their eyes to the sonic boom problem and resigned themselves to at least having the overseas market'. Even Maxwell at the FAA admitted to the PAC that no solutions had been found for Concorde's problems; development costs and the sales price were increasing, but so were airline orders.

As the CIA also acknowledged in October 1966, Concorde did exist and was apparently on schedule. Orders had increased from fifty-four to a tentative sixty-four since August, and the project had assumed a high order of diplomatic political importance. The CIA observed:

Charles Carpenter
Tillinghast Jr
(b. 30 January
1911, d. 25 July
1998), lawyer,
businessman,
investment banker
and chairman of
Trans World Airlines.

> General de Gaulle continues to view the Concorde as an important step in demonstrating the technical competence required of a major power. He sees the project as a means, also, to enhance French prestige, particularly vis-a-vis the US and has taken a personal interest in it. The French government's determination that the project be completed, despite growing British disenchantment because of mounting costs, also stems from Gaullist assertions that France's independent foreign policy has not harmed its friendship with its allies.

As another high French official put it, 'For technological, commercial, and also political reasons, our European countries cannot allow themselves to sink to the level of mere subcontractors.'

Both the CIA and the FAA's chief official in Europe, Raymond Malloy, continued during the remainder of 1966 to stress Concorde's political and technological importance to the French for enhancing national prestige.

TWA president Charles Tillinghast was even more bullish. He told the PAC on 7 December 1966 that Concorde could indeed be a real threat, although it had lousy seat-mile economics, and that TWA would love to skip the Concorde. He maintained that if the American SST fell further behind, TWA would have no choice but to opt for the Anglo-French aircraft. Tillinghast estimated that TWA could afford at the most an eighteen-month lag, and

Just some of North American Aviation's studies for a US SST. *(North American)*

warned the PAC: 'The British and French are in. They may have been silly to have done it. They are in. They are going ahead. I think anyone who has a tendency to write off the Concorde as a lot of flop is being very unrealistic. Its economics are considerably less than sensational but it will fly; it will fly well.'

McNamara and McKee agreed at the 10 December PAC meeting that it was a fair assumption that Concorde would be produced, either through a joint Anglo-French effort or, if that should fail, by the French alone. However, even the prospect of a Concorde ultimately flying never really struck fear in the hearts of most PAC members – at least not enough fear to accelerate the SST programme. McNamara flatly declared that the US was unduly concerned and that both Concorde and the American SST were sure to face serious technical problems and resulting delays. McCone and others agreed.

The PAC's fourth and final interim report to the president emphasised the technical and economic superiority of the American SST, and observed that many aircraft development problems typically do not become apparent until the prototype stage. The committee expected significant delays with Concorde, and predicted little performance improvement, given the aircraft's small engine thrust and resulting limited range. They also claimed that Concorde's estimated direct and total operating costs were, respectively, 25 per cent and 15 per cent higher than those of the American SST and were increasing rapidly.

In 1967, following the selection of the Boeing-General Electric swing-wing model as the American SST's design at the very end of 1966, the whole US decision-making structure for the SST programme began to change.

Status of the American Designs

The Lockheed L-2000 was Lockheed Corporation's entry into the SST competition. Like Boeing, Lockheed had done a number of 'paper studies' on various SST designs, starting in 1958. They sought an aircraft with cruise speeds of around 2,000mph, with take-off and landing speeds that compared to large subsonic jets of the same era. Lockheed also desired an aircraft whose centre of pressure could be managed throughout the entire speed range. They knew a variable-geometry, swing-wing design could accomplish this goal, but felt it was too heavy; however, they preferred a fixed-wing solution. In a worst-case scenario, they were willing to design a fixed-wing aircraft using fuel for ballast.

Early designs followed Lockheed's tapered straight wing much like the type used on the F-104 Starfighter, with a delta-shaped canard for aerodynamic trim. The problem was that in wind-tunnel tests the shift in the aircraft's centre of pressure was substantial. A delta wing was substituted which alleviated a portion of the movement, but it was not deemed sufficient. By 1962, Lockheed arrived at a highly swept, bat-wing design featuring four engine pods buried in the wings and a canard. The improvement was closer to their goal, but still not optimal. By 1963, they extended the leading edge of the wing forward a bit to eliminate the need for the canard, and reshaped the wing into a double-delta shape with a mild twist and camber. This, along with careful shaping of the fuselage, was able to control the shift in the centre of pressure caused by the highly swept forward part of the wing developing lift supersonically. The engines were shifted from being buried in the wings to individual pods slung below the wings.

The new design was designated L-2000-1 and was 223ft long with a narrow-body, 132in-wide fuselage to meet aerodynamic requirements, allowing for five-abreast passenger seating in coach class and a four-abreast arrangement in first class. A typical mixed-class seating layout would equal around 170 passengers, with high-density layouts exceeding 200 passengers.

The L-2000-1 featured a long, pointed nose that was almost flat on top and curved on the bottom, which allowed for improved supersonic performance, and could be drooped for take-off and landing to provide adequate visibility. The wing design featured a sharp forward inboard sweep of 80°, with the remaining part of the wing's leading edge swept back 60°, with an overall area of 8,370sq. ft. The high-sweep angles produced powerful vortices on the leading edge which increased lift at moderate to high angles of attack, yet still retained stable airflow over the control surfaces during a stall. These vortices also provided good directional control as well, which was somewhat deficient with the nose drooped at low speeds. The wing, while only 3 per cent thick, provided substantial lift due to its large area, which, aided by vortex lift, allowed take-off and landing speeds comparable to a Boeing 707. Additionally, a delta wing is a naturally rigid structure which requires little stiffening.

The aircraft's undercarriage was a traditional tricycle type with twin-wheeled nose gear. Each of the two six-wheeled main gears utilised the same tyres used on the Douglas DC-8, but which were filled with nitrogen and at lower pressures.

To provide an optimum entry date into service, Lockheed decided to use a beefed-up turbofan derivative of the Pratt & Whitney J58. The J58 had already successfully proven itself as a high-thrust, high-performance jet engine on the

---

Two views of the mock-up of the Lockheed L-2000 SST, as revealed in the *Lockheed Star* staff magazine for 27 June 1966, showing the nose in both landing and cruise positions. The paper said, 'the 1,800mph transport will compete for world traffic supremacy in the 1970s against the British-French Concorde.' *(Lockheed Aircraft)*

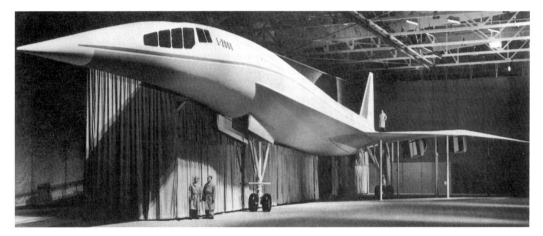

top-secret Lockheed A-12 – and subsequently on the Lockheed SR-71 Blackbird. Owing to its being a turbofan, it was deemed to be quieter than a typical turbojet at low altitude and low speed, required no afterburner for take-off and allowed reduced power settings. The engines were placed in cylindrical pods with a wedge-shaped splitter, and a squarish intake providing the inlet system for the aircraft. The inlet was designed with the goal of requiring no moving parts, and was naturally stable. To reduce the noise from sonic booms, rather than penetrate the sound barrier at a more ideal 30,000ft they intended to penetrate it at 42,000ft instead. It would not be possible on 'hot days' (usually over 80°F), but on normal days this would be achievable. Acceleration would continue through the sound barrier to Mach 1.15, at which point sonic booms would be audible on the ground. The aircraft would climb precisely to minimise sonic-boom levels. After an initial level-off at around 71,500ft, it would cruise climb upwards, ultimately reaching 76,500ft. Descents would also be performed in a precise way to reduce sonic-boom levels until subsonic speeds were reached.

By 1964, the US government issued new requirements regarding the SST programme which required Lockheed to modify their design, by now called the

L-2000-2. The new design had numerous modifications to the wing; one change was rounding the front of the forward delta in order to eliminate the pitch-up tendency. To increase high-speed aerodynamic efficiency, the wing's thickness was reduced to 2.3 per cent, the leading edges were made sharper, the sweep angles were changed from 80/60° to 85/62°, and substantial twist and camber were added to the forward delta; much of the rear delta was twisted upwards to allow the elevons to remain flush at Mach 3.0. In addition, wing/body fairings were added on the underside of the fuselage where the wings are located, allowing a more normally shaped nose to be used. To retain low-speed performance, the rear delta was enlarged considerably; to increase the payload, the trailing edge featured a forward sweep of 10°. The new nose reduced the overall length to 214ft while retaining virtually the same internal dimensions. Wingspan was identical as before, and despite the thinner wing, the increased wing area of 9,026sq. ft allowed the same take-off performance. The aircraft's overall lift-to-drag ratio increased from 7.25 to 7.94.

During the course of the L-2000-2's development, the engine previously selected by Lockheed was no longer deemed acceptable. During the time frame between the L-2000-1 and L-2000-2, Pratt & Whitney designed a new afterburning turbofan called the JTF-17A, which produced greater amounts of thrust. General Electric developed the GE-4 – an afterburning turbojet with variable guide-vanes – which was actually the less powerful of the two at sea level but produced

The interior mock-up of the Lockheed L-2000, showing the 3-2 seating. What is noticeable is the very small size of the aircraft's windows. *(Lockheed Aircraft)*

more power at high altitudes. Both engines required some degree of afterburner during cruise. Lockheed's design favoured the JTF-17A over the GE-4, but there was the risk that GE would win the engine competition and Lockheed would win the SST contract, so they developed new engine pods that could accommodate either engine. Aerodynamic modifications allowed a shorter engine pod to be used, which utilised a new inlet design. This inlet featured minimal external cowl angles and was precisely contoured to allow a high-pressure recovery using no moving parts and allowed maximum performance with either engine option. To allow additional airflow for noise reduction or to aid afterburner performance, a set of suck-in doors was added to the rear portion of the pod. To provide mid-air braking capability for rapid deceleration and rapid descents, and to assist ground braking, part of the nozzle could be employed as a thrust reverser at speeds below Mach 1.2. The pods were also repositioned on the new wing to better shield them from abrupt changes in airflow.

The additional thrust from the new engines allowed supersonic penetration to be delayed until up to 45,000ft under virtually all conditions. Since at this point the possibility of supersonic overland flight was still an option, Lockheed also considered larger, shorter-ranged versions of the L-2000-2B. All designs weighed exactly the same, with a new tail design, changes to the fuselage length, extensions to the forward delta, increased capacity and variations in fuel capacity. The largest version featured capacity for 250 domestic passengers, while the medium version featured transatlantic capability with 220 passengers. Despite the fuselage length changes, there was no appreciable increase in the risk of the aircraft pitching upwards too far (over-rotation) on take-off.

By 1966, the design took on its final form as the L-2000-7A and L-2000-7B. The L-2000-7A featured a redesigned wing and a fuselage lengthened to 273ft. The longer fuselage allowed for a mixed-class seating of 230 passengers. The new wing featured a proportionately larger forward delta, with greater refinement to the wing's twist and curvature. Despite having the same wingspan, the wing area was increased to 9,424sq. ft, with a slightly reduced 84° sweepback, and an increased 65° main delta wing, with reduced forward sweep along the trailing edge. Unlike previous versions, this aircraft featured a leading-edge flap to increase lift at low speeds, and to allow a slight down-elevon deflection. The fuselage, as a result of greater length, changes to the wing design and attempts to further reduce drag, featured a slight vertical thinning in the fuselage where the wings were, a more prominent wing/body 'belly' to carry fuel and cargo, a longer nose and a refined tail. Since the aircraft was not as directionally stable as before, it featured a ventral fin, located on the underside of the trailing fuselage. The L-2000-7B was extended to 293ft, utilising a lengthened cabin and a more pronounced upward-curving tail to reduce the chance of the tail striking the runway during over-rotation. Both designs had the same maximum weight of 590,000lb, and the aerodynamic lift-to-drag ratio was increased to 8:1.

American Designs Begin to Take Shape

A slimming down of the proposed models resulted in North American NAC-60 and Curtiss-Wright efforts being dropped from the programme, with both Boeing and Lockheed asked to offer SST models meeting the more demanding FAA requirements and able to use either of the remaining engine designs. In November, another design review was held, and by this time Boeing had scaled up the original design into a 250-seat version, the Model 733-290. Owing to concerns about jet blast, the four engines were moved to a position underneath an enlarged tailplane. When the wings were in their swept-back position, they merged with the tailplane to give a delta-wing planform.

Both companies were now asked for considerably more detailed proposals, to be presented for final selection in 1966. By then, Boeing's design was the 300-seat Model 733-390. Both the Boeing and Lockheed L-2000 designs were presented in September 1966, along with full-scale mock-ups. The Boeing SST mock-up included both overhead storage with restraining nets for smaller items, as well as large drop-in bins between sections of the aircraft. In the main 247-seat tourist-class cabin, the entertainment system consisted of retractable televisions placed between every sixth row in the overhead storage. In the thirty-seat first class area, every pair of seats included smaller televisions in a console between the seats. The windows were only 6in in diameter due to the high altitudes the aircraft flew at maximising the pressure on them, but the internal pane was 12in in diameter to give an illusion of size.

Boeing predicted that if the go-ahead were given, construction of the SST prototypes would begin in early 1967 and the first flight could be made in early 1970. Production aircraft could start being built in early 1969, with the flight testing in late 1972 and certification by mid-1974.

A lengthy review followed, and on 31 December 1966, Boeing was announced as the winner. The design would be powered by the General Electric GE-4/J5 engines. Lockheed's L-2000 was judged simpler to produce and less risky, but its performance was slightly lower and its noise levels slightly higher.

The Boeing design was considered more advanced, representing a greater lead over Concorde and thus more fitting to the original design mandate. In the

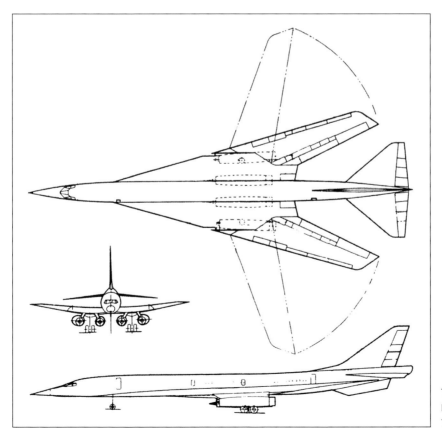

The 203ft 10in-long Boeing Model 733-197.

end, Boeing eventually changed its advanced variable-geometry wing design to a simpler delta-wing similar to Lockheed's design, but with a tail. If Lockheed had built its simpler design, it might have flown by 1971. The new Boeing design was also smaller, seating 234, and known as the Model 2707-300. Work began on a full-sized mock-up and two prototypes in September 1969, now two years behind schedule.

A promotional film claimed that airlines would soon pay back the federal investment in the project, and it was projected that SSTs would dominate the skies, with subsonic jumbo jets – such as Boeing's own 747 – being only a passing fad.

The PAC did not formally meet again after December 1966. SST decisions now became more programmatic, centring on relations with contractors and on technical problems – especially on the fact that the winning swing-wing design was not economic and on the two-year reassessment by Boeing resulting in the firm selecting a new fixed-wing SST design in 1969. High-level and wide-ranging policy discussions on such issues as overall design selection, the sonic boom, economic performance and project financing were infrequent. In the same vein, American officials began to view Concorde more passively, and discussions about its threat diminished considerably. The FAA continued to monitor Concorde's development, but the intelligence effort became less focused and more irregular, and the CIA's role diminished. In addition, the usefulness of the raw intelligence on foreign SST programmes from the CIA and the State Department was questionable, since this data usually added little to what was already known publicly.

Then, on 27 April 1967, Lyndon Johnson announced funding for an American SST:

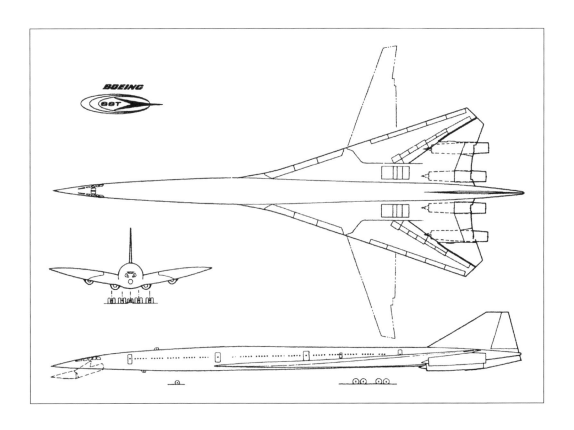

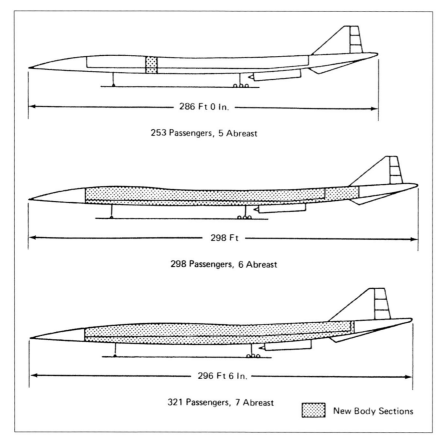

286 Ft 0 In.

253 Passengers, 5 Abreast

298 Ft

298 Passengers, 6 Abreast

296 Ft 6 In.

321 Passengers, 7 Abreast   ▦ New Body Sections

Even Boeing's own departments got mixed up as to how each design was designated – according to one of their own releases relating to the 2707 but shown with drawings of the SST: 'Aircraft range and payload requirements vary from airline to airline due to individual route and traffic conditions. The basic design of the 2707-300 airplane is such that accommodation of these varying requirements can be made through changes in the body length and width, while retaining commonality of most of the remaining components.'

Today I am pleased to announce that this Nation is taking a major step forward in the field of commercial aviation.

I am authorizing the Secretary of Transportation to sign the contracts for the prototype construction of a commercial supersonic transport. I am also sending to the Congress on Monday a request for $198 million to finance the Government's share of the next phase of the development of this transport aircraft. These funds and this action will help to bring the supersonic transport from the drawing boards into the air for prototype testing and evaluation.

This new prototype test phase is the culmination of many months of a resourceful and intensive design competition. Out of that competition two firms were selected to proceed with the development of the aircraft – the Boeing Company for the airframe, and the General Electric Company for the engines.

This project, in which I have been proud to participate, is an outstanding example of creative partnership between your Government and American industry. That partnership is evidenced by the arrangements which will carry the project through to its next phase:

• The Government will continue to share in the cost of development with industry.
• The airlines and the manufacturers will invest substantial capital in this project.

Although the promise of the supersonic transport is great, the program still carries high technical and financial risks. Industry's willingness to share those risks is a clear sign of its confidence in the program. This participation will also help assure that sound business judgments are exercised throughout the development of the supersonic transport.

With a successful program, the Government will recover its investment with interest. The taxpayers of this Nation will benefit.

The impact of the supersonic transport program will be felt well beyond our own shores. Jet aircraft have already brought the world closer to us. Commercial supersonic transports – traveling at 1800 miles an hour or even faster – will make South America and Africa next-door neighbors. Asia will be as close to us as Europe is today.

Only by sustaining the highest levels of business-Government cooperation will we reach that stage of progress. Only through that cooperation can we achieve the goals which I affirmed at the beginning of this program: the development of a supersonic transport which is
- safe for the passenger;
- superior to any other commercial aircraft; and
- economically profitable to build and operate.

During 1967 and 1968 the dominant American scepticism about Concorde seemed continually confirmed. By the middle of 1967 the FAA was receiving more news of Concorde delays. British and French Concorde officials appeared to regret their old confident predictions regarding deadlines and costs. A group of American aviation experts who visited Concorde facilities in the summer of 1967 reported increases in gross weight, limitations in basic engine size and diminished fuel capacity. Malloy too called attention to these problems and to Concorde's increased noise. By November 1967 even TWA, whose chief executive had stressed Concorde's competitive strength to the PAC the previous December, was, in Maxwell's words, 'not at all enchanted with the Concorde'. TWA decided not to reserve additional Concorde delivery positions and told Maxwell that it might even drop the six positions it held if the aircraft's performance dropped even further.

Boeing Starts to Talk to the World

Clearly by this time – with the presidential announcement and the further disparaging reports about European efforts – Boeing were confident enough to think that they were well on the way. In a flurry of press releases they started off by explaining the background to their designs, and that their product was filled with good-neighbourliness:

Two United States supersonic transport (SST) prototypes now under development at The Boeing Company's Seattle facility will be the forerunners of a new generation of 1,800-mile-an-hour passenger jetliners.

The Federal Aviation Administration (FAA) signed a contract with Boeing in May 1967 for prototype construction.

The plane Boeing has designed will take off fully loaded at about the same speed and in less runway than a fully loaded Boeing 707 requires. Its landing-approach speed with the variable-sweep wings set forward at 20 degrees also will be about the same as current big jets.

During subsonic flight the American SST's wings will be swept to an intermediate position; with the wings in this setting the airliner will cruise efficiently at speeds equal to those of subsonic airliners. For supersonic flight the SST wings, hinged on giant pivot bearings, will be swept to 72 degrees, allowing the big plane to sweep through the air at almost three times the speed of sound.

The ability to climb quickly after takeoff and to approach for landings at low power ensures less noise at airport communities, additional sound-reduction features built into the engines mean even quieter operation.

The FAA announced 31 December 1966 that the Boeing SST design had been chosen winner in the three-year government competition. General Electric Company's design was picked for the huge SST engines.

Most of the SST will be built of titanium alloy of 90 per cent titanium 6 per cent aluminum and 4 per cent vanadium.

The Boeing design evolved from a study of nearly 500 different configurations. Boeing's first study paper on the supersonic transport was written in 1952; a continuous SST project was established in 1958.

This was followed up later with details as to how the plan would proceed:

The Boeing Company's commitment to the US supersonic transport program is backed by more than $800 million in company-owned building and equipment resources located at 14 major industrial sites across the nation.

More than 75 per cent of the company's investment in these resources is oriented toward airplane work. Boeing also has access to six airfields. Nine of the industrial sites and four of the airfields are located in the Pacific Northwest, near the Boeing Developmental Center where two SST prototypes will be built.

The Developmental Center is a 108-acre complex located across a highway from Boeing Field International in Seattle. Its more than 1,700,000sq ft of covered work space contain laboratories, developmental shops, offices and a high bay assembly area for construction of the prototypes. A new, 87,000sq ft titanium plant, the most modern of its kind in the aerospace industry, and a 65,000sq ft control development building have been placed in operation at the Developmental Center. A substantial amount of new equipment also is being acquired. In addition, the SST program will derive multi-project support from existing Boeing facilities, particularly those in the Seattle area.

Boeing's central fabrication complex, representing an initial investment of more than $110 million, is located in Auburn, Washington, about 17 miles from the Developmental Center. The complex consists of more than three million square feet of space for machining, processing and spar-milling in support of all Boeing programs.

Company laboratory and test facilities are concentrated primarily around Boeing Field. These include wind tunnels, mechanical and propulsion laboratories and engine test stands. Additional engine test facilities are located at the company's Boardman, Oregon, test site.

Boeing production sites in Seattle, Renton and Everett, Washington, are located near airfields. To supplement these fields and provide a site for crew training and flight testing, Boeing has leased the use of Grant County Airport, Moses Lake, Washington, although SST flight test activity will be centered at Boeing Field and Edwards Air Force Base, California.

Under a heading of 'Profit Potential of SSTs in Commercial Operation', the news bureau of the Boeing Company explained their thinking:

A study shows that the US SST can be operated at a profit using the same fare levels and incentive fare practices in effect for current subsonic jet fleets.

The Boeing study assumed airlines would use routes and operating techniques to prevent sonic booms over populated areas. The study indicated that even with flights at supersonic speed restricted to routes over the oceans and unpopulated areas such as the polar regions the 300-passenger US SST would be the cost productive airliner available during the next several decades.

An airplane's productivity is determined by how far and how fast a certain number of passengers can be moved. The US SST will triple the speed of today's subsonic aircraft on long range overwater routes and will carry up to 300 persons in air-conditioned comfort along air corridors some 12 miles above the Earth.

One US SST will be almost as productive as four 707s − or 500 DC-3s. According to study results the 300-passenger SST also will be about 75 per cent more productive than the 747 superjet equipped with 440 seats.

Forecasts indicate the total free world passenger air traffic will increase six-fold between 1968 and 1990 while the International traffic will increase eight-fold during the same period. The daily number of North Atlantic crossings would jump from about 250 in 1968 to 2,100 in 1990 if the only available jet transports were subsonics of the 707 class. Even if everyone crossed the Atlantic in 747 superjets there still would be about 700 crossings each day.

With overseas flights divided between SSTs and super jets, the study shows there would be a daily average of about 200 crossings by the subsonics and 600 crossings by the SSTs. The supersonics will utilize air space about 30,000ft above that used by the subsonics and they will use it only about one-third as long. A complementary fleet of SSTs and superjets can keep the air traffic density at about the same level in the 1980s as it is today − although eight times as many passengers will be moved.

The almost-final version of the Boeing 2707-300.

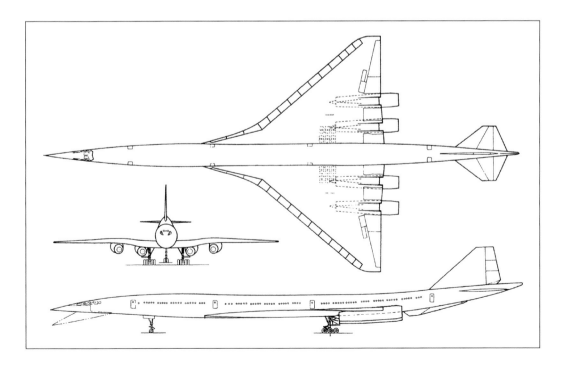

In addition, the study points out that the SST's great speed will make it possible to schedule flights throughout the day, and not just as certain departure fixes to take advantage of midnight to 6 a.m. curfews in effect at most airports. Peak traffic periods for long distance flights will level off.

Passenger preference for supersonic flight is expected to produce high load factors for several years after SSTs first enter commercial service, just as passenger preference for subsonic jets produced high load factors when the 707s first joined airline fleets. Later on, as SST service becomes more common, the great productivity of the SST will offset the steady increase in labor costs which will affect operating expenses of the subsonic jet transports more than it will affect the SST's operating costs.

Historically, with the passage of time, labor costs steadily increase because of inflation, wage increases and other factors. Because the SST is more productive per hour of labor, it is less sensitive to wage escalation pressures than subsonic jets.

The Boeing news bureau also went into details as to the funding of the prototypes:

The final version of the Boeing 2707. Gone were the swing wings, replaced by a double delta similar to the Lockheed and Concorde design.

The nationwide government-industry SST prototype development program which will have a projected $20 billion benefit to the US economy by the end of the 1980s will cost an estimated $1.283 billion by the time two prototypes have completed 100 hours of flight testing.

Money for the prototype program is being advanced by the US government, the customer airlines and the manufacturers. The government is contributing 90 per cent, less risk money provided by the airlines, and the manufacturers are providing 10 per cent, plus certain commercial and capital expenditures not covered by government contract.

For costs above a target incentive point, the government's share would be reduced to 75 per cent and the manufacturers' share would be increased to 25 per cent. The 75/25 split would go into effect at the point at which Boeing had spent $625 million on the airframe and General Electric $284 million on the engines.

A breakdown of the $1.283 billion prototype development phase cost shows that the government will contribute $1.051 billion, the airlines $59 million and the manufacturers $173 million. The $173 million includes the manufacturers' regular 10 per cent share of their contract costs ($62.5 million for Boeing and $28.4 million for GE) plus 25 per cent of a possible $328 million above the target incentive point.

However, these figures do not include costs during earlier phases of the program, or facilities and other expenditures on the part of the manufacturers.

The government contributed $291 million to the US SST design competition which concluded with the selection of Boeing and General Electric to build the prototype aircraft and their engines. Boeing's and General Electric's share of the design competition costs were $17 million. This brings the overall cost for the competition and development phases of the SST program to $1.591 billion (including $308 million spent during the competitive design phase).

The total spent by Boeing and its suppliers will come to about $210 million when all program expenditures and facilities are considered. General Electric will spend about $94 million in cash prior to production. The total manufacturers' contribution, then, will be $334 million. Additionally, the airlines have deposited $22.4 million in the US treasury for delivery positions reserved with the government, making their total investment $81.0 million.

The contract under which the prototype development program was launched states how federal money will be repaid. Boeing and GE will make royalty payments at a rate which will return all invested funds to the government by the sale of about the 300th airplane.

After the investment has been repaid, royalty payments will be made on the sale of additional aircraft to allow the government a return on its investment.

Department of Transportation and Boeing economic studies indicate a minimum market for 540 US SSTs. Under the royalty schedule in the contracts, the government will be repaid all invested funds plus a return of more than $1 billion on the sale of 500 aircraft.

Concorde is Rolled Out

In Toulouse, with over 1,100 guests present, the first prototype Concorde was rolled out on 20 September 1968 – which was unfortunate for them in the publicity stakes, for Soviet troops in Czechoslovakia stole the headlines in the next day's papers. The aircraft was designated Concorde 001. With the British Concord prototype almost complete, British technology minister Anthony

Wedgwood Benn announced at Toulouse that from now on the British aircraft would also be spelt 'Concorde'. The 'e', he said, stood for 'excellence, England, Europe and entente'. It was said the overall shape, aerodynamics, flight controls, propulsion and auxiliary systems made Concorde a generation ahead of any other form of civil transport.

In the US, the FAA and its SST contractors worked strenuously to counter the resulting publicity from the unveiling. Boeing contacted twenty media organisations in Washington DC – including representatives from the Washington dailies, the three major television networks, *Time*, *Newsweek* and the *Wall Street Journal* – to supply them with background information and a picture of the newly designed American SST.

Although the American aircraft manufacturers such as Boeing could hardly repudiate publicly their pro-SST position, their interest was obviously not in the commercial success of Concorde, which may have captured a significant market share at the expense of subsonic transports.

Still, the Americans could not deny Concorde's progress, and by mid-1968, SST programme director Maxwell once more started to refer to the Concorde threat in promoting the SST programme. In late June 1968, he told Congressman Philip Philbin (Democrat, Massachusetts) that Concorde was making progress, a first prototype was being readied for flight in France, and a second was being built

The roll-out of the first Concorde at Toulouse was attended by the UK Minister of Technology Anthony Wedgwood Benn and the French Minister of Transport Jean Chamant, both seen on the right of the picture, about to cut the ribbons. *(BAC)*

Anthony Neil 'Tony' Wedgwood Benn (b. 3 April 1925), formerly the 2nd Viscount Stansgate.

in Great Britain and was nearly complete. Maxwell reminded the congressman that the British and French governments had committed over $2 billion to Concorde in the form of subsidies, loans and loan guarantees and that it could possibly enter commercial service in the early 1970s, 'three to four years ahead of our US SST'. Two months later, Maxwell declared, 'too much emphasis has been placed on Concorde problems and not enough on Concorde progress'.

During the Concorde project, Morien Morgan tirelessly worked through problems, both technical and political, to see the programme to its conclusion. Alternating with his French counterpart, Robert Vergnaud, he chaired the Concorde oversight committee from 1963, when work began in earnest, to 1966, when prototype construction was well advanced. Given the aircraft was the first of its sort, the relatively rapid progress from design to construction is notable (testing and certification took much longer, however). Morgan noted:

> I became convinced – in this I have been reinforced of late by the impressive way in which Concorde is ploughing through the prototype flying phase – that in aeronautical design and research a combination of Gallic fervour and British phlegm produces pretty impressive results by any standards. It is a combination well worth preserving.

McNamara Quits – and Environmental Concerns Start to Surface

Robert McNamara grew more and more controversial after 1966. His differences with the president and the joint chiefs of staff over Vietnam strategy became the subject of public speculation, and frequent rumours surfaced that he would leave office. In early November 1967, his recommendation to freeze troop levels, stop the bombing of North Vietnam and for the US to hand over ground fighting to South Vietnam was rejected outright by President Johnson. McNamara's recommendations amounted to his saying that the strategy of the US in Vietnam that had been pursued to date had failed. Largely as a result, on 29 November that year, McNamara announced his impending resignation and that he would become President of the World Bank.

The president's announcement of McNamara's move to the World Bank stressed his stated interest in the job and that he deserved a change after seven years as Secretary of Defense, much longer than any of his predecessors or successors.

Others give a different view of McNamara's departure from office. There are strong suggestions that he was asked to leave by the president – a subject that McNamara himself was always vague on. When interviewed for an oral history project in 1975, the interviewer said: 'The record in the Library on your resignation is fairly complete but will be closed for some time. Could you comment for the record on the reasons for your resignation and some of the controversy generated by it, especially assertions that you were being fired or forced out.'

McNamara replied:

The last question you ask relates to my resignation from the administration. First let me emphasize again that my recollection of those years is dim. I have no documentary evidence of the sequence of events. The President's records, even when they are ultimately released, will probably chronicle the period fully, so what I have to say now is subject to whatever modification the records later indicate is appropriate.

As I recall the sequence of events, it began in this fashion. In the summer of 1967, George Woods, then the president of the World Bank, told me that he would be retiring in the fall, although he stated the date of his retirement could be significantly deferred; and he wished to recommend me as his successor. I told George that the presidency of the Bank was a job that particularly interested me. I emphasized, however, that I had given no consideration to what I was going to do when I left the department, and that I would not wish, under any circumstances, to leave the government except at a time acceptable to the President even though I had stayed far beyond the time I had initially planned to stay.

I then reported the conversation with George Woods to the President. He asked me my views, and I repeated to him the points I had made to George. The President said he didn't want me to leave, but, as I had served nearly seven years, he could recognize the necessity of my thinking of leaving. In any event,

Engineers work on one of the undercarriage units between test flights. *(BAC)*

he wanted to be sure that when I did leave, to use his words, 'I had anything I wanted.' I believe he meant exactly that.

The President and I had worked closely together throughout his entire term. He knew of my deep respect and affection for him. He knew of my loyalty to him; and I felt his respect for me, and his desire to advance my interests. It is true that my views on Vietnam policy, views relating to the level of bombing, the level of troop support, the necessity for moving more rapidly toward a political settlement were increasingly diverging from those of others in the administration. And I think perhaps that fact advanced the time of my departure by a few months. It may have influenced the President; but I never had any feeling then that I was fired, as was alleged in the press; and I've seen no evidence since that was the case.

McNamara served as head of the World Bank from 1 April 1968 to June 1981. Just at a time when he was about to leave governmental circles the opposition to the US SST project was becoming increasingly vocal. Environmentalists were just starting to become an influential group, voicing concerns about possible depletion of the ozone layer due to the high-altitude flights, and about increased noise at airports and from sonic booms.

The latter became a most significant rallying point, and fed in to the American scepticism about SSTs in general, especially after the publication of the anti-SST paperback *S/S/T and Sonic Boom Handbook* by William A. Shurcliff.

6

Wiggs, Nixon, Shurcliff and *S/S/T* and *Sonic Boom* Handbook

In 1963 the centre-left *Observer* newspaper in the UK published an article entitled 'The Supersonic Threat' that was based on Dr Bo Lundberg's previously little-known study 'Speed and Safety in Civil Aviation'. Lundberg's purely speculative conclusions were that sonic booms generated by fleets of supersonic passenger aircraft would produce effects varying from annoyance to severe physical shock, breaking windows and cause structural damage to buildings.

Bo Lundberg, a former test pilot, was Director General of Flygtekniska Försöksanstalten – the Aeronautical Research Institute in Bromma, Sweden. His studies, which contained increasingly politically orientated titles, included 'Is Supersonic Aviation Compatible with the Sound Development of Civil Aviation?' published in 1962; 'Aviation Safety and the SST' published in January 1965; 'Supersonic Aviation, a Test Case for Democracy' also published in 1965; and 'The Menace of the Sonic Boom to Society and Civil Aviation' in May 1966.

Director General of Flygtekniska Försöksanstalten, Dr Bo Lundberg.

Would the structures of the aircraft be safe at such heights? Would there be catastrophes arising from hailstones? Would radiation have disastrous effects, particularly on pregnant women? Also, what about the sonic boom? Surely it would be intolerable to have to live with that terrible noise? The questions he asked were perfectly valid – but they were still just speculative. He also reminded the profit-conscious airlines that the passengers had not been asked, 'Do they wish to be shot through the air rather than flown?' He offered a grim Swedish warning to the manufacturers: 'Supersonic transports cannot be built without introducing a host of similar features simultaneously. An aircraft designer can normally do a great deal to minimise foreseeable risks – but he can do nothing about the risks that he fails to foresee.'

This was the first time Lundberg's predictions reached an audience beyond scientific and engineering academia but they certainly roused the rabble. 'He is the director of a scientific institute ... he was a test pilot ... this MUST be true!' *Observer* readers responded, in the main not unsurprisingly, expressing the standard left-wing view that this would be an 'intolerable price for ordinary citizens to pay for the transportation of privileged business travellers' and a flurry of correspondence to the paper ensued. A Mr D.W. Rowell wrote that he would support an anti-Concorde movement, if only someone would organise it. Richard Wiggs, a teacher from Letchworth, Hertfordshire, quickly responded, inviting people to write to him. Wiggs gave up teaching to become the full-time organiser of the Anti-Concorde Project and was soon claiming to have the support of thousands of people, including university professors.

Lundberg had protested about the upcoming SSTs at the Montreal Conference of 1961, and now tried to protect the Innuit as much as the well-heeled inhabitants of London and New York when there was talk of operating SSTs over sparsely populated areas, including the Arctic, by writing in the *Washington Post*: 'The suggestion that SSTs should fly over sparsely populated areas seems to me a ruthless proposition. If sonic booms are unbearable for people in the cities, they are equally unbearable for people in the country.'

The Arrival of Wiggs

Richard John Wiggs was, by all accounts, a left-wing, anti-establishment neo-Luddite. He protested against so many things that he could almost be called a 'professional complainer'. When called up for National Service in 1948, he registered as a conscientious objector. He was an early participant in the Campaign for Nuclear Disarmament and marched to the Atomic Weapons Research Establishment at Aldermaston in Berkshire. One of the hand-written placards made by Wiggs read: 'Four minutes' warning: just in time to boil an egg.' In 1960, he joined the left-wing philosopher and social critic Bertrand Russell's Committee of 100 which, disillusioned with the political inefficacy of marching, had begun a campaign of

Richard John Wiggs (b. 4 June 1929, d. 5 July 2001).

non-violent civil disobedience. Wiggs took part in the 'sit-down' demonstrations at Grosvenor Square in London, protesting against the US Polaris missile.

Nevertheless, the UK press loved his outpourings and gave him and his campaign both a platform and many column inches. Wiggs' idea was that the Anti-Concorde Project would collate and publish the scientific information available about the sonic boom, airport noise and astronomical fuel use. The project would also publicise what it saw as facts about the economics of Concorde: that the aircraft could not be operated at a profit, and that the research and development costs, funded entirely by taxpayers' money, would never be recovered, in order to provide an elitist form of travel for the lucky few.

In 1971, Wiggs wrote the book *Concorde: The Case Against Supersonic Transport* with a foreword provided by legendary left-wing Labour politician Michael Foot.

Wiggs was prone to florid tirades in the press – on one occasion in a paid advertisement in *The Times* he called Concorde 'a classic example of the Frankenstein syndrome; a monstrosity has been created which is beyond both the intentions and the control of its creators and which is revealed as an anti-social menace!' Unfortunately, this particular attack misfired because Prime Minister Harold Wilson chose the same day to announce a general election which lessened the impact somewhat.

After the appearance of the first Anti-Concorde Project advertisement in *New Scientist* magazine, Professor John Tileston Edsall, a biochemist of Harvard University, began corresponding with Wiggs. A few months later, Edsall, together with Dr William A. Shurcliff, physicist and senior research associate at the Cambridge Electron Accelerator, founded the Citizens' League Against the Sonic Boom (CLASB) on 9 March 1967 with just nine members. Andrew Wilson, author of *The Concorde Fiasco*, wrote: 'The League adopted the same propaganda techniques as the Project with astounding success.'

Both British and American anti-SST groups supported and co-ordinated their actions, in spite of what would be considered now the very rudimentary means of communication – mainly telephone and surface mail. The Citizens' League sent funds to Richard Wiggs' movement and the two leaders exchanged letters and information.

Citizens' League Against the Sonic Boom

Publicly, the incentive to form CLASB appears to have been derived from Dr Shurcliff's concern over government publications regarding the acceptability of the sonic boom. CLASB operated out of Dr Shurcliff's home at 19 Appleton Street in Cambridge, Massachusetts, and he himself conducted most of the campaign, which publicly appeared to have been, in the main, personally funded. Shurcliff was quoted as saying: 'From the start I and other members made it clear that I must stick very close to the most pedestrian truth; I was to indulge in no colourful writings; no rudeness, and I was to document all major statements.'

Founders of CLASB
Prof. William
A. Shurcliff
(b. 27 March 1909,
d. 20 June 2006).

It was claimed that CLASB was to lead a 'better kind of protest', but that ideal was not upheld for long. Shurcliff claimed that CLASB had 5,000 members from all parts of the USA, and that he made a deliberate point of maintaining personal contact with them. To put this into context, especially as CLASB claimed to be speaking on behalf of all citizens of the USA, this membership was a microscopic part of the overall population of 203.5 million people in 1970, as documented by the census that year.

Shurcliff stated that no dues were required; financial support was derived from periodic requests for contributions and was soon registering an income of $25,000 a year. With his sister and a few colleagues, the professor mailed the press, television and radio throughout America with regular factsheets and bang-zone maps. They lobbied Congress and appeared on the television.

Dr William A. Shurcliff earned a BA from Harvard in 1930, a PhD in 1934, was called to Washington in 1942 to work as a senior technical aide for the Manhattan Project and was promoted to head of the Technical Intelligence Group. This was the effort, led by the US with participation from the UK and Canada, which resulted in the development of the first atomic bomb during the

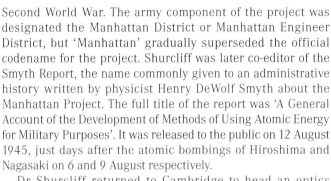

Prof. John Tileston
Edsall (b. 3
November 1902,
d. 12 June 2002).

Second World War. The army component of the project was designated the Manhattan District or Manhattan Engineer District, but 'Manhattan' gradually superseded the official codename for the project. Shurcliff was later co-editor of the Smyth Report, the name commonly given to an administrative history written by physicist Henry DeWolf Smyth about the Manhattan Project. The full title of the report was 'A General Account of the Development of Methods of Using Atomic Energy for Military Purposes'. It was released to the public on 12 August 1945, just days after the atomic bombings of Hiroshima and Nagasaki on 6 and 9 August respectively.

Dr Shurcliff returned to Cambridge to head an optics laboratory at the Polaroid Corporation, a company run by his former classmate Edwin H. Land, and his inventions led to a large number of patents.

Edwin Herbert Land was a scientist and inventor, best known as the co-founder of the Polaroid Corporation. Among other things, he invented inexpensive filters for polarising light, a practical system of in-camera instant photography and his retinex theory of colour vision. His Polaroid instant camera, which went on sale in late 1948, made it possible for a picture to be taken and developed in sixty seconds or less. What is less well known is that Land worked closely with Richard Bissell of the CIA and Clarence 'Kelly' Johnson of Lockheed Aircraft on both the U-2 and A-12 aircraft projects.

In the early 1950s, Land took part in the succession of studies at Massachusetts Institute of Technology (MIT) that helped to spur the formation of Lincoln Laboratory for air defence and to focus attention on the need for direct overhead surveys of the Soviet Union. Land was on the steering committee of the Technological Capabilities Panel of 1954, led by James R. Killian of MIT. The panel produced a timetable for US development of intercontinental and intermediate-range missiles.

Land headed the TCP project on intelligence. In 1954, he worked with James Baker and others on the design of cameras for aerial reconnaissance photography of the Soviet Union. He also played an important role in two assignments to the CIA: development of the U-2 by the CIA instead of the USAF, and firm control of the interpretation of its photographs. The programme involved co-operation of Itek and many other firms. One of these, Eastman Kodak, provided a thin film for the U-2 cameras that allowed more pictures per flight. As it was understood that it was only a matter of time before the secret

Shurcliff's boss
at the Polaroid
Corporation, Edwin
Herbert Land
(b. 7 May 1909,
d. 1 March 1991).

of the U-2 was broken, development of US spy satellites began soon after, going into high gear in 1958. The first successful Corona satellite returned pictures in a re-entry capsule in August 1960, less than four months after a U-2 was shot down over Sverdlovsk.

Land was involved in a number of so-called 'black' projects – that is classified military/defence projects, unacknowledged publicly by the government, military personnel and defence contractors, which were highly classified and denied to exist until ready to be announced to the public. Indeed, it was Land who proposed to CIA Director Allen Dulles that the agency should fund and operate the U-2. He was a member of the President's Science Advisory Committee (PSAC) from 1957 until 1959, a Consultant-at-Large of different PSACs from 1960 until 1973, and also a member of the President's Foreign Intelligence Advisory Board from 1961

Left: Democrat politician Edward William Proxmire (b. 11 November 1915, d. 15 December 2005). Proxmire was to head up the campaign against the American SST and was also to create the Golden Fleece Award, which was designed to focus media attention on projects he felt were self-serving and wasted taxpayers' dollars. One winner of the Golden Fleece Award, Ronald Hutchinson, was so outraged that he sued Proxmire for defamation in 1976, and later settled out of court. In a number of circles his name has become a verb, meaning to obstruct scientific research unfairly for political gain.

Left: Richard Milhous Nixon (b. 9 January 1913, d. 22 April 1994) was the thirty-seventh President of the USA.

until 1977. In many of these roles he worked closely with Secretary of Defense McNamara. Land died on 1 May 1991, and it is alleged that his personal assistant immediately shredded all his personal documents.

It was from this high-ranking defence background that Dr Shurcliff came – a background that clearly had deep and lasting relationships built on a bedrock of leaving no paper trails of documentation.

Publicly, the purpose of CLASB was to oppose the sonic boom and halt the construction of all commercial supersonic transports, both in the USA and abroad. To this end, a massive information dissemination campaign was launched, directed primarily at the taxpayer, the media and Congress. Dr Shurcliff's aim was to change public policy through public outrage. By demonstrating the potential damage to property and health caused by sonic booms, the economic inefficiency and unfeasibility of supersonic transportation, and the strain placed on the tax dollar by the increase in government funding of Boeing's SST, CLASB hoped that supersonic travel would be prohibited in the USA.

The publicly stated aims and activities of CLASB principally consisted of gathering newspaper and magazine articles, books and reports related to the SST and using this information to prepare factsheets, newsletters and handbooks to influence the opinions of individuals and institutions. One early effort was a *Citizens' League Against the Sonic Boom Handbook*.

The media was originally identified as the most expedient means of reaching and influencing the public. CLASB initially focused its campaign on newspapers,

Below: John Anthony Volpe, US Secretary of Transportation, who was in office from 22 January 1969 to 2 February 1973.

radio and television, and so the attitude of the press changed from pro-SST to anti-SST.

Congressmen and other government officials, especially those connected with the FAA and the DoT (two agencies directly involved with the development of the SST), were also contacted. Some members of CLASB lobbied in Washington against the appropriation of additional funds for Boeing's SST.

Much of the scientific information used by Dr Shurcliff was based on the works of Dr Bo Lundberg. Senator William Proxmire was also an early opponent of the SST and was one who had always been convinced that the supersonic transport was a waste of taxpayers' money, so it was understandable that there was a mutual coming together – he too latched on to the greatly claimed 'noise pollution'.

Another Change of President

In a three-way race between Richard Milhous Nixon, Hubert Humphrey and independent candidate George Wallace, Nixon defeated Humphrey by nearly 500,000 votes to become the thirty-seventh President of the United States on 5 November 1968. He was inaugurated on 20 January 1969.

As Nixon was sworn in it seemed that he had inherited some of the most difficult problems any president had had to face: troubled cities, racial tensions, disaffected youth and the running sore of Vietnam. Ordinary Americans could be forgiven for wondering if the republic would tear itself apart under the stress of civil and racial tension. Technological virtuosity allied to fiercely acquisitive capitalism made the USA the richest and most powerful country in the world, but if deep social and political divisions were the price for riches and power, many believed it was too high. American technology was in the hands of corporations with a vested interest in maintaining the tempo of their business activity, without worrying too much about the socio-political consequences. The Vietnam War was to symbolise this, since the conflict seemed to add a great stimulus to the industrial-military complex. Technology seemed to be an out-of-control juggernaut and Americans of all political persuasions were questioning the machine.

James Montgomery Beggs was Under-Secretary of Transportation under Richard Nixon. He headed the ad hoc committee on the SST, and later went on to head NASA.

There was one cause which could unite them – pollution of the environment. The physical as well as the social destruction of the American dream had emerged as a factor in the presidential election. Americans who would never dream of joining a demonstration on Vietnam, and who deplored extremes of all kinds, could make their feelings known about the spoilage of their continent. The SST, waggling its swing wings like an enormous 300ft-long insect in Boeing's Seattle workshop, became the symbol of pollution, and united all those who were uneasy about America's progress.

It was known that Nixon supported an American supersonic airliner, but political opinion would not automatically accept one, and the public's view would be crucial. The whole issue depended on federal funding and each time the president sought a budgetary allocation, the issue could be aired by those who hated the whole idea of supersonic transport.

Less than a month after taking office – on 7 February 1969 – President Nixon introduced John A. Volpe as Secretary of Transportation at a White House news conference; then, on 19 February, he sent a memorandum for James Beggs, Under-Secretary of Transportation:

Concorde 001, F-WTSS, is seen at low level over Paris, the Seine and the Eiffel Tower in June 1969. *(BAC)*

I am establishing an ad hoc committee to review the Supersonic Transport program in line with the recommendations given to me by Secretary Volpe.

I hereby appoint you the Chairman of this Committee. The other members of the committee will be: Mr Rocco Siciliano, Under Secretary of Commerce; Dr Robert C. Seamans Jr, Secretary of the Air Force; Mr. John Veneman, Under Secretary of HEW; Mr Russell Train, Under Secretary of the Interior; Mr Richard G. Kleindienst, Deputy Attorney General; Mr Arnold Weber, Assistant Secretary of Labor; Ambassador U. Alexis Johnson, Under Secretary of State; Mr Paul Volcker, Under Secretary of the Treasury; Dr Henry Houthakker, Member, Council of Economic Advisers; Dr Lee A. DuBridge, National Science Adviser; Mr Charles W. Harper, Deputy Associate Administrator of NASA.

The activities of this committee should be coordinated closely with the Bureau of the Budget. The composition of the working panel was made up of:

1. Balance of Payments and International Relations Panel – Representatives from Treasury (Chairman), Commerce and State.
2. Technological Fall-Out Panel – Representatives from the Office of Science and Technology (Chairman), Department of Defense, and NASA.
3. Environmental and Sociological Impact Panel – Representatives from HEW (Chairman), Interior, and Office of Science and Technology.

4. Economics Panel – Representatives from the Council of Economic Advisers (Chairman), Labor and Commerce.

The committee called upon the services of a number of witnesses: Dr Arnold Moore, Director of the Naval Warfare Analysis Group at the Center for Naval Analyses; Gerald Kraft, President of Charles River Associates; Najeeb Halaby, President of Pan American Airways; Robert Rummel, Vice-President of Trans World Airlines; Harding Lawrence, President of Braniff Airways; Karl Harr Jr, President of Aerospace Industries Association; William A. Shurcliff, Director of CLASB; and Elwood R. Quesada, chairman of the board and President of the L'Enfant Plaza Corps and former head of the FAA.

Clearly, most of these witnesses were well versed in what had gone before. The one obvious 'no-sayer' amongst the witnesses was Dr Shurcliff, and somewhat surprisingly the one major 'name' missing from the committee was Robert McNamara. However, given the link already proven between him and Shurcliff via Edwin Land, one has to wonder if Shurcliff was acting as McNamara's remotely controlled mouthpiece.

Soliciting airline views on behalf of the Beggs committee, the FAA asked for views on the probable market for Concorde and how that market might be affected if the US programme continued as planned or if a decision was made to delay it. Writing to John H. Shatter, a Thompson Ramo Wooldridge executive who was to be the new FAA administrator, Beggs entered the now standard blind alley: 'The English are very anxious to talk to us regarding possible collaboration between their Concorde effort and our SST effort. The competitive nature of this entire supersonic transport area would, of course, change if the English decided to join us in some kind of a joint effort.' On the same subject, Beggs told Volpe, 'I believe that the present inquiry is just another in a series of attempts by the English to get a better deal from us than they have with the French.' One of the airline replies

The first British Concorde 002, G-BSST, took to the air on 9 April 1969, a month after its French counterpart. (BAC)

came from Najeeb Halaby, now President of Pan American, who not unexpectedly urged continuation of the programme as planned in the face of the European and Soviet competition.

One group that did have a view on the SST question was the White House Office of Science and Technology (OST). First, in a letter to Beggs, OST Director Lee A. DuBridge judged the competition of French and Russian SSTs to be far less serious than had been thought two years previously. Second, in a report by the OST's own ad hoc SST review committee, the balance-of-payments arguments in favour of the US SST were dismissed and 'substantial doubt' was cast on the commercial viability of Concorde and the Tu-144. For those and other reasons, the OST committee recommended a withdrawal of government support from the US SST programme.

The Beggs committee produced no consensus for or against the programme. Once more there were conflicting views on the balance-of-payments issue. On the foreign relations impact of the US decision, the relevant panel report warned that American actions apparently designed to scuttle Concorde would undoubtedly lead to an adverse political reaction in Britain and France. US noise standards might bar Concorde from major American airports, 'which would undoubtedly doom the Concorde program and so Britain and France should be kept informed of US noise developments'.

The State Department agreed, adding that there was no overriding foreign policy reason for going ahead with, delaying or cancelling the SST programme. However, a delay would ease the time pressure on the Concorde builders, possibly enabling them to reduce the noise of the aircraft. This would be important for the USA, 'since at present it looks as if the United States, France and the UK will become involved in quite serious differences over the operation of the Concorde in US airspace'. Also, a delay would enable the two sides to discuss their programme schedules.

The report that landed on the president's desk in March 1969 was very different to what he had expected; thankfully it was confidential, and not surprisingly Nixon decided to withhold it from public discussion for as long as possible. Its assumptions would clearly dictate the debate that could decide the fate of the American programme, challenging the validity of the economic arguments and giving official voice to the fears of the environmentalists.

The committee having turned down their thumbs on the American scheme hoped they could kill all SSTs if America withdrew from the race, since it was in a strategic position to down its competitors, with its grip on the world civil aviation industry. The possibility had to be considered that the biggest passenger market in the world would be denied to Concorde.

The president's immediate action was shrewd. He shifted responsibility for the SST programme to the Department of Transportation in April, whose job was to 'advance the transportation art', embracing roads and railways. Not only would this prevent a conflict of interest with the FAA, but it would shelter the SST from congressional sniping. A new Office of Supersonic Transport was set up, headed by William M. Magruder, an ex-test pilot who had headed Lockheed's abortive SST design team in the 1960s.

His task was not made easier by the failure of Boeing to reach specifications with the Dash 200 swing-wing design. The company had outlined plans for yet another attempt at an SST a few weeks before Concorde's first flight. This undermined confidence in the programme, with people wondering if more good money would follow the funds already spent. The federal government had nothing to show for three years' work and expenditure; it did not have even the politically advantageous position of the French and British governments, who knew that the taxpayers were so far committed that it would be a waste of money to turn back. It was to be Magruder's job to pilot the Boeing to success, and he was going to need as much nerve to weather the political turbulence of the environmentalists as if he was flying a new prototype.

On 23 September 1969, Richard M. Nixon spoke at 9.04 a.m. in the Roosevelt Room at the White House:

> The purpose of this briefing, which will be conducted by Secretary of Transportation Volpe, is to make a major announcement with regard to the future of American leadership in air transport.
>
> I think all of us are aware that for 50 years the United States has led the world in air transport. The decision that we announce today means that we will continue to maintain leadership in this field.
>
> The supersonic transport is going to be built. The question is whether in the years ahead the people of the world will be flying in American supersonic transports or in the transports of other nations. And the question is whether the United States, after starting and stopping this program, after stretching it out, finally decides to go ahead.
>
> This has been a very difficult decision in terms of a very spirited debate within the administration and also within the Congress as to the proper priority for funds.
>
> I have made the decision that we should go ahead. I have made it first because I want the United States to continue to lead the world in air transport. And it is essential to build this plane if we are to maintain that leadership.

Crowds gather around for the roll-out of the first British Concorde at Filton. *(BAC)*

I have made the decision, also, because in another sense this means that through this plane we are going to be able to bring the world closer together in a true physical and time sense. This plane, which will fly at 1,700 miles an hour, will mean that in the year 1978, when it will fly commercially – the prototypes will fly in 1972 – but in the year 1978 when it will fly commercially, that Tokyo will be as close to Washington DC, as far as hours are concerned, as London is today. And, in another sense, Argentina will be as close – the furthest tip of Latin America – to Washington DC as London is today. This is a massive stride forward in the field of transport and I think all of us want the United States to move forward in this area.

There are arguments that the Secretary will be able to answer with regard to the technical features of the plane. After listening to all of those arguments, I am convinced that the technical factors can be solved and that we should move forward. And the decision is that now we do go forward and that the first prototype will be flown in 1972 and that the United States will continue to lead the world in air transport.

I want to congratulate at this time not only the Secretary of Transportation, who has felt very strongly within the administration that we should go forward with this decision, but to the leaders – particularly from the State of Washington where the planes will be built, I understand, in the first instance, although this art will spread around other parts of the country, and I am sure subcontracts will cover the whole country, as I understand – to Governor [Daniel] Evans, to Senator [Henry M.] Jackson, to Congresswoman [Catherine] May, to Congressman [Thomas M.] Pelly, and also to the Representative from the Appropriations Committee of the House, Mr Bill Minshall of Ohio – certainly he has an interest in aviation, being a pilot himself, and has long felt that we should go forward.

With strongly conflicting advice within the Nixon administration, another report from a panel of outside technical 'experts' headed by Richard Garwin of IBM that eventually surfaced as being extremely negative and funding problems were among the factors that delayed a presidential decision on the American SST during 1969. Looming large were differing assessments of the Concorde threat. The committee's report was released on 30 October of that year, only after Congressman Reuss of Wisconsin threatened to invoke the Freedom of Information Act, accusing the executive branch of attempting to keep the unfavourable aspects of the reports confidential. The Garwin Report itself became the subject of a long court battle when Boston attorney Peter Koff, acting on behalf of CLASB, Friends of the Earth, the Sierra Club and the American Civil Liberties Union, brought a suit under the Freedom of Information Act, a case that was still not settled when the report was voluntarily released in August 1971.

At the time of the Nixon announcement, flight testing of prototypes of both Concorde and the Soviet Tu-144 was well under way. Now that the two competing SSTs were in the air, there was an added urgency in the continuing US assessments of their impact on the market for the US SST. The FAA came up with some interesting numbers. Sales of more than 200 Concordes or Tu-144s could be expected if these aircraft had a lead of four or five years over the American machine. The president's announcement had placed the in-service date for the US SST at 1978, so if Concorde met its certification date of late 1972, the Anglo-French machine would indeed have a lead of at least five years over the American product.

Between 1973 and 1978, about 240 Concordes could be delivered. Production of the American SST would begin in 1978, with Concorde production estimated to be 500 by the end of 1990. During their monopoly period the Concordes would fly high-density routes at high-load factors, enabling their airlines to recover their investments in three to four years. Assessing the impact of the Tu-144 was difficult, but since the Soviet aircraft was similar in size and schedule to Concorde, sales were likely to come from the estimated Concorde market. The Soviet airline Aeroflot, as principal user of the Tu-144, could require about 130 aircraft, on the assumption that there would be no sonic-boom restriction on domestic flights.

The ad hoc committee's report shook Congress. There was fury on the Hill. A member of the Sub-Committee on Appropriations, Congressman Yates, was 'amazed that President Nixon approved the request for the SST. The Committee, which consisted of many of the ablest people in his Administration, recommended overwhelmingly in favor of suspending work on the project.' He pointed out that the $750 million limit promised by President Kennedy in 1963 had almost been reached and future estimates showed an overspend; he warned the president that, 'This is the logical time to call a halt to the program and I shall try to strike out the appropriation by my Committee'.

Nixon was asking for increased funds, giving the anti-SST lobby a chance to attack. When his request for $96 million reached the Senate in November, Senator William Proxmire acted. His concern, apart from federal funds being poured into what he saw as a white elephant, was that commercial pressures would force the sonic boom upon people once the SST was flying. FAA chiefs conceded under the senator's questioning that 'pressures from the people who want to use this airplane for profit ... may drag it into that market, which one might identify as east to west over populated areas'. The president did nothing to allay the fear of a boom carpet across the US when he was seen telling a group of children on television that one day they would be able to travel from Los Angeles to New York in less than two hours.

After tough infighting, a compromise was agreed with the anti-SST lobby, and a token cut of $11 million was imposed on the president's request for funds, whilst the SST survived in the Senate and the House. It must have looked to Boeing, the pro-SST lobby and the president that the remaining $500 million needed to put the 2707-300 into the air would come through safely.

Clearly Shurcliff was not happy with the results contained in the reports of the ad hoc committee he had participated in, nor was he pleased with the decision of the president. It was time to take his views to the people in the same manner Wiggs was doing in the UK.

Shurcliff's Book

Shurcliff's publication, *S/S/T and Sonic Boom Handbook*, is a strange concoction of high science, scaremongering, selective partisan choices of information, quasi-scientific theory and written sleight of hand that is all surrounded by a framework of factual reporting – and was probably the single document that killed off the American SST and fatally damaged Concorde.

The February 1970 publication was based on the earlier *Citizens' League Against the Sonic Boom Handbook* and, as far as can be ascertained, only differs from the earlier publication by the inclusion of material taken from the Nixon ad hoc committee, to which Shurcliff was one of the witnesses called. It was followed by Richard Wiggs' much less effectual *Concorde: The Case Against Supersonic Transport*.

It is said that Shurcliff sent 10,000 free copies of his shocking pink-and-black-covered book to congressmen, administration officials, newspapers and even to the president himself, but I have been unable to trace who paid for this. Boeing executives and FAA officials discovered their copies in plain paper wrappers.

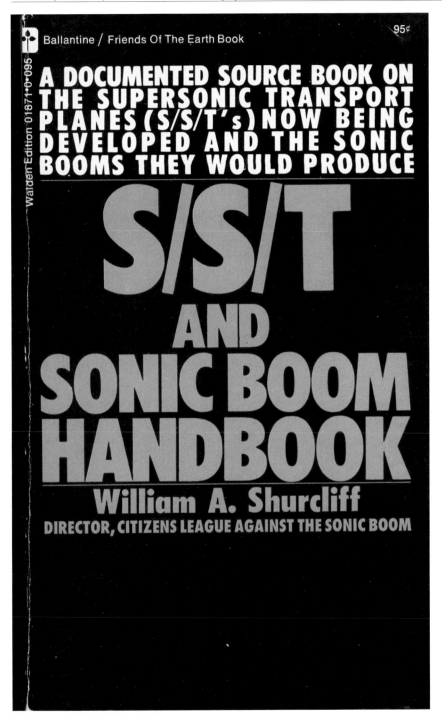

Shurcliff is quoted as saying, 'I mailed them in brown paper wrappers, with no return address indicated, to increase the chance that the mailroom clerk would not collect and burn them.'

Given the targeted circulation, this work deserves looking at in some detail. The book starts innocently enough, explaining what the author sees as the $64 billion question:

Airplane builders here and abroad are enthralled in a grandiose dream: the dream of building $64,000,000,000 worth of supersonic transport planes. They dream of revolutionizing long-range travel, improving the respective countries' balance of payments, creating more than 200,000 jobs, gaining prestige, and reaping handsome profits.

But to many people the dream is a nightmare. They dread the sonic booms the supersonic transport planes would produce, and estimate that the sonic booms would startle hundreds of millions of people each day and damage at least a million houses a week. They expect that such planes would be dangerous and almost prohibitively expensive. They believe that widespread use of the planes would hurt, rather than help, the balance of payments, and they are convinced that the project as a whole would be a financial failure and would leave the taxpayers out-of-pocket to the tune of about $5 billion.

Here in the USA where there is as yet no supersonic transport plane but only a mass of drawings and reports prepared by Boeing Company and associated manufacturers, the issue is a simple one: Should our Government push the Boeing project and support it with billions of dollars? Or should the project be dropped?

Shurcliff then proceeds to explain what SSTs are, what the sonic boom is and then cites examples of sonic-boom damage:

BAC and Aérospatiale marked the occasion of achieving Mach 2 in an understated way – with a postcard!

Concorde
FLIGHT NEWS

ISSUE No. SPECIAL

DATE **4 NOV 1970**

Mach 2 was attained for the first time today, by aircraft 001 flying from Toulouse. **Sustained flight 53 mins.**

Issued by the
BAC-AEROSPATIALE JOINT SALES ORGANISATION

M. Mendels (Aerospatiale)
K.W. Turner (BAC)

With visor down, G-BSST is seen above the clouds before heading off for another routine supersonic phase to the flight during testing. *(BAC)*

Ottawa, Canada. Late in 1959, at the Uplands Airport at Ottawa, an F-104 supersonic fighter plane flew at 500 feet altitude above the multi-million-dollar terminal building, producing a sonic boom that broke most of the windows, twisted metal window frames, and jarred loose the insulation cemented to the underside of the roof. The damage was estimated at $500,000 (*Mechanix Illustrated*, October 1965).

Oklahoma City. In the mid-1950s a military plane flew low over the Will Rogers Terminal at the Oklahoma City Airport and delivered a sonic boom that caused $500,000 damage (Congressional Record, June 10, 1968).

Colorado Springs. On May 31, 1968, an F-105 plane flew at supersonic speed 500 feet above the Air Force Academy at Colorado Springs, Colorado. The sonic boom broke $50,000 worth of windows and showered broken glass onto persons attending graduation ceremonies. Fifteen persons were injured (*New York Times*, June 1, 1968).

White Sands, New Mexico. In January 1965 at the White Sands Missile Range, New Mexico: Gordon Bains, director of the nation's SST program, was telling newsmen that many persons who claimed their property had been damaged by sonic booms were only imagining the damage. 'I believe there's a great deal of psychology in this', he explained, when – WHAM! A jet fighter pilot in an F-104 broke through the sound barrier at an altitude of only 500 feet. The booming shockwave which followed blew out two 7 by 12 feet plate-glass windows ... (*Parade*, January 17, 1965).

The 40psf sonic boom ... knocked out a store front and windows all over town. It also dislodged a ten pound window screen that hit an FAA official on the head ... no one knows yet how much damage was done (*Mechanix Illustrated*, October 1965).

Palmdale, California. A minor disaster at Palmdale, California, was described thus: in Air Travel for June 1967: 'The only sonic boom I ever experienced close at hand scared the bejeezus out of me and a number of other newsmen who had been flown by North American Aviation to Palmdale (near Los Angeles) for the flight demonstration of a new supersonic fighter aircraft. The pilot, eager to give the assembled reporters and photographers a reasonably close view of the plane, made a supersonic pass over the field at a little too low altitude and shattered most of the plate glass windows and doors of the airport terminal building.'

Kelowna, British Columbia. On August 6, 1969, a US Navy F4 acrobatic plane accidentally exceeded the speed of sound while flying at 300 feet altitude above Kelowna, BC, with the result that 'about 75% of the windows in an eight-block area of downtown Kelowna were reduced to shards. Damage was estimated at $250,000. Seven persons were cut by flying glass. Heavy plate-glass windows splintered and pieces flew into the streets. Glass went all over the place' (*Toronto Globe and Mail*, August 8, 1969).

Reading this, it all sounds terrifying. The reader may then spot that the aircraft that caused all this mayhem were flying at ridiculously low heights. Shurcliff goes on:

These disasters were caused by sonic booms having 10 to 20 times the overpressure that SSTs would produce when flying at prescribed altitude. They have nothing to do with the SST problem – except in the unlikely event that an SST pilot, in some emergency, flies his plane at supersonic speed at lower-than-permissible altitude over a city.

So if, as Shurcliff himself admits, they have nothing to do with the SST problem, why put it all in unless he is stating information for the purposes of scaremongering? This example is typical of the contents of the rest of the book – and of the comments of some participants of Nixon's ad hoc committee.

Shurcliff continued to stack up his 'evidence'. Under the heading 'Types of damage' he said:

> In general, sonic booms from SSTs have done many kinds of damage. They have cracked and shattered glass windows; cracked plaster walls and dislodged loose plaster; cracked masonry; cracked highly strained foundations of buildings that were poorly constructed or were situated on ground that had undergone settlement; cracked various kinds of brittle objets d'art and fragile antiques; jiggled and vibrated shelves, causing dishes, tumblers, and vases to jiggle sidewise and fall onto the floor and break; set off burglar alarms; triggered rock slides and avalanches.

Whoa! One moment – back the truck up! '... SSTs have done many kinds of damage'? The actual date of Shurcliff's first document is not known, but when the paperback came out, in February 1970, America had no SST and Concorde had only gone supersonic for the first time on 1 October 1969 and had not yet crossed the Atlantic – so just when had all this damage been done?

McNamara's Influence

It is not until the reader reaches the section on damage estimates that the influence of Robert McNamara really appears – analysing data to an inch of its life in the manner of the Whiz Kids:

> Suppose the SST proponents' dreams come true: supersonic flight over land is permitted, the people of the world are prosperous and are willing to pay extra-high fares to travel by SST, and large numbers of SSTs are built and put into use. Specifically, suppose the USSR sells 200 of its Tu-144 SSTs, the British and French sell 400 Concordes, and Boeing Co sells 1,200 of its B-2707-300 SSTs (making about $64 billion worth of SSTs in all). How much damage would these planes' booms do to buildings?
>
> No exact answer can be given, but a rough estimate can be made using the damage-payment figures listed in Chapter 4. Suppose each of the 1,800 SSTs makes many trips a day, traveling 9,000 miles a day at supersonic speed. This makes a total of (1800) x (9000) = 16,200,000 SST-supersonic miles a day. Let us assume that half of these miles – 8,100,000 – are over land. If the bang-zone width is 50 miles, the total number of square-mile-booms will be (8,100,000) x (50) or about 400,000,000.
>
> How much damage would these booms do to buildings? First, let us convert the square-mile-booms to man-booms. Then we can use the actual-damage-payments figure of $600 per million man-booms, based on the major sonic boom tests discussed in Chapter 4. If on the average there are 100 persons per square mile (which may be typical of much of the USA in 1990), the total number of man-booms per day will be (400,000,000) x (100) = 40,000,000,000. At $600 per million, this amounts to (40,000) x ($600) =$24,000,000 damage per day.
>
> Think of it! A global damage of $24,000,000 per day! To the best of the writer's knowledge, pro-SST persons have never published an estimate of the world-wide daily damage to buildings. Instead, they state repeatedly that a typical boom should not damage a well-made building. But actual sonic boom tests conducted at enormous expense in Oklahoma City and elsewhere have shown that each

million man-booms leads to about $600 damage to houses. The $24,000,000-per-day damage figure is a result of applying simple arithmetic to this figure.

The figure is certainly only an approximate one. In different countries, houses are constructed differently. They may be more vulnerable – or less vulnerable – than houses in Oklahoma City or Chicago. Costs of repair, too, may differ in different countries. But if the figure is wrong, it may well be wrong by being too low – because the main sonic boom tests mentioned were conducted with average overpressures of about 1.3 to 1.7psf whereas the SSTs are expected to produce booms of 2.0 to 3.5psf overpressure.

Pro-SST persons have claimed that, after a while, most of the easily damaged window panes and plaster walls will have been broken and thereafter the damage rate will decrease. But others point out that this may not be true, for two reasons:

(1) The boom overpressure is highly variable, so that a window pane that has withstood hundreds of 2.0 to 3.5psf booms may nevertheless break when eventually hit by a 6psf superboom.

(2) There may be a cumulative effect such that an initially sturdy plaster wall will gradually deteriorate under repeated sonic booming and eventually will crack.

What does $24,000,000 worth of damage imply physically? At $120 per cracked plaster wall – (a very rough guess) – and $12 per broken window, it could imply, for example, 50,000 ruined plaster walls and 500,000 broken window panes – with $12,000,000 left over to cover damage to ceilings, masonry, dishes, and the like.

Such a figure for window-pane breakage is reinforced (within an order of magnitude) by the special study of window-pane breakage at the Edwards Air Force Base tests where the carefully-confirmed breakage rate was found to be 0.127 panes per million pane-booms. Multiplying this by our global estimate of 40,000,000,000 man-booms per day and assuming that typical houses have about 10 panes per occupant, we find that about (40,000) x (10) x (0.127) or about 50,000 panes would be broken each day. If, instead, we use the 0.5 panes-per-million-pane-booms figure applicable to the village adjacent to Edwards, we arrive at a figure of about 200,000 broken panes per day.

Think of the work involved in filling out perhaps 500,000 damage claims per day! Think also of the efforts of the people who must process the claims. The number of jobs created in the building of the SSTs might be surpassed by the number of jobs created in processing the claims and repairing the broken windows and cracked walls.

G-BSST is prepared for another flight. *(BAC)*

Right: The flight from Paris Orly was handled by Air France operations, and appeared on their dispatch board like any other flight. Concorde was integrated into the airport traffic without any special treatment. (*Aérospatiale*)

Below: On 12 December 1971, France's President Pompidou boarded a Concorde for a trip to Lajes Air Force Base in the Azores for a meeting with US President Nixon. (*Aérospatiale*)

HOR	ORE	LIGNE	POST	T	IM	PROVEN	DAL	PAX
1550	Δ1720	AF0017		N	JO	NCE		09/075
1610		AF0315				MAN		
1610		AF0817		N		LHR		
1615		AF2310				ORN		
1645	★1945	AF0653		N	JL	LIN		
1700	★1800	AF0526		N	JQ	BCN		
1700	Δ1725	AF0751		F	RR	TXL	03/018	TML
1700	★1520	AFVOIO	HAN			FCO	TRANSALL	
1710	★2115	AFAT2006		N	JN	CMN		
1715	★1800	AF0797		F	RA	FBUCPH		RSV
1715		LH0114		X		FRA		
1720	Δ1700	AF0004		T	CK	LAX	13/119	
1730		CONCORDE		C	SS	LGS		
1745	H	AF0500		F	RV	LIS	02/047	
1745		AF0717		F	RL	BUDPRG		
1800	Δ1745	AH1420		N	EA	ALG	11/126	
1800		BE0018		Y		LHR		
1810		AF1512		F	RG	BIA		
1810		ATAF0602		F	CZ	OUD		
1820		AF0713		F	RT	BEGZAG		

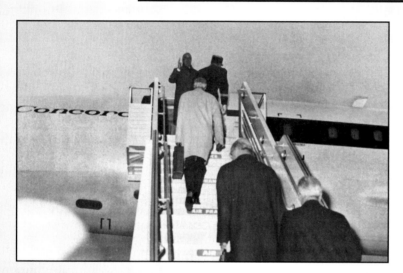

Meeting of the Presidents

Below: Concorde 001, with President Pompidou on board, is seen taxying out past the main terminal to Runway 27 at Orly. (*Aérospatiale*)

Above: Concorde 001 seen on the ramp at Lajes Field, parked behind Air Force One. *(Aérospatiale)*

Left: Before embarking on Air Force One for his trip back to the USA, Nixon spared a few minutes for an unscheduled inspection of Concorde with Portugal's Prime Minister Marcello Caetano. When shaking hands with Aérospatiale's President Ziegler he somewhat ruefully said, 'I wish we had built it', and later told journalists, 'I have one quote for you: We will build it one day. We'll start late but we'll catch up'. *(Aérospatiale)*

Right: While at Lajes Field, Ziegler and test pilots Jean Franchi and Jean Pinet met with interested Pan American and TWA aircrews and showed them over Concorde. The tour to the Azores confirmed what was already known: Concorde operation could be easily integrated into the normal traffic of a major international airport. *(Aérospatiale)*

As can be seen, Shurcliff – or was it McNamara? – extrapolates data that was already built on a series of suppositions to a point where the reader forgets that what they are reading is really just a forward 'projection' and thinks of it as a fact. He also casually uses phrases like 'within an order of magnitude' that most people would have difficulty understanding, yet uses calculations based on it. By definition, 'an order of magnitude' is a number rounded to the nearest power of 10 – a highly flexible amount – and yet Shurcliff happily uses it to demonstrate numbers to three-decimal-place accuracy! The reader becomes browbeaten with lines of zeroes and almost impenetrable arithmetic that is impossible to do – or check – in one's head as one reads it. There is almost no choice but to take the easy way out and accept it.

Twisting the Truth – aka Bullshit Baffles Brains!

Shurcliff dedicated a whole chapter to what he saw as 'The Dangers in SST Flight'. Much of what he writes is couched in a highly condescending tone that is just stating the blindingly obvious to anyone who knows anything about aviation.

'Fire; Much of the fuel will be stored in the wings; many different tanks will be used; the tanks are to be interconnected by large numbers of pipes, valves, and an elaborate system of pumps for transferring fuel from one tank to another, to maintain balance of the plane.' Well, yes, but so what? As a statement that is true for just about every large aircraft built since around 1935.

Under a section on hail, he writes:

Discussing possibilities of SSTs colliding with birds and hailstones, FAA engineers stated: The most critical of such materials at supersonic speeds is likely to be hailstones. A review of meteorological literature on hailstone observations and theory of development indicates that little reliable information is available concerning what sizes and densities can be expected in the high altitudes. One difficulty is that of determining hail size in the air. There is ample evidence that hailstones occur at high altitudes, with convective cloud tops up to 70,000 feet.

Over an eight-year period, USAF aircraft are reported to have experienced 272 damaging hail encounters. Forty-six percent of these encounters occurred above 20,000 feet, with maximum height at 44,000 feet. Pilots have reported hailstones of possibly three to five inches between 29,000 and 37,000 feet.

OK, so hail occurs at all altitudes and over eight years USAF aircraft collided with hailstones 272 times; it sounds frightening – but wait. If that was 272 times in 272 flights, it is deadly with a certainty of collision. However, if that was 272 times in, say, 6 million flights, then whilst still dangerous, the risk is one impact every 22,059 flights! Shurcliff often does this: he makes a statement but fails to put it into context by providing all the information. In a section entitled 'Poor visibility' this appears:

Traveling at 1,800mph, a Boeing SST would cover one mile in two seconds, and 10 miles in 20 seconds. If atmospheric conditions limit a pilot's vision to less than 10 miles, he can see no farther ahead than the distance to be traveled in the next 20 seconds. The angular width of vision is limited also. In moderate haze the pilot may be flying virtually blind. Persons who know that hundreds of near-misses occur each year in crowded airspace, and know that occasional fatal collisions occur, find this prospect unpleasant. In 1966, pilots reported 462 near-misses, and the true number has been estimated at 5,000 per year. In 1968 a total of 2,230 near mid-air collisions were reported, according to the FAA (*Aviation Week*, October 6, 1969).

An item of artwork that well represents the thinking of the day – the day being the late 1950s. Twelve engines push this tri-finned, Union Flag-bedecked delta airliner to the fringes of space – apparently above the limits of atmosphere.

Someone, somewhere made this model of the Barnes Wallis Swallow SST from the mid-1950s in the colours of Pan American. A later design from this incredibly innovative designer was suggested as being capable of travelling from London to Sydney in just five hours! *(both Simon Peters Collection)*

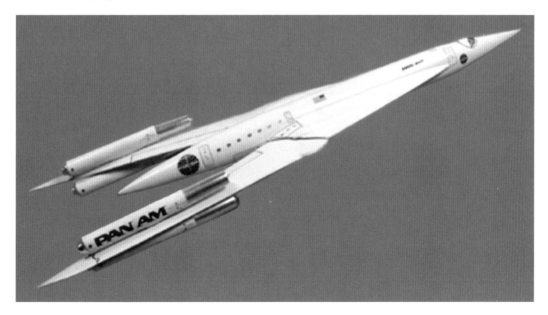

One of the many versions of the early Boeing SST designs, this one being the Model 733-179, believed to be the smallest of all the Boeing design concepts. Again, the artist gives the impression that the aircraft is flying almost 'above the atmosphere'. *(Simon Peters Collection)*

An artist's impression of the Boeing SST in full Boeing corporate colours entitled as with the design above 'USA/ SUPERSONIC'. The main aircraft is shown with the wings fully swept, while the machine in the bottom of the picture, supposedly coming in to land, is seen with the wings swept fully forward. *(Simon Peters Collection)*

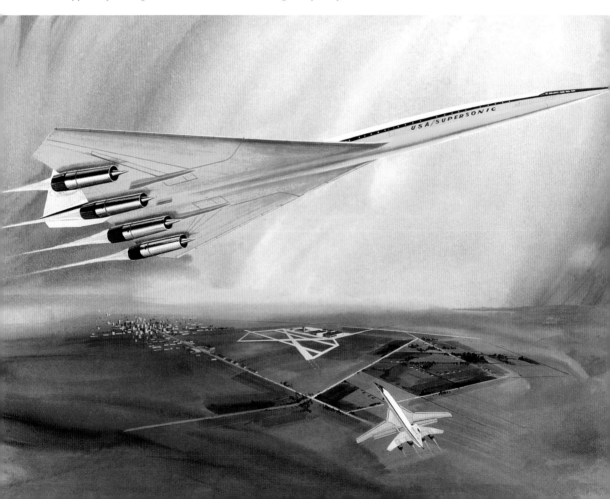

The Boeing SST soon passed from artist's impression to full mock-up, as seen here in full corporate colours with the wings extended in the take-off and landing position with 20° of sweep. The man on the floor close by the aircraft gives a sense of scale. *(Simon Peters Collection)*

The mock-up of the main cabin of the Boeing SST. *(Simon Peters Collection)*

Another view of the Boeing SST mock-up in Seattle, this time from the rear. From this view the 'wasp-waisted' change in fuselage diameter is noticeable. In the background on the right is another mock-up – this time of just the flight-deck area with a droop nose that bent in two places. *(Simon Peters Collection)*

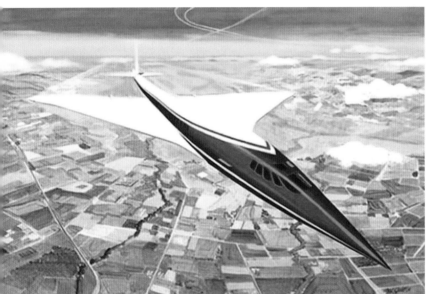

From the Boeing SST evolved the non-swing-wing design, tentatively designated the Boeing B-2707. Although not shown on the early artwork above, this design was to be fitted with forward canards just aft of the flight deck. *(Simon Peters Collection)*

Boeing went to the expense of constructing a full mock-up of this design as well, complete with an apparently fully equipped flight deck. *(Simon Peters Collection)*

The Soviet Union issued all sorts of artwork and mock-ups before cutting metal on the Tu-144. The artwork right is typical of the period, showing the machine in the colours of the state airline Aeroflot and minus the forward canards that were later fitted. *(Simon Peters Collection)*

The Tu-144 entered limited services with the Russian state airline, but technical and aerodynamic problems meant that it prematurely retired. *(Simon Peters Collection)*

In the early 1970s the Tupolev OKB began work on the creation of a second generation, SST-2. Tupolev decided in 1973 on the development of the Tu-244, using as the base the experience acquired by the Soviets, Europeans and Americans in their different SST programmes. It came to nothing. *(Simon Peters Collection)*

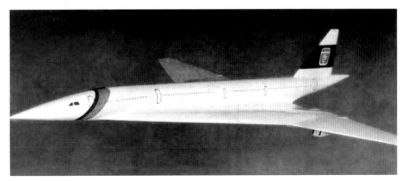

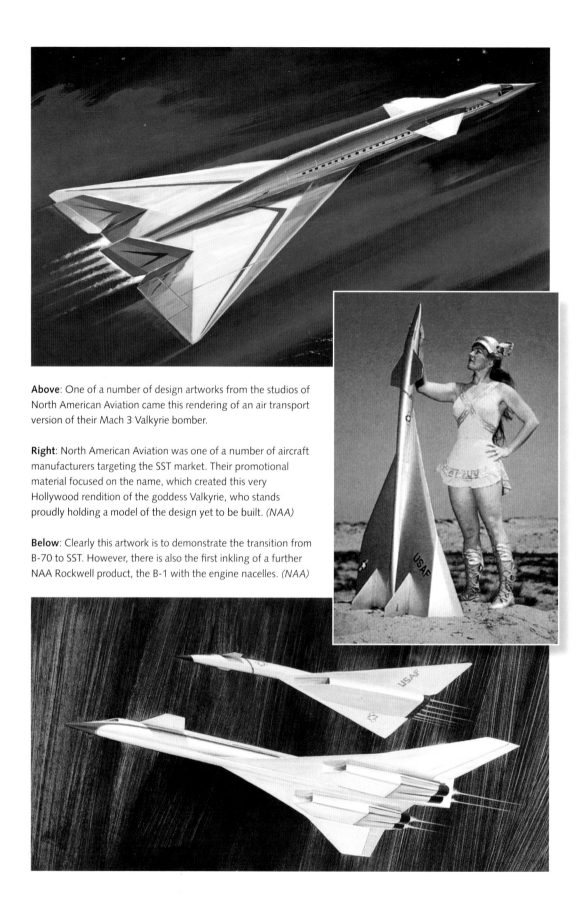

Above: One of a number of design artworks from the studios of North American Aviation came this rendering of an air transport version of their Mach 3 Valkyrie bomber.

Right: North American Aviation was one of a number of aircraft manufacturers targeting the SST market. Their promotional material focused on the name, which created this very Hollywood rendition of the goddess Valkyrie, who stands proudly holding a model of the design yet to be built. *(NAA)*

Below: Clearly this artwork is to demonstrate the transition from B-70 to SST. However, there is also the first inkling of a further NAA Rockwell product, the B-1 with the engine nacelles. *(NAA)*

Above: Perhaps a little far-fetched, but the point is made in this XB-70 illustration, putting the travelling businessman in the SST version with his transport at meteoric speed. The beaker/flask would suggest that the drawing was done while NAA was still having thoughts of chemically augmented powerplant – or perhaps it is the world's largest Martini! *(NAA)*

Below: The full-scale mock-up of the Lockheed 2000 SST.

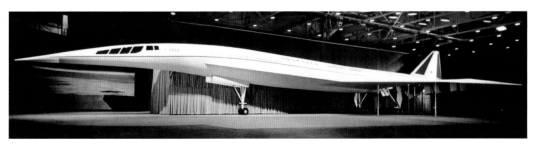

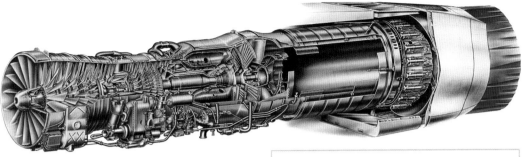

Left: Concorde G-BSST seen making a low and fast pass of its birthplace, Filton, just outside Bristol. *(BAC image C777)*

Above: A highly detailed artwork of one of Concorde's Olympus engines. *(Rolls-Royce Ltd, Bristol Engine Division, E131009)*

Right: British Airways made great use of the Mach 2 concept. This is the face of the short-lived Miami–Washington–London service.

Below: A stunning night-time picture of one of the early Concordes. Somehow the darkness makes the shape of the wing even more noticeable.

Above: G-BOAD in the early British colour scheme. *(Simon Peters Collection)*

Below: An unidentifiable British Airways Concorde over Manhattan. *(British Airways)*

Opposite top: A truly incredible picture of one of the British Airways Concordes just at the point of lift-off. *(British Airways)*

Opposite bottom: 'Express Meals' and light and healthy options were provided for Concorde passengers. The meal on the left is a beautiful lobster salad and dressing. The finest fresh fruits and cheeses were supplied on a linen-lined tray with china by Royal Doulton. British Airways Concorde originally offered a two-tray meal service. On the right is the dessert half-tray with liqueur glass, dessert, Concorde chocolates, cup and saucer, silver-plated knife, dessert spoon and teaspoon. Such was the shortage of space aboard Concorde that the cheeses were offered from the silver tray on to small china plates.

AEROSPATIALE and B.A.C.
send you their best wishes for the New Year

As part of the 'end of year report', the team from *Concorde Flight News* sent out this New Year's card showing Air France and British Airways Concordes. Close inspection of the original shows that they were both French-registered machines!

The Air France
Concordes
somehow always
managed to look
stylish.

The flight deck of Air France Concorde Foxtrot Alpha.

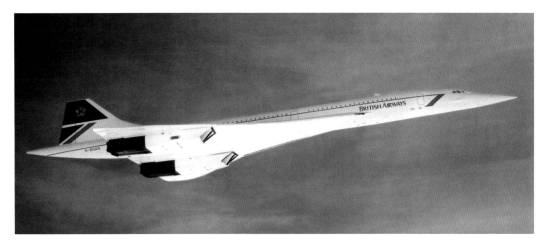

G-BOAG in the 1980s British Airways colour scheme. *(British Airways)*

Air France F-BTSD in the thankfully short-lived 'Pepsi' advertising scheme. *(Air France)*

The classic Concorde shot – nose on, sleek and stylish. *(British Airways)*

Above: When Her Majesty Queen Elizabeth II travelled on Concorde the interior was changed to provide a suite. *(British Airways)*

Right: BOAC's Concorde promotional material was just as the aircraft – sleek and stylish.

Below: 'Sunsets are so beautiful that they almost seem as if we were looking through the gates of Heaven,' Sir John Lubbock, 4th Bt. *(British Airways)*

TIME/CONCORDE

➤ **BOAC**

What does he expect, the cockpit to be fitted with rear-view mirrors? If linear visibility (angular or otherwise) had anything to do with the safety of any given flight, then no flying would take place at all at night or in any clouds. In fact, regulations do exist to take this into account – Visual Flight Rules (VFR) – which allow a pilot to operate an aircraft in weather conditions generally clear enough to allow the pilot to see where the aircraft is going. This is the basis of the Private Pilot Licence. No airline pilot operates under such rules – they are all qualified to fly under Instrument Flight Rules (IFR). Federal Aviation Regulations (FAR) in the USA define IFR as 'Rules and regulations established by the FAA to govern flight under conditions in which flight by outside visual reference is not safe. IFR flight depends upon flying by reference to instruments in the flight deck, and navigation is accomplished by reference to electronic signals.'

The Type-28 nacelle is installed with a pair of Olympus 593 engines in the test cell of the French test centre at Saclay. *(SNECMA)*

A rear view of the Type-28 nacelle for Concorde, showing the reheat ring, the multi-flap primary nozzle and the movable buckets for exhaust jet modulation and reversing. *(SNECMA)*

Test pilots Brian
Trubshaw (left)
and André Turcat,
following the
maiden flight of
Concorde 002.

Of course, Shurcliff reveals none of this to his readers, for it repudiates his rationale. Immediately after this, he goes on to describe the air-to-air collision of the second North American XB-70 Valkyrie:

> Poor visibility has been blamed for one of the world's most dramatic airplane crashes – the June 8, 1966, crash of the unique, 250-ton supersonic bomber XB-70 piloted by Al White. The crash was described in detail in the *Life* of November 11, 1966, and the February 1967 *Readers Digest*; 'With limited vision from inside the XB-70's long, reptilian nose, White could not watch the other planes ...' A photographic plane collided gently with the XB-70, then 'pitched upward, rolled sharply to the left and somersaulted ... slicing the big plane's two vertical fins. The XB-70 turned upside down, and ... a big piece of the left wing broke off.' The XB-70 struck the ground. It 'made a terrible explosion and an enormous plume of smoke came up'.

Again Shurcliff is selective with what he tells the reader. 'White could not watch the other planes ...' Well of course he could not – he was leader of the formation, and it is standard operating procedure for any formation leader to provide the course, altitude and speed of the formation; all others participating were supposed to be watching and formating on the XB-70. However, again, one has to question the reasons for this inclusion. Airliners, SST or otherwise, never fly in close formation, so why include the details of the XB-70 crash unless just for sheer sensationalism?

Thus so it goes on. Shurcliff sets up a series of unlikely scenarios that, although possible, were remote in the extreme. In 'Loss of pressure in main cabin' there is more scaremongering:

> In a subsonic plane, if cabin pressure is lost while at moderate altitude, crew and passengers don oxygen masks and suffer no harm. But in an SST, the situation is quite different: the altitude is so great (about 65,000 feet), and the outside air pressure there is so low, that should the plane lose its pressure, sudden 'boiling of the blood' would occur, producing unconsciousness of crew and passengers

within about one minute. Oxygen masks would not avail. A disastrous crash would be unavoidable. Loss of pressure would occur, for example, if several windows of the plane were to be blown out, or a small bomb blew a hole a few feet in diameter in the side of the plane. The air-pressure-maintenance system is designed to maintain at least a barely livable pressure if a small opening (one-foot diameter or less) occurs in the side of the plane, e.g., if one small window is blown out.

The fact is that several windows being blown out, or a small bomb blowing a hole a few feet in diameter in the side of the plane, could equally apply to a subsonic airliner, as has been tragically proven, but this point is not made to the reader.

If it was not for the fact that the reader was being seriously misled, large parts of this chapter could be classed as amusing. He continues:

Inability to 'Hold' for Long Periods – Subsonic planes, using relatively little fuel per hour, can hold for hours near a crowded airport, awaiting permission to land. If the chosen airport is closed because of a storm or an accident, the subsonic plane can fly to some other airport – perhaps 500 or 1,000 miles away, if necessary. But the SST uses in the order of a half ton of fuel per minute, and can ill afford to take off with any greater reserve of fuel than is absolutely necessary. Thus its ability to hold over an airport, or to be diverted to a distant airport, is restricted. The Concorde's fuel reserve guaranteed by the manufacturer – for flight from Paris to New York – is only '30 minutes over alternate'.

Limited Number of Airports Available in Emergency – Because SSTs require very long runways and specially strengthened surfaces (to take the enormous weight and landing impact), relatively few airports can accept an SST. Thus the number of secondary, or emergency, landing sites is small. The Boeing SST will require 10,300 feet (almost two miles) for take-off.

Incompatibility with Other Kinds of Planes – With its high speed, high altitude of cruise, poor maneuverability, and limited fuel reserves, the SST is in many ways poorly compatible with, or incompatible with, other types of planes – as regards routes, headway separations, holding patterns, landing priorities, and other obvious categories such as pilot training and airplane servicing. Extra expense and perhaps extra danger may be involved.

The huge XB-70 seen in formation with other fighters, moments before one collided with it – an event so dramatically described by Shurcliff. I have only one problem with this: when do airliners ever fly this close together? (USAF)

Before starting the high-incidence trials, Concorde 001 was fitted with an anti-spin parachute which had been checked in flight for proper operation at speeds up to 165 knots. This parachute was aimed at pitching Concorde's nose down in case of difficult recovery from a high-incidence condition. *(BAC)*

These three points may have been reasonably correct when referring to the Boeing designs, but are incorrect when referring to Concorde, which was specifically designed to fit in with existing traffic patterns and airports.

Pilot Strain – The strain on the SST pilot will be enormous. The number of tasks he must perform, their novelty, and the requisite speed of execution are impressive. Even on conventional transport planes the strain is great. In 1966 there were six instances in which a pilot on duty on the flight deck of a commercial plane suffered sudden incapacitation from cardiovascular disease. In the last eight years, 14 commercial transports crashed during training flights. The strain on an SST pilot must be exceptionally great: he is handling a more cumbersome and complicated plane, relying on a greater array of automatic (and often invisible) equipment, with need for quicker decisions. Presumably he will be well aware that a crash may mean loss of a $50,000,000 plane, liability for perhaps $60,000,000 in lawsuits by the heirs of the victims, and glaring publicity throughout much of the world.

Inadequate Testing – When testing small planes, produced at reasonable cost, a test pilot can put the plane through its paces with gusto. Besides trying out all the recommended flight conditions and maneuvers, he can try some extra-curricular tests, such as flying through bad storms, diving steeply, stalling, landing cross-wind, or deliberately making a hard landing with exaggerated bounce. He can find whether the plane holds up well even when abused.

But the SST pilot, realizing that the prototype plane may be worth $250,000,000 and that to build a replacement would take a year or two, must be careful not to make the extreme tests that would be of such interest. If some design error is found in a small plane, the manufacturer can modify the design quickly and produce and test additional planes. But to modify an SST could be a major undertaking, slowing down the whole program by months or years and causing large financial loss.

These two parts are incredibly offensive to both pilots and engineers alike. To imply that any pilot would take into account the value of the aeroplane and/ or public liability while flying is just plain wrong. Likewise to suggest that any aircraft manufacturer tests its products differently – dependent on the value of what is being tested – is also incorrect and offensive. In fact BAC/Aérospatiale built a number of prototypes and pre-production Concordes just to be able to perform such tests and assess performance.

Expected Number of Crashes – 'Qualified observers ... foresee the loss of two B-747 jumbo jets during the first eighteen months ... after that plane becomes operational,' according to the Washington DC Insurance News Letter Inc (*New*

York Times, September 15, 1968). This estimate is based on past experience with new types of airplanes. The SST, having far more radical design features than the jumbo jet, may be expected to have an even more ominous record in the first years of service.

Well that encourages confidence in air travel! No aircraft ever built can be guaranteed 100 per cent safe – there is always a risk, as there is with every aspect of living; the trick is to reduce that risk down to an acceptable level. To write in this manner – along with the darkly foreboding '... may be expected to have an even more ominous record ...' – is scaremongering again.

As to be expected, a large chunk of the book relates to the effect of SSTs on the environment. After all, the supersonic transport aroused the opposition of a growing environmental coalition, because of its level of pollution, its level of noise around the airports, and the human and environmental impact of the sonic booms it created by surpassing the speed of sound. Again, though, Shurcliff presents what can only be called at best 'half truths' to his readership:

> The engine roar at landing, too, will be great. The Concorde, for example, will land at 180mph with an upward tilt of 10.8 degrees and with engines on full. According to *Aerospace Technology* (of May 20, 1968, p.53), the Concorde 'may show a rather startling 124PNdB figure during approach, primarily because its engine inlets cannot be choked'. (The symbol PNdB stands for perceived noise, in decibels.) The decibel is a logarithmic unit. By way of illustration: 50PNdB corresponds to the amount of noise in a typical quiet living room, 90PNdB corresponds to the noise beside an expressway on which trucks are going by at high speed, and 120PNdB is almost unbearably loud.
>
> What loudness is acceptable? In January of 1969 the FAA circulated a proposed regulation (Docket 9337, Notice 69–1) suggesting an ideal goal (ceiling on noise at airport) of 80EPNdB and proposing to limit noise of the very heavy (600,000lb) subsonic planes to about 108EPNdB. (The distinction between PNdB and EPNdB is slight, and too technical to explain here.)

What Shurcliff does not say is that the sound intensity of the PNdB varies roughly as the inverse square of the distance from the source. This means that for each doubling of the distance from the point of sound, the 'hearer' can expect a 6dB reduction in the noise level. In simple terms, standing right by the side of a highway the traffic roar is deafening, but move away and the noise level drops away sharply.

He also comes across as arrogant and elitist, implying that his readership has a lower intelligence than him with the often used 'too technical to explain here'.

Regarding the level of noise around the airports, Concorde was designed to respect the noise regulations of the 1960s. The aircraft was slightly over the new regulations (FAR-36) imposed by the FAA in 1973 for all the aircraft to be built after 1974. However, it made less noise than the Boeing 707 and, according to the Environmental Protection Agency, over 90 per cent of American airliners exceeded the new limitations. Thus, the take-off and landing pattern, utilising Concorde's high rate of climb and manoeuvrability, had shown that the ground noise could be cut by as much as 60 per cent.

The sonic boom heard on the ground in a corridor 50 miles wide is, in fact, caused by the sudden change in pressure associated with the shock waves trailed by the plane. This phenomenon was absolutely not new, since air force aircraft already generated sonic booms both in America and in Europe. At the same time, Congress voted the credits to build a fleet of supersonic bombers such as the B-1 swing-wing bomber.

If people accepted the nuisances and the damage occasioned by the military flights as the 'price for liberty', they did not show the same benevolence regarding civil supersonic machines. In America, in France and in Great Britain, the governments organised tests in order to assess the effects of the sonic booms and to reassure their populations with scientific observations.

One of my favourite pieces of 'confusing the reader into giving up' and one that has caused me endless arguments with chemists and mathematicians can be found in Shurcliff's section on 'Contamination of Upper Atmosphere':

> Dr V.J. Schaefer, world-famous atmospheric physicist and Director of Atmospheric Sciences Research Center at Albany, New York, worries lest a fleet of SSTs, discharging in the order of 150,000 tons of water vapor daily (from fuel combustion) into the upper atmosphere, produce 'global gloom' (*This Week*, August 11, 1968, p.4). The President's SST ad hoc Review Committee believes that by raising the humidity in the upper atmosphere, the SSTs 'would alter the radiation balance and thereby possibly affect the general circulation of atmospheric components'.

A further explanation on the same theme is given by quoting extracts from the ad hoc committee review:

> The widespread use of supersonic transports will introduce large quantities of water vapor into the stratosphere. The weight of water vapor released is about 40% greater than the weight of the fuel consumed. Four hundred SSTs flying four trips per day might release an amount of water vapor per day that is 0.025% of that naturally present in the altitude range in which the flights occur. The introduction of this additional water vapor into the stratosphere can produce two effects which may be important:
> 1. Persistent contrails might form to such an extent that there would be a significant increase in cirrus clouds;
> 2. There could be a significant increase in the relative humidity of the stratosphere even if there were no significant increase in the extent of cirrus cloudiness.
>
> Both effects would alter the radiation balance and thereby possibly affect the general circulation of atmospheric components. Of greater significance may be the local contamination one can expect from a high concentration of flights over the North Atlantic. If half the activity is concentrated over 5% of the earth's surface, local contamination would be ten times larger than calculated above on a global basis or about 0.25% per day of the naturally present water vapor. However, the local concentration of water vapor from flights on crowded routes may spread out rapidly and be of no real significance.

'The weight of water vapor released is about 40% greater than the weight of the fuel consumed'? Sounds like one of the holy grails of alchemy has been discovered here! How can that be? I am no chemist, but I am aware that there must be a conservation of mass throughout the combustion process. In simple terms, what you put in you get out; nothing can be 'destroyed' – or multiplied.

Then I realised that the key word here is 'fuel'. To the man in the street, 'fuel' is the petrol you put in the tank of your car – or in the case of a modern airliner, kerosene. However, to a chemist, that is just only one component of 'fuel', the other part being oxygen.

The type of jet turbine engines fitted to Concorde – and that were going to be fitted to the American SSTs – burn one of two main grades of turbine fuel. 'Jet A-1', a kerosene grade of fuel suitable for most turbine-engined aircraft, is produced to a stringent internationally agreed standard, has a flash point above 38°C (100°F) and a freeze point maximum of -47°C. It is widely available outside the USA. The other is 'Jet A', which is a similar kerosene type of fuel, produced to an ASTM International specification and normally available only in the USA. It has the same flash point as Jet A-1 but a higher freeze point maximum (-40°C).

The display in the cabin of Concorde showing the Mach number at every instant of the flight was highly praised by guest passengers. Mach 1.99 … 2.00 … 2.01 … in sequence for veteran airman and television star Arthur Godfrey (top), Colombia's Director of Civil Aviation Jorge Barco (centre) and Mme Guena, the French Transport Minister's wife (bottom).

Now, I have no intention of insulting my reader by saying that this is 'too technical to explain here', but what follows *is* technical, so please stay with me!

The basic chemical make-up of kerosene is $CH_3(CH_2)10CH_3$ – it is a mixture of hydrocarbons of this formula, but has no specific molecular formula, with twelve to fifteen carbon hydrocarbons that typically contain between six and sixteen carbon atoms per molecule. There is no oxygen in it, so in order to combust, it has to have oxygen supplied from an external source – the atmosphere. Shurcliff states that the water vapour released was 40 per cent greater in weight than the fuel consumed – water has a chemical make–up of two hydrogen molecules and one oxygen molecule. Part of the increase in weight can be explained by the changes in molecular structure – and therefore atomic weight – brought about by combustion, the remainder being brought about by addition of oxygen extracted from the atmosphere. Of course, Shurcliff explains none of this – he just quotes the 40 per cent increase for it 'looks better'.

Hazards to Passengers and Crew

It is in this area that Shurcliff excels. He throws everything into the mix to terrify the reader:

> There is an urgent need to carefully evaluate the inherent operational and environmental hazards that will be encountered while accelerating from zero to Mach 3 and cruising at supersonic speeds in a hostile environment. Passengers and crew will be vulnerable to a number of potentially serious physical, physiological, and psychological stresses associated with rapid acceleration, gravitational changes, reduced barometric pressure, increased ionizing radiation, temperature changes, and aircraft noise and vibration.
>
> Man cannot tolerate acceleration loads above 4 to 5g. Visual disturbances occur between 3 and 4g. At 5g. loss of consciousness occurs. Turbulent flight may cause brief linear acceleration of 10 to 12g. which could cause fractures in unrestrained persons. Angular accelerations in turns and linear-angular accelerations during turbulent flight are important causes of motion sickness. Under cruise conditions the SST's exterior skin temperature will approach 260°C. Therefore, it is necessary to insulate the cabin and to install refrigeration, whereas subsonic jets require heating at cruise altitudes because the external temperature is approximately 55 degrees below zero centigrade.
>
> Ozone is present in a concentration of about 8ppm [parts per million] at 65,000 feet. There is ample evidence that ozone is a highly toxic substance which must not be allowed to enter the plane.
>
> A doubling of the present flight altitude reduces ambient air pressure from one-fifth to one-thirtieth that at sea level. Therefore, in order to maintain current cabin pressures equivalent to an altitude of 7,500 feet, pressurization of the SST must be increased by approximately 2.5psi above subsonic jets. A loss of pressure at 65,000 feet would result in all aboard losing consciousness within fifteen seconds.
>
> The radiation hazard would be approximately 100 times greater than at ground level. A flight crew exposed for 600 hours annually will accumulate 0.85rem (roentgen-equivalent-man) from this source alone. When this value is compared with the Maximum Permissible Dose of 0.5rem for the general public, the question arises whether SST crews should be placed in the category of radiation workers and kept under close surveillance. The advisability of allowing pregnant women, especially in the first trimester, to travel in these

planes, and of limiting diagnostic x-rays for individuals who fly SSTs, will also need to be considered. Much higher rates of exposure associated with solar flares are to be avoided by utilizing a warning network which will permit the pilot to descend to safer altitudes. Criteria should be developed to guide prospective passengers afflicted with chronic diseases, for whom the environmental stresses which might conceivably be encountered could be detrimental to their health. Lastly, special consideration should be given to the bio-instrumentation of flight crews in view of experiences in manned space flight which have demonstrated the occurrence of serious loss of insight and judgment which accompany stress such as hypoxia or fatigue. At the earliest indication of malfunction of the aircraft, especially in its pressurization, temperature control, or oxygen systems, the aircraft must be brought down to safe levels as quickly as possible either by the crew or by the automatic pilot. The health and welfare of crews and passengers are incomparably more dependent on the proper functioning of equipment for the SST than for subsonic aircraft.

en vol à bord de
in flight aboard   **Concorde 02** ➤

Vendredi 1er juin 1973

Caviar Frais d'Iran
Vodka Moscowskaia

Aiguillettes de Canetons Nantais
au Poivre Vert

Mousseline de Céleri
à la Crème

Crottins de Chavignol

Dacquoise aux Fraises

Dom Perignon 1964   Café
Château Batailley 1965   Liqueurs

During the 1973 Paris Air Salon a refined passenger service was provided by a mixed Air France and Aérospatiale cabin crew to selected guests during a series of demonstration flights. For the record, the menu of the first lunch served at Mach 2 speed aboard Concorde 02 is illustrated to the left, suggesting a typical meal for Concorde passengers in 1975, leaving Europe at 10 a.m. and landing in New York … at 8.30 a.m. local time!

Just in case the reader had not been terrified enough, Shurcliff rammed the point home, stating that it had been suggested that women of child-bearing age might be advised to avoid such high-altitude flights. SST hostesses, likewise, should perhaps be beyond child-bearing age, and all crew members should be classified as 'radiation workers', with their doses and flight hours controlled accordingly.

Dr S.R. Mohler, Chief, FAA Aeromedical Applications Division, has indicated that SST crews would run the risk that radiation 'may shorten the life span by 5 to 10% and the gross signs of aging may appear earlier than would otherwise be anticipated'. Other possible results of exposure to radiation, according to Dr Mohler, are damage to sperm cells, bone marrow, lung tissues, kidney tissues, and the lymphatic system – and leukemia.

Shurcliff Attempts to Justify his Case

Let us start with the question of need. Would the SST fill an important need? The proponents say it would. They say that a 1,800mph SST would reduce the flight time across the North Atlantic from 5½ hours (by jumbo jet) to 2½ hours and would reduce the flight time across the Pacific from 10 hours (by jumbo jet) to 6 hours. This is important, they claim. Much time would be saved by high-paid businessmen, dealings with Europe and the Orient would be facilitated, and international trade and goodwill would flourish.

But what really counts is door-to-door travel time. Traveling by SST instead of jumbo jet, a businessman going from a hotel in New York to a hotel in London would reduce his over-all travel time from 9 hours to 6 hours. Going from a hotel in San Francisco to a hotel in Tokyo he would reduce the over-all travel time from 14 hours to 10 hours.

Thus the saving in door-to-door travel time would be only about 30%. And this saving would be made at the price of eliminating time for rest and sleep, and complicating the 'biological clock' problem. Also, SST fares might be 20 to 40% higher than jumbo jet fares. SSTs would be less comfortable than jumbo jets, and less safe.

The saving in time afforded by the SST might be offset by various mundane circumstances such as: delays in highway traffic en route to the airport; delays at the airport (ticket problems, customs, baggage bottleneck, wait for permission to use runway); delays while waiting to land; delays in recovering luggage; delays en route to hotel.

Once again, Shurcliff states facts but then twists them by not saying that his argument concerning the saving in time afforded by the SST being offset by the delays he lists also applies to subsonic air travel, thus completely negating his argument.

Consider purchase. How many SSTs will actually be purchased? The price, $52 million and perhaps $60 to $80 million, is as great as the cost of building a first rate college or medical center. Few airlines could scrape up enough money to buy one such plane without borrowing from Wall Street. (What kind of SST service will an airline provide if it owns only, say, four SSTs? What happens when one of the four has mechanical or electrical trouble and is out of service for a week?) Which Wall Street financing institution will want to lend hundreds of millions of dollars to airlines that today are flying with 48% of the seats empty, are engaging in cut-throat competition, and at best barely manage to keep out of the red?

What about the foreign airlines that, it is claimed, would buy hundreds of the Boeing SSTs? Where would they obtain the billions of dollars needed?

Yet again, Shurcliff's argument is incomplete, for his claims apply equally to subsonic aircraft as well as SSTs.

Let us now take up balance of payments. How many Boeing SSTs are sold to foreign airlines; will this really help the US balance of payments? A resounding No is given by the financial experts on the President's SST ad hoc Review Committee. The large sum of money paid by those foreign airlines for the purchase of the Boeing SSTs would be more than offset by the even larger sums paid to those airlines by US tourists (for airplane tickets to Europe, say) and by the additional billions of dollars those tourists would spend abroad for hotel rooms, food, and luxury purchases. Even the advocates of SSTs agree that sales of Boeing SSTs would be disappointingly small unless the speed of the SST stimulates millions more people to travel. Who will these people be, that travel in extra-fare planes? US citizens, mainly. Thus the more SSTs are sold to foreign airlines, the more our balance of payments will be hurt – by US citizens buying flight tickets from the foreign airlines and making purchases abroad.

Pro-SST persons reply to this by saying: 'But the Anglo-French Concorde SSTs will be flying then. Isn't it better to have the tourists fly in a Boeing SST than in a foreign SST?' There are two answers to this. First, there is excellent prospect that the Anglo-French Concorde project will be dropped. The plane has basically poor economics, there are no firm orders for it (and only 74 positions), and its price has escalated to more than $20,000,000. The take-off and landing noise would be intolerable at many major airports and its sonic boom would be intolerable over land, over islands, and perhaps over main shipping routes. The British Cabinet has already stated that the project may be re-examined or dropped if costs increase by 15% more (the costs are already about four times the original estimate). Second, the Boeing SST is not expected by its proponents to replace the Concorde but to supplement it – that is, to result in sales of many hundred additional SSTs. This would result in an even greater outflow of US dollars as the increasing numbers of our citizens flocked to foreign countries and spent large sums there.

Below left: British government ministers also made a point of flying in Concorde. Frederick Corfield, the Minister for Aerospace, looks over one of the test positions. *(BAC)*

Above: On the left is John Davies, the Secretary of State for Trade and Industry. On the right is Lord Carrington, the Secretary of State for Defence. *(BAC)*

In this section Shurcliff is again twisting the facts somewhat; he is also starting not only to plant the seeds of protectionism but to spark the flame of some kind of ban against Concorde as well.

> Consider the little detail of insurance. Who would insure the SSTs? If a fully loaded SST were to crash, the damage claims for loss of passengers' lives could reach $50 million, and the loss of the plane itself would represent an additional $50 million. What insurance firm wants to gamble $100 million on a plane that admittedly contains dozens of radically new engineering features, requires two miles of runway, takes off at 220mph, and is especially vulnerable to clear air turbulence, hail, lightning, and sabotage?

This is yet another red herring. There are no specific insurance items that apply just to an SST. Indeed, it could be claimed by the same rationale that Shurcliff is using, that there is a greater exposure to insurance risk in carrying around 400 people aboard a Boeing 747.

> Now consider creation of jobs. SST proponents claim that the Boeing SST program would create 50,000 jobs directly and 150,000 jobs indirectly, and this would be a great benefit to the country. But experts on the SST ad hoc Review Committee dispose of this claim by pointing out that the more Boeing SSTs are built, the fewer subsonic planes would be built; in creating jobs building SSTs, we would be destroying jobs building jumbo jets and air busses. Also, the jobs created would be concentrated in professional, managerial, skilled, and semi-skilled occupations which in a period of full employment, when these skills are in short supply, may prove inflationary. Very few unskilled workers will be required.
>
> Creating jobs is never a problem. *The Wall Street Journal* pointed out on February 9, 1967, that creating new jobs is a poor excuse for embarking on a vast new project: 'By that reasoning we should go around breaking windows so somebody could have the job of replacing them.' The problem is to create jobs that result in real benefit to the country and give employment to persons who badly need work. The SST project fails on both counts. (Cannot any reader think of a hundred projects more deserving of support than an extra-fare airplane that could not be allowed to fly at cruising speed overland?)
>
> Finally, there is the emotional question of prestige. Would we not suffer serious loss of prestige if we allowed some other country to build a faster plane than we produce? Could we abide seeing our President forced to travel in a foreign-built plane? The SST ad hoc Review Committee has answered these arguments by saying, in substance: if the British and French wish to build an uneconomic plane, then let them! Let them be the ones to find that SSTs are expensive, dangerous and unnecessary. Let them be the ones to reap the harvest of protests over take-off noise and sonic boom. Our aviation industry is second to none. We do not have to apologize for declining to pour billions of dollars into a doomed project —a multi-billion dollar boomdoggle.

Two items that are possible indications of Shurcliff's own bias can be found – the first in his 'Conclusions':

> Why should the public (95 or 98% of whose members would never fly in an SST) be forced to provide billions of dollars for an inefficient, unnecessary plane that could destroy peace and quiet throughout much of the civilized world?

Both Concorde and the Boeing 747 were heavily promoted on world tours. *(BAC)*

The second is in the explanatory note preceding Appendix Four:

> The main content is the set of four reports by the Committee's working panels. These four reports are presented here in full. A summary prepared by the Department of Transportation staff is not included here, since a majority of the Committee members issued statements declaring that the summary was biased and misrepresented the views of the panels.

In other words, although he was forced to admit that it existed, he did not like the views that report contained, and, as it went against his own case, he was not going to include it!

The Long Hot Summer of 1970

The environmental cause was picked up by the Sierra Club, the National Wildlife Federation and the Wilderness Society. The project also suffered political opposition from the left, which disliked the government subsidising the development of a commercial aircraft to be used by private enterprise.

Halaby attempted to dismiss these concerns, stating: 'The supersonics are coming – as surely as tomorrow. You will be flying one version or another by 1980 and be trying to remember what the great debate was all about.'

Nixon himself continued to lobby Congress on 2 February 1970:

> In this first year of the new decade, we have been working to establish a firm basis for a balanced national aeronautics and space program which is compatible

with our national priorities, goals and resources and which insures continuing progress throughout the decade. 1970 has been a year of transition from past successes to new challenges ...

From our aeronautics activities have come substantial contributions to continued US pre-eminence in civil aviation, major improvements in aeronautical services, and impressive developments in a sound SST program. This year has seen the initiation of new military aeronautics programs that will enhance our national security. We must consider other new means to insure that our national aeronautics program is given the opportunity and encouragement to contribute to our national well-being.

I am pleased to transmit to Congress this report of our national aeronautics and space activities during 1970. I take this opportunity to express my admiration for the men and women whose devotion, courage and creativity have made our aeronautics and space progress a source of national pride.

As the lobbying pressures intensified, Boeing took the unprecedented step of working with BAC and Aérospatiale (by then Sud had become part of Société Nationale Industrielle Aérospatiale) in the face of the common anti-SST enemies. In October 1970, the three companies agreed to exchange environmental information, and in January representatives of the three companies met to discuss environmental and other issues. The Seattle team sought environmental data from Concorde flight testing and suggested a number of further actions that would help their case in the US. Tupolev participation in the next joint meeting should be considered, the forthcoming appearance of the Tu-144 at that year's Paris Air Show should be publicised and influential Americans such as Senator Barry Goldwater and astronaut Neil Armstrong should be invited to fly in Concorde and comment favourably on it. The January meeting was followed the next month by a joint BAC-Boeing press conference in London, nominally addressing 'Concorde and the environment', but in fact embracing environmental aspects of supersonic transports in general. William Strang of BAC and H.W. 'Bob' Withington of Boeing joined forces to argue that, relatively speaking, supersonic transport aircraft would be environmentally friendly – except perhaps on noise.

The threat of competition from the British and the French was by now of little consequence in the battle to save the American supersonic transport. Far bigger issues were already set to decide the outcome. Even Boeing, despite its influential network in Washington DC, could not have resisted the environmental pressure that led to the cancellation of the SST project, although the country had already invested $1 billion in it. However, the balance of forces now bent in favour of the anti-Concorde side. The environmental groups resorted to large-scale methods of lobbying. They organised advertising campaigns in the media. *The New York Times* devoted many articles to the SST issues. In March, it published the advertising feature: 'SST airplane of tomorrow breaks the windows, cracks walls, stampedes cattle, and will hasten the end of the American wilderness.'

Generations of urbanised Americans had survived on the subconscious belief that the great wild frontier of opportunity lay just beyond every city highway. The grim consequences of supersonic flight were listed under thirteen headings in highly emotive prose with particular concentration on the sonic boom, whose 'enormous vibrations' would disperse the Newfoundland fisheries, affect the nervous, endocrine and reproductive systems, and even damage unborn children.

People were invited by the advertisement to believe that they were 'locked in a small room, and the walls and ceiling are closing on us' and were warned that the SST typified 'the sort of thinking that will lead our species into an unnecessarily short and miserable life'. On one of six mailing slips at the top of the advertisement, readers were invited to mail the president, opposing the SST on the grounds that, in words that sound very like those of Richard Wiggs, 'Growth for the sake of growth is the ideology of the cancer cell'.

This sort of propaganda was highly effective and the average American might have been forgiven for thinking that the SST was a metallic outrider of the apocalypse, trailing in its terrible wake not just earth-shattering sonic booms but widespread skin cancer and the fourth ice age.

There was no shortage of eminent scientists to support theories that the SST could trigger off one global catastrophe after another. None of these theories could or would be dismissed lightly by the US administration, and the government's scientific agencies found themselves landed with the impossible task of allaying fears by having to prove the impossible. If a hypothesis – no matter how fantastic – had been propounded that the SST might radically upset the environment in some particular way, then, according to the critics, the implication was so serious that the supporters of the SST would have to prove absolutely beyond any scientific doubt whatsoever that this was not the case. This was clearly an impossible task with some of the wilder assumptions.

The environmental case against the SST was admitted by many of its proponents to be based on the slenderest of evidence, but some of the charges were potentially very damaging. The debate grew to alarming proportions over the hypothetical damage that the supersonic airliner might inflict on the planet, but the undeniable damage being caused by industrial pollutants and motor-car exhausts was strangely relegated to the background. Shurcliff was remarkably quiet about the vehicle plants in Detroit that continued to turn out thousands of motor cars a week, which burnt millions of gallons of petrol to produce the greatest pollution problem any country had known in history up to that

Concorde is coming. *(BAC)*

time. Perhaps, through Shurcliff, this was McNamara's way of protecting his old employers.

Although the pollution caused by the internal combustion engine was only too apparent, and scientifically documented, to tackle it was a bigger political task than hitting the troubled SST. The aircraft became the symbol of the evils of runaway technology, very conveniently assisted by the patriotic fact that the immediate threat was from the foreign Concorde and Tu-144.

Boeing Walks the Tightrope

Concorde seen on the ground in the company of a Qantas 707 and a Super Air DC-8. The environmentalists often claimed that Concorde was much louder than these two subsonic jetliners; in fact on the EPNdB scale they were all virtually equal. (BAC)

The Boeing Aircraft Company found itself walking a very fine line in trying to protect its own product against the lurid claims made by the environmentalists whilst at the same time making the European effort appear to be suffering from exactly the same 'faults' that the environmentalists were complaining about. They did it by the clever use of the phrase 'US SST'. Their news bureau issued a statement entitled 'SST Environmental Issues' with a number of headings:

Water Vapor – Speculation about supersonic transports creating contrails at high altitude has led some persons to fear that a permanent cloud cover will be formed with possible adverse effects on global temperatures.

Actually, at the cruise altitude of the US SST – 60,000 to 70,000ft – contrails are rarely formed. The temperature and relative humidity are not right most of the time. During the past decade, military pilots have flown supersonic airplanes hundreds of thousands of hours at high altitude. Still, vapor trails above 60,000ft are rare. Most contrails occur at the 30,000 to 40,000ft altitudes where subsonic jet transports operate today.

All indications are that the SST's effects on the upper atmosphere will be negligible. Two scientific groups – the National Research Council of the National

Academy of Sciences, and the Office of Meteorological Research – have studied the situation and reported there will be no appreciable disturbance of the Earth's normal atmospheric balance by a fleet of SSTs making 1,600 flights each day (NAS Report 1350, dated 1966).

The study by the National Academy of Sciences showed that 400 SSTs, each making four flights a day, would produce about 150,000 tons of water. Although this sounds impressive it is about the same amount of water injected into the stratosphere by a single large cumulonimbus cloud in the tropics, and is dispersed over vast areas.

A comprehensive study by the Science Policy Research Division of the Library of Congress (Sept. 21, 1970) came to the same conclusion: No detectible impact on the environment or on global weather patterns.

Carbon Emissions – Turbojet engines produce carbon monoxide – about half as much as an automobile engine, per pound of fuel burned. Hydrocarbon emissions, seen as black smoke, indicate inefficient burning of fuel; the latest jet engines do not smoke. No visible carbon emissions are expected from the SST's engines when the airliner enters commercial service in the late 1970s.

The SST engine with its high-temperature combustors will be one of the most efficient powerplants ever built. The smoke-free exhaust is estimated to contain some particles of solid material and some oxides; however, the quantity of toxic gases such as carbon monoxide (CO) is estimated to be smaller than those generated by internal combustion engines on buses and automobiles. Measurements of the exhaust gas composition of the SST engine are currently being made, and the results will be compared with the theoretical calculations for subsonic jet engines and automobiles.

The SST will have far less detrimental effect on the quality of the environment than any means of transportation developed to date. A study by Professor R.F. Sawyer of the University of California at Berkeley shows that carbon monoxide and hydrocarbon emissions for even today's jet engines during cruise conditions are less than one per cent of average automobile emissions. Put another way, a fleet of 500 SSTs, even if all flew at the same time, would emit about the same amount of pollutants per mile as 1,500 typical automobiles.

Noise and Sonic Boom – The SST engines – ample power will permit these sleek airliners to rise quickly over the community on takeoff. Thus the engine roar will be less than today's jets at the standard measuring point – usually 3½ miles after the takeoff run begins. Using today's yardsticks for measuring sound, the US SST will be quieter than today's jets on both climb-out and approach.

On landing, the plane's design (wide span with separate tail and high-lift devices) will give excellent low-speed handling characteristics, allowing the pilot to cut power for landing. In addition, he can adjust the engine inlet to block the turbine whine from coming out the front of the engine. The plane will be noisier on the runway than today's jets, but research and testing are being pushed to find technical solutions to this problem.

Sonic booms created by the SST will not be heard because supersonic flights will not be made over populated areas. At the SST's cruise altitude of about 65,000ft, the maximum amount of overpressure produced is from 2 to 2.5psf. This is comparable to the change in pressure experienced by rising 50ft in an elevator. It could not break windows. But the pressure change is sudden and probably would be annoying to people under the flight path, so Federal Air Regulations prohibit boom-producing speed over land areas south of the Arctic Circle. Over oceans, the boom will go largely unnoticed and will not harm marine life in any way.

Radiation Exposure – Everyone is exposed to natural radiation. People living in Denver receive nearly three times as much radiation a year as people in New

'The first production Concorde approaching flight readiness ...' So went the caption to this photograph taken at Toulouse with airframes 3, 5 and 7 closest to the camera. *(BAC)*

York. A three-fold increase sounds big but three times practically nothing still doesn't amount to much. In some areas of the world natural radiation is as high as 12,000 millirems per year (100 times the US average). People live there about as well as anywhere else.

Supersonic flights at 65,000ft would increase the radiation dose by a factor of three because the thinner atmosphere won't soak up as much of the radiation. The result is a stand-off: An average passenger on an SST would be exposed to three times the radiation that subsonic passengers would, but only for one-third as long.

During periods of solar flare activity (usually on 11-year cycles) the additional radiation from a major solar flare could increase this exposure rate. However, US satellite systems regularly monitor solar flare activity and if a significant event occurred, there is plenty of time to divert to a lower altitude.

In Conclusion – The protection of our environment has become a highly vocal issue in recent months – and rightly so. Past management of our air, water and soil resources has not been adequate.

However, environmental protection should not become merely an emotional issue, but should be a continuing part of technical advances in any field. In this spirit, the SST will be the first aircraft designed with the environment in mind.

The SST will have no appreciable effect on the atmosphere. Its sonic boom will not be heard anywhere over land areas. It will present no radiation hazard to the traveler. Water vapor emissions will be less than normal fluctuations in stratospheric water content. What the SST will do is provide a new, high-speed transportation system around the world – a long-range rapid transit system for the 1980s.

The Fight Goes On

The case against the SST could be divided in two: the micro-environmental issues dealing with the more immediate and measurable consequences for the environment, sonic boom, engine noise and immediate air pollution; and the larger geo-physical issues which are much more difficult to measure and assess, such as oxygen balance, toxic additives to the atmosphere, weather modifications owing to the effect of water vapour and radiation hazards due to ozone layer depletion. These latter issues have caused the most controversy, the difficulty being that it is impossible to say that any given physical change has absolutely no effect.

Almost every change in nature produces another change, however infinitesimal. Estimates can be made of probabilities of radical and dramatic change, and as more knowledge is gained these estimates can be made more reliable. In assessing supersonic flight in the atmosphere it can be shown that specific effects are relatively trivial in comparison with the same effects from other sources, but it is impossible to be absolutely certain of every consequence, even though the probabilities indicate that the effects will be negligible.

In face of the determined attack on the SST by the environmentalists, the plane makers became alarmed. At Seattle 3,600 skilled workers were already preparing the Dash 300 prototypes for construction. A giant mock-up was being assembled in an attempt to try to stem the rising tide of criticism. However, like the Anglo-French project, as each month went by the cost began to rise.

Some subcontractors lost their nerve and decided to pull out of the project of their own accord, because of budgetary uncertainties and the mounting public campaign. If the SST was shot down, the Avco Corporation, Aerojet General Corporation and Tool Research did not want to crash and burn with it.

The politicians and anti-SST campaigners redoubled their efforts. The popular mood was turning against the SST and needed to be translated into votes which could effectively kill the project by cutting off its annual appropriation. To take on the government, the anti-SST pressure groups allied themselves into a single confederation in the summer of 1970, into the new 'Coalition Against the SST', to fight the president's request for $290 million needed to keep Boeing at work on the Dash 300. Marshalling all the paraphernalia of American lobbying, the coalition aimed at sixty key senators. For some reason the resources of the aircraft industry and the FAA seemed impotent in resisting the challenge.

In an NBC documentary, William Magruder was certainly flying in the wrong direction, blandly telling the nation:

> The SST program is perhaps the only and certainly one of the few programs in which the taxpayers can invest their dollars and receive, as a partner in their investment, all of their money back plus one billion dollars in profit through royalties, and at the same time undergird our economy in America to the tune of better than twenty billion dollars over a twelve-year period.

Looking straight at the camera over the desktop model of the Boeing 2707-300, the ex-test pilot told them:

> Now this economy improvement is what's going to allow us in the United States to do these housing, education, transportation and environmental improvement programs that are so necessary. So the SST is good for Americans.

To most of his audience the SST seemed positively harmful, and the credibility gap yawned between plane-makers and public. The anti-SST coalition concentrated on the one indisputable irritant connected with the new era of commercial aviation – the sonic boom. Whatever assurances the FAA, Magruder or even the president himself gave that the SST would not boom over America, the suspicion was deeply planted that once the SST got off the ground it would one day, in a sneaky way, boom all the way from Los Angeles to New York. To the environmentalist image-makers it was a case of telling the public: no money – no boom. The cards demanding an end to the SST filled the in trays of Congress.

In May 1970 the Appropriations Committee of the House of Representatives rejected an amendment to delete $290 million from SST funds and thus voted to continue funding for the SST. Nixon passed on his congratulations on 12 May:

> I congratulate the House of Representatives for having very wisely reversed their earlier position on the SST, and I strongly urge the Senate to reconsider promptly its earlier vote.
>
> The Congress has today taken an important first step on behalf of thousands of workers across the country who have been engaged in the SST program – and whose vital skills and experience might otherwise be lost to the Nation.
>
> It has been a mark of America's greatness through the years that this Nation has been willing to explore the unknown, to maintain technological leadership, and, in so doing, to contribute enormously to the progress of civilization.
>
> I reaffirm a pledge made earlier: that the SST will not be committed to production until all environmental concerns have been thoroughly satisfied. I hope the Members of the Senate will find persuasive the same considerations that moved the House, and that when it comes before them they also will give it their approval.

On the other side of the English Channel, airframes 2, 4 and 6 were also approaching completion at Filton. *(BAC)*

The administration fought skilfully. On 27 May it persuaded the House of Representatives to vote in favour of the SST appropriation of $290 million, having wrapped up the SST's requirements into the total budget of the Department

of Transportation. To halt the project now on a vote in the House would have brought the whole of federal funding for roads, railways and airports in the USA to a standstill.

The Senate was a different matter. In the late summer of 1970, a Senate subcommittee opened up a lengthy series of public hearings into the SST – the ammunition in the ad hoc report was particularly valuable.

Witnesses were called from all over the world, including, from Britain, journalist Mary Sheila Goldring of *The Economist*. Goldring was an economist who graduated from Lady Margaret Hall, Oxford University. She turned to journalism in the late 1940s and joined the staff of *The Economist*, where she became the aviation correspondent and was well known for her sustained and trenchant critique of the development programme for the Anglo-French Concorde. Goldring later became *The Economist*'s business editor, rising to the rank of deputy editor alongside Norman McRae. Given Goldring's performance at the hearings, some irate aircraft manufacturers' representatives muttered darkly that she should be sent to the Tower immediately on return.

Mary Sheila Goldring OBE, aviation correspondent for *The Economist*.

Goldring and *The Economist* had led a vitriolic campaign against Concorde for many years. For example, the leader in the edition of 31 July 1965, attacked stridently: 'And yet the charade goes on; another round of sour criticism, another week of cuts in Government spending and Concorde officially still survives. Unofficially, most people have written it off as dead.' Goldring was fond of labelling Concorde as a 'bad aircraft' – whatever that meant. She pointed out: 'Extreme American caution, despite huge resources, despite careful research, should be a warning that supersonic airliners that can pay their way are not things designed on the back of an envelope.' Those words have a strange echo with those of Robert McNamara. Maybe this is not that surprising when one looks at other phrasing: 'Someone must call the bluff; the Concorde supersonic airliner will not be built. This is no sourpuss guess; it is the consensus of opinion among the men closely connected with the project.' One has to wonder, did she have confidential information from the top of BAC or was information being fed to her from other sources?

Goldring was later to claim in 2003: 'I said Concorde would be an expensive mistake. I was right.'

As the witnesses were called by the chairman, Senator Proxmire, the case against the SST programme was relentlessly pursued. The environmental arguments were paraded and economic arguments were torpedoed by a group of leading economists, headed by Professor Samuelson of MIT, who stated: '...even if the SST had no adverse effects upon the environment in the forms of sonic booms and contamination of the atmosphere, it would be an economic and political disaster.' Professor J.K. Galbraith of Harvard dismissed the balance-of-payments arguments as something that was 'strictly fraudulent and should detain no one. What is certain is that the SST will cost a great deal of money that is needed for other things.'

Najeeb Halaby did his best to defend the SST, telling the committee that the nation had to pay the price for staying in front:

> Failure to support the supersonic transport program will ultimately mean that we run the risk of relinquishing world leadership in aviation as we already have in shipping. In view of what is already happening around the world in the production of steel and textiles and automobiles, there is compelling reason to hold fast to the production advantages we have in aeronautical technology.
>
> The whole anti-SST movement was not without its dangers. One of the terrifying things to one who is dependent on technology is that there seems to be abroad a feeling of anti-technology, technology is the devil that has caused

every problem that we have in the United States today. But my only resource, the only resource for American industry in the future is to improve technology, without damaging the environment, so that we can meet the payrolls, can keep the ride going at a low price, can increase the size of the market.

Halaby also played the patriotic and anti-Soviet card: 'That is the real threat we face, and, of course, if there is no Concorde, if there is no US supersonic, for which I think most of the world's airlines would wait, then the Tupolev is the only SST.'

On 3 December 1970 the Senate took their final vote on the appropriation after a three-hour attack led by Senators Proxmire, Nelson and Muskie. The voting rejected the appropriation of $290 million by fifty-two votes to forty-one – a much larger majority against the bill than had been expected. The SST was almost dead.

Whilst the press and the Coalition Against the SST celebrated their notable triumph as the 'victory of common sense over blind technology', the administration fought back and tried to exploit the conflict between the House which had passed the appropriation and the Senate that had rejected it.

Nixon went on record on 5 December:

The action of the US Senate in disapproving the SST is a devastating mistake, both because of its immediate impact and because it will have profound long-range consequences for this country, I urge both Houses of Congress to reverse this action.

Because of our transition from a wartime to a peacetime economy we are experiencing substantial unemployment in the aerospace industry. The Senate's action means the loss of at least 150,000 jobs in that and other industries.

Another immediate impact results from waste. The SST prototype phase is now 50% complete. Halting work now – and destroying a development effort well on its way to completion – would be a waste of nearly $700 million of our national resources. It would be like stopping the construction of a house when it was time to put in the doors. There is another aspect to this waste: It would cost nearly $278 million in contract terminations under the present law to simply close down this project – only slightly less than the $290 million being sought at this time to continue the program.

Most important, taking a longer range view, halting the SST now could well be a mortal blow to our aerospace industry for years to come. The research and development and the accomplishments of this industry have been major factors in giving the United States a superior position in the field of technology. We must not abandon this national advantage now.

Beyond the effects on the aerospace industry, the SST program will have an extremely important impact on our whole economy. It will have a deep effect on our balance of payments and on the tax revenues coming into our treasury.

I am well aware of the many concerns that have been voiced about the possible effects supersonic transports might have on the environment. I want to reassure the Congress that the two prototype aircraft will in no way affect the environment. As for possible later effects, we have an extensive research project under way to insure against damage. Further progress on the part of the United States in the SST field will give this country a much stronger voice with regard to any long-range effects on the environment than if we permit other nations to take over the entire field. And this they will surely do if we retire from this project now. The SST is an airplane that will be built and flown. This issue is simply which nation will build them.

Throughout the history of aviation, the United States has been first in this field. If the action of the Senate is not reversed, our country will be relegated to second place in an area of technological capability vital to our economy and of profound importance in the future.

I believe that the Senate's unfortunate action can be and should be corrected.

Five days later, on 10 December, the president held a press conference during which he was asked about the delay in releasing the ad hoc committee and Garwin reports. A member of the press corps asked:

Mr President, you have had at least two reports on the supersonic transport prepared at your direction. Both of those reports have been kept secret. Now a group of conservationists and others are in court asking that one of these reports be made public, and the Attorney General is arguing against this, trying to keep this document kept secret.

I am wondering if you could tell us why the public should not know what is in that report in view of the fact that you support the continuing expenditure of hundreds of millions of dollars.

Nixon replied:

I have no objection to the substance of reports being made public. The problem here is that when reports are prepared for the President, they are supposed to be held in confidence and some of those who participate in the making of those reports have that assurance.

Now, with regard to the SST, I have satisfied myself, after long deliberation and considering both of these reports, that the arguments with regard to the environment could be met, that this prototype should be built.

What is involved here is not just 150,000 jobs which will be lost if we don't build it, not just the fact that billions of dollars in foreign exchange will be lost if we do not build it; but what is lost here is the fact that the United States of America, which has been first in the world in commercial aviation from the time of the Wright brothers, decides not just to be second but not even to show.

Now not out of any sense of jingoism but because this plane is going to be built, because it's going to bring, for example, Asia, not only Japan but China, in the last third of this century 3 hours from the West Coast to Asia – I think the United States should build it, and I believe that we can answer the arguments of the conservationists.

However, the SST was not quite dead. Congress and Senate leaders reached an agreement to fund the Boeing project for a further ninety days, until a newly elected Congress could make the final decision. It was purgatory for the men in Seattle who knew that their livelihoods were at stake.

The administration prepared for the last round – but their opponents already scented a significant victory for democracy, achieved by a movement started by a small group of citizens. Where the 'Peace Campaign' had failed, the anti-SST campaign had begun to succeed. Moreover, if they were going to preserve America from the SST, this meant making the whole world safe from the monsters.

After complicated congressional manoeuvring, including a filibuster by Senator William Proxmire, a compromise was reached under which SST funding was extended until 31 March 1971. The SST's defence rested with Nixon, who threw his full personal weight behind the closing stages of the lobbying. Overwhelmed by their mailbags, the level of public debate and by pressures from wives who were particularly attuned to the ecological issues, the Senators voted against the SST funds.

On 18 March the House voted 215 to 204 on what was termed the Proxmire Amendment to delete all SST funds, and on 24 March the Senate followed suit by defeating by 51 votes to 46 an amendment to restore the funds. America's SST was dead, leaving the world SST market to the Anglo-French Concorde, and perhaps the Soviet Tu-144.

A press statement was released by the White House on 24 March:

> Today's action by the Senate in disapproving funds for continued development of the supersonic transport prototypes is both distressing and disappointing. It represents a severe blow not only to the tens of thousands of workers affected, and to their families, but also to the United States' continued leadership position in the aerospace industry. More deeply, it could be taken as a reversal of America's tradition of staying in the vanguard of scientific and technological advance.
>
> I am determined that this vote on the SST will not be a shift in basic direction. It is a setback, but we will remain on a continuing course of exploration and development in those areas in which America traditionally has taken the leading role, and from which so much has flowed to the benefit of mankind.
>
> It has always been America's pride, and the source of much of our strength, that we have constantly reached out toward new horizons in the search for knowledge – not from a chauvinistic desire to be number one, but from the conviction that we must continue to develop the countless new benefits that flow from exploration of the unknown. Development of the SST has been a part of that proud, creative, and deeply humanistic tradition. Though the Congress has declined to continue helping fund this development, I shall strive to ensure that the tradition is maintained.

Just how large a role the Boeing Aircraft Company played in this saga can be gauged by a personal telephone call Richard M. Nixon placed on 25 March. White House records show that the president spoke at 4.50 p.m. from the Oval Office to employees of Boeing in Seattle, Washington, and Wichita, Kansas:

> I know this is a deeply disheartening moment for all those of you who have worked so hard and so long to make the American SST a reality. And I am sure that your disappointment is compounded not only of uncertainty about what it means for your own personal future, but also of distress that a project in which you believed has been turned down by the Congress.
>
> I share your disappointment, and I simply want to take this opportunity to express to you personally my thanks for all that you have done over the years to bring this project so close to completion and also my determination that the remarkable combination of skills and talents your team represents should not be lost to the Nation.
>
> Each time I fly in Air Force One – a Boeing plane – I am reminded of the role Boeing has played in making America the world's leader in commercial aviation. Throughout the world, the 707, the 727, the 737, and now the giant 747 have become symbols of America's leadership. I am counting on you here at Boeing to remain a dynamic force in our determined effort, even in the face of this defeat for the SST, to maintain that leadership.
>
> The reason I fought so hard to keep the SST project alive was that I believe deeply that America must remain in the vanguard of scientific and technological progress – the kind of progress your team represents, and to which you have been dedicated. Congress action on the SST has come as a severe blow to us all. But I am determined that America must and will continue

pushing outward the horizons of the unknown. I am also determined that we must and will make full use of the most valuable resource we have as a nation – the skill, the dedication, and the imagination of its people, such as you on the SST team, who have made our advances possible in the past and on whom we depend to go forward in the future.

As an FAA history of the time somewhat ruefully recorded:

Those intent on changing the patterns of government spending, its close cooperation with large corporations, and its determination of national priorities had selected the SST as their chief target. But most of all, the advanced airliner became the symbol of America's past response to its environment. The ecology movement, needing a clear-cut victory to establish itself as a credible political force, turned the SST into a suitably grotesque dragon, which it slew in heroic combat.

The *Los Angeles Times* admitted that it had 'became the symbol of resistance to the so-called military-industrial complex, a symbol of resistance to technological spoliation of the environment, even a symbol of distaste for President Nixon'.

Attention turned to the Anglo-French effort. Now that the Americans had decided to opt out of the SST race, would they force the others out too? The indications over noise were ominous. The British maintained a nervously respectful silence; the French reacted differently. On 25 March 1971, General Henri Ziegler, President of Aérospatiale, issued a statement. With French temerity he said that the future always disproved the beliefs of reactionaries. He pointed out that should the US

The visors on the pre-production examples provided a very restricted view forwards when in the 'full-up' position. *(BAC)*

The variable air-intake geometry to the Concorde Olympus engines produced 75 per cent of the total thrust in cruising flight. *(BAC)*

deny Concorde landing facilities, there were other parts of the world like Europe, Asia, Australia, Africa and South America. The general ended his statement by declaring resolutely, 'The Concorde programme must be pursued with more energy and confidence than ever.'

Others saw it differently. In an exuberant 'Success!' note to CLASB members on the demise of the American SST on 8 April 1971, Shurcliff added a postscript: 'I will be writing to you in a few weeks as to our revised aims, foremost of which is to stop the Anglo-French Concorde.' He advised Senator William Proxmire that the league was now focusing its efforts on 'shooting down the Concorde'. His target was not only Concorde, however. In CLASB newsletter 39A, released on 22 June, he reported that members had voted unanimously to continue to work to help stop both the Anglo-French machine and the Soviet Tu-144.

So the battle was nowhere near over.

7

Certification

It was not just the environmentalists who were trying to stop Concorde – the FAA also played its part, initially to prevent an exchange of information and then latterly as a method of preventing US airlines from operating the type. This revolved around the issuance of an American 'type certificate' for the aircraft. While the French and British national certificates of airworthiness for Concorde enabled the two national airlines to operate the aircraft, an American type certificate, issued by the FAA, was required before any US airline could do the same.

Type Certification

Anglo-American talks on safety aspects of supersonic transports began before the launch of the Concorde project. In April 1961, at the request of the British Air Registration Board (ARB), officials of the board met with FAA staff in Washington to discuss potential problem areas. Since design features of the aircraft were unknown then, only general discussions were possible.

Once the Anglo-French agreement to develop a supersonic transport was signed, Sud and BAC lost no time in considering airworthiness certification, both to co-ordinate British and French requirements and to plan how US certification should be approached. In December 1962, in Paris, the SST committee of directors of the two companies decided first to agree on a joint Anglo-French approach on regulations, and then open discussion with the FAA. In the meantime, contact with the FAA was to be maintained to ensure that 'nothing detrimental to us was being done'.

This comment is particularly noteworthy, for it shows that 'the other side' were highly suspicious that what may well have happened before could happen again. Indeed, this appears to be confirmed in one of Stephen Enke's reports to the PAC-SST, where he noted that approval of Concorde, 'as in the case of the earlier Comets', might 'long be delayed by the US'.

With strong echoes of what was to happen later with Concorde as we shall see, Sir Basil Smallpeice, Managing Director of BOAC, explains what happened in 1958:

> We ran into difficulty over the Comet 4 with the authorities, who would not authorise us to land the aircraft because of the noise it was alleged to create. We produced evidence that the noise level in 'perceived noise decibels' was not materially higher than that of large piston-engined aircraft.

It seems that political forces were at work here, possibly because Pan American Airways were frantically trying to get their own new Boeing 707 jet into service in the autumn of 1958.

Sir Basil Smallpeice (b. 18 September 1906, d. 12 July 1992).

G-BBDG's cabin
was devoted partly
to instrumentation
and partly to
passenger seating
as part of the
certification
process. Some seats
were fitted with
air-temperature
probes, as seen on
the left.

Sir Basil again:

We brought as much pressure to bear on the Port of New York Authority as we
could, through the Ministry in London and the British Embassy in Washington.
As a first stage we succeeded in getting approval for Comet 4 training flights but
not – repeat not, they emphasised – for commercial service flights. I felt that
they would be bound to give way on our Comet 4 application in due course – but
probably not until the fifty-ninth minute of the eleventh hour. So we went ahead
full speed with our Comet 4 pre-service flight-training and other preparations as
though there were no obstacles in our path.

    I was already determined to get to New York in our first aircraft as soon as
possible. I wanted to see what I could achieve with the Port Authority with a
BOAC Comet 4 actually sitting on the ground in New York – previous Comet
4 visits having been made with aircraft still belonging to de Havilland. The
Ministry did not rate very high my chances of success in getting early Port of
New York Authority permission for scheduled public services, but I decided to
go all the same.

On Tuesday 30 September, ahead of schedule, de Havilland delivered not just one
Comet to BOAC but two. Sir Basil decided to take advantage of the delivery and
conceived the idea that, as they now had two aircraft, BOAC could inaugurate the
world's first transatlantic jet service with a flight in both directions on the same
day, passing one another in the mid-Atlantic:

On the Wednesday we alerted the press and took them across on Thursday, 2
October. For their purpose we dubbed our westbound training flight to New York
that day a pre-inaugural flight. Next morning, I met the Port Authority. After the
meeting, there was nothing to do but return to our office on Fifth Avenue, and
try to possess ourselves in patience until we heard the results.

    While waiting in New York on the Friday for the Port Authority decision I
was turning over in my mind the organising complexities of a double inaugural,
when suddenly, about 5 o'clock, word came that a letter was on the way. It was
10 o'clock at night in London. There was still time to alert them for a possible
flight next day.

It seems that the Port of New York Authority caved in – possibly through fear of retaliation by London banning the Pan Am 707 services:

> So, on Saturday, 4 October, 1958, BOAC made aviation history by operating the first transatlantic jet service ever – and, to cap it, both ways on the same day. Capt Tom Stoney, our Comet flight manager, in command eastbound, took the aircraft up to 1,850ft while still inside the perimeter fence of the airport, at which point he throttled back to reduce the noise level within limits acceptable to the authorities.

Back to Concorde; this early, if wary, contact included further consideration as to the sharing of information between the Ministry of Aviation and the FAA. The level of trust between the two countries – or lack of it – especially considering their supposed 'special relationship', was remarkable. In January 1963, Lucian Rochte, SST programme manager in the FAA, warned that care should 'be exercised in selecting the specific areas for exchange of technical information', since the British officials might be able to speak for their manufacturers in making such commitments. In April the framework of discussion was widened, with the first conference between officials of the FAA, the ARB and the French Secrétariat General de l'Aviation Civile (SGAC) to develop international certification standards for supersonic transport aircraft.

The work continued during 1964, when much effort went into two joint meetings: an Anglo-American conference in Washington DC in March and a tripartite conference in Paris in June. At the Washington meeting the supersonic transport was one of three items on the agenda. Najeeb Halaby and Julian Amery co-chaired the final plenary meeting, during which there was agreement to the exchange of non-competitive information and to the further tripartite meeting. This meeting, the US delegation was told, was to exchange views and non-competitive information on airworthiness, 'system-worthiness', sonic boom and airport noise limitations, and operational factors. The FAA approach to the tripartite meeting was cautious. Its team were told: 'The delegation will refrain from indicating firm views on any of the problem areas which are to be discussed at this meeting.'

This instruction was followed by the US delegation, which was heavily outnumbered by the British and French representatives – and almost overwhelmed by the amount of working papers produced for the meeting by the host partners.

The Paris meeting was important in marking the start of a formal programme, known as FAUSST (Franco-Anglo-US SST), intended to unify certification requirements on both sides of the Atlantic. Timing presented an immediate obstacle, however. From the French and British view, firm design decisions on Concorde were now due, and a number of TSS 'firm standards' had been drafted by the regulators, who were pressing the FAA to indicate whether the Americans would accept these standards as a basis for US certification. The American view was that no commitment could yet be made on standards; the FAA's own tentative SST airworthiness objectives and standards had yet to be discussed with US industry. A programme of further co-operative action was agreed on, and the FAUSST meetings continued over the next few years.

In September 1964, an FAA team led by Halaby spent a week in England for what he described as 'intensive and extensive discussions' with senior government officials and industry managers involved in the Concorde programme. On their return Halaby reported a disagreement between the officials and the companies in both countries over the wisdom of requesting FAA type certification of Concorde. He noted that while the companies required answers on important design features, the ministries were reluctant to let the FAA have free access to

The second production Concorde, G-BBDG, left London on 7 August 1974 for a month of hot-weather trials and demonstration flights in the Middle East. On the first leg Tehran was reached in three hours, thirty-three minutes, crossing Europe subsonically and accelerating to Mach 2 over the Black Sea. After a few hours at Tehran, where Concordes are now a familiar sight, 'DG continued with a hop of 1hr 8min – just long enough to make it worthwhile to go supersonic again – to Bahrain which was to be the main hot trials base. A highlight of these technical trials was the carriage on 17 August of a hundred passengers, in addition to crew, at Mach 2 for two and a half hours. This was believed to be the first occasion when a hundred passengers ever travelled supersonically together. *(Both BAC)*

design information. This disagreement had been resolved by 15 July 1965, when General André Puget and Sir George Edwards on behalf of their companies signed an official application to the FAA for a type certificate for Concorde.

Though the procedures for type certification were essentially technical matters – the FAA had first to establish technical requirements and then be satisfied that the aircraft could meet them – General McKee, although only just sworn in as the new FAA administrator, was clearly very aware of the wider political issues the formal application raised. He lost no time in warning the State Department that there were a number of potentially serious problem areas ahead in the Concorde certification process. The State Department, after a more detailed briefing from the FAA, spelled out the implications in a letter to Charles Cary, the agency's head of international aviation affairs:

There is no doubt that should the Concorde fail to qualify for a United States type certificate or should there be a great delay in receiving such certificate, the ire of the British and French would be great indeed. The political repercussions which would result from a United States refusal to certificate the Concorde after its having been certificated by the British and the French aviation authorities would undoubtedly be enormous, no matter how good our technical justification for such.

Thus the FAA should stay closely in touch with Concorde developments, the department added, and the British and the French should be promptly advised of any Concorde characteristics that might prevent its qualifying for a US type certificate. At this stage, America's views should be stated in a low-key manner.

It was Raymond Malloy, successor to George Prill as the FAA's man in Brussels, who conveyed the low-key views to the British and French regulators in February 1966. 'It appears that we should now begin preparation for the first meeting on the Concorde certification.' The FAA's list of possible problem areas had grown to twenty-three topics: cockpit view, emergency evacuation of passengers, runway length, fuel reserves, noise-abatement procedures, centre-of-gravity control, controllability, crashworthiness, reliability of systems, new materials, structural loads, speed margins, de-icing and ten specific propulsion items.

A series of type board meetings (TBMs) to discuss certification issues were held throughout 1966 and 1967, and the FAA canvassed the views of US airlines holding Concorde options. At the roll-out of the first prototype Concorde at Toulouse on 11 December 1967, Pierre Satre and William Strang complained to Malloy of the serious problems in the FAA certification processes – they were not clear and, as they stood, they would delay Concorde development. Malloy agreed to set up a joint meeting in Brussels a week later with the companies, the ARB and SGAC to discuss the problems. At that meeting, Satre argued that the production design characteristics of Concorde were already chosen, and since the first eighteen aircraft – for Air France, BOAC and Pan American – must all be to a common standard acceptable to the FAA, it was imperative that the final FAA requirements be made known as soon as possible. The FAA in turn complained about the slow progress in issuing the Anglo-French TSS standards, which the agency needed for comparison, and that both sets of standards were continually changing. After a wide-ranging discussion, they agreed on a six-point statement of ground rules that defined the schedule for the approval of standards.

FAA certification of Concorde was to prove a long, drawn-out affair. In July 1968, Malloy reported on progress to the deputy administrator, adding a caustic comment on the practical problems facing the British and French in their efforts to complete the TSS standards:

There has been evidence of inconsistent organization, overlapping, repetition, and the ever-present problem of translating the half that are in French into English. It should be borne in mind that, on the manufacturers' side, the Filton Division of the British Aircraft Corporation has not engaged in a civil transport certification program since the Britannia program in the mid-1950s, and Sud has not been involved in a type certification since the Caravelle was certificated in 1958, thus both companies show evidence of being out of practice. This confusion is being augmented by the inputs of a number of committees, airlines, IATA [International Air Transport Association], IFALPA [International Federation of Air Line Pilots' Associations], plus two ministries and three airworthiness authorities.

Concorde 02,
F-WTSA, painted
in Air France
colours on one
side and British
Airways colours on
the other, is seen
outside the United
Airlines base at San
Francisco during
the October 1974
proving flights.
(BAC)

Concorde 02 seen
at Los Angeles
Airport during the
October 1974
proving flights. The
Aérospatiale flight
crew comprised
André Turcat,
Firector of Flight
Test Operations;
Jean Pinet, pilot;
and Michel Rétif,
chief flight engineer.
They were joined
in Lima by Pierre
Dudal, an Air France
captain acting as
check pilot for the
French Certification
Agency. In-flight
cabin service and
ground support
were supplied by
British Airways
(from London to
Los Angeles) and
Air France (from Los
Angeles to Paris),
who took advantage
of this opportunity
to further their
preparation for
the entry into
commercial service
of their Concorde
fleet at the end of
1975. (BAC)

An important milestone on the road to US certification was the ninth type board meeting, held in Paris in December 1968, which represented the completion of first-round evaluation of Concorde and the presentation by the FAA of the proposed basis for Concorde certification to the French and British authorities. The draft validation programme document marked the start of the legal process of obtaining US certification. At that time twenty-seven technical problems had been resolved and twenty-nine remained open. Concorde was about to begin to prove its airworthiness in an exhaustive flight-test programme.

Technical meetings between the FAA and the British and French Concorde makers and regulators continued to thrash out the details of the special conditions that were to be applied before the aircraft could receive its US type certificate. Along the way, development of the United States SST was dropped in March 1971, and Pan American and TWA cancelled their Concorde options in January 1973, as Sir George Edwards had part expected.

As the airworthiness negotiations continued, the Flight Simulator for Advanced Aircraft at the NASA Ames Research Center in California proved an invaluable resource in exploring the performance of the aircraft, establishing appropriate standards and assessing flight-test methods.

American views about Concorde grew more complex during the Nixon administration, which began in January 1969. On the one hand, doubts continued, despite the success of the Concorde flight; reports on payload, fuel consumption and aircraft sales were pessimistic. Similarly, also about this time, an inter-agency ad hoc review committee, which President Nixon established to examine the whole American SST programme, like the now-defunct PAC and the 1963 Black-Osborne Report, did not take Concorde very seriously. One member, Under-Secretary of the Treasury Paul Volcker, believed that Concorde posed no serious threat to American leadership in aviation, that it would not create a burden on American balance of payments, and that it should not be 'an overriding factor in the consideration of our SST project'.

However, at the same time respect for Concorde as a potential rival was increasingly voiced and the Nixon administration generally viewed Concorde much more favourably than its predecessors.

On 2 March 1969, Concorde prototype 001, registered as F-WTSS, was now packed with 10 tons of test instruments. Its first flight from Toulouse had been delayed for several days due to bad weather, but at 1540hrs, and captained by chief test pilot André Turcat, Concorde 001 started its first take-off run. With afterburners lit, the four Olympus 593 engines briskly accelerated the aircraft, and after 4,700ft of runway and at a speed of 205 knots Captain Turcat, flying manually throughout, rotated 001. The aircraft climbed steeply away accompanied by two chase aircraft, one taking film and the other to serve the calibration of Concorde's airspeed indication systems. For this historic flight the landing gear was left in the down position and the 'droop-snoot' nose left lowered. Accompanying André Turcat that day were co-pilot Jacques Guignard and engineer observers Henri Perrier and Michel Rétif. At 1608hrs Concorde 001 made a perfect landing.

By early April 1969 the French prototype had completed eight flights and had flown a total of ten hours, and on 9 April, British Concorde 002 (G-BSST) made its first flight from Filton. Concorde 002's crew for that flight were chief test pilot for commercial aircraft BAC, Brian Trubshaw, co-pilot John Cochrane and Brian Watts, the engineer observer. After carrying out the specified test items G-BSST made its approach to RAF Fairford, which had been equipped as the main Concorde flight test centre. With both radar altimeters failed, and the crew being 35ft above the landing gear, Brian Trubshaw made an impeccable landing. One experienced American observer characterised the British prototype's performance as 'good, standard, easy takeoff'.

In mid-August Transportation Secretary John A. Volpe, who had emerged as an important SST advocate now that the FAA and the SST programme were part of his department, reported to President Nixon that the Concorde test-flight phase was 'progressing satisfactorily, with British confidence holding firm'. On 1 October, the French prototype flew at supersonic speeds for the first time. It was the aircraft's forty-fifth flight. One SST programme official remarked that in spite of sceptical views from the ad hoc review committee, Concorde and even the Russian Tu-144

SST had been successful. The SST Office believed that Concorde would be 'a viable commercial aircraft' and would be operational in 1973.

Then, on 6 October 1969, issue 7 of *Concorde Flight News* proudly announced, 'Concorde flew at supersonic speed for the first time on 1st October. This was the 45th flight of aircraft 001 and the sixth since flying resumed on 21st September. M. André Turcat and M. Jean Pinet who were at the controls reported that handling and thrust margins were satisfactory.'

In the interest of historical accuracy, the editors somewhat amusingly stated: 'Readers in the air transport industry will perhaps point out that this is not the first time a commercial passenger aircraft has exceeded Mach 1' – adding that a DC-8 on test achieved the distinction eight years ago. 'It can at any rate be said that this is the first time in the Western world that it has been protracted and deliberate!'

The event they were referring to was when, on 21 August 1961, during a routine certification test flight, Douglas chief pilot William Magruder flew the aircraft faster than the speed of sound, making the DC-8 the first commercial jet transport to break the sound barrier. After climbing to an altitude of 52,090ft, the DC-8-42 series aircraft attained a maximum speed of Mach 1.012 or 660mph while in a controlled dive through 41,088ft. The purpose of the flight was to collect data on a new leading-edge design for the wing.

It was not long before BAC and Sud-Aviation let others fly Concorde. On 11 November 1969, Captain Paul Roitsch of Pan American, Captain Maurice Bernard of Air France, Captain Vernon Laursen of TWA and Captain James Andrew of BOAC all evaluated the handling qualities of the aircraft during subsonic and supersonic flight and gave an assessment of the developments which were necessary to ensure that Concorde could be operated on their routes by airline pilots of average ability without the need for excessive training.

The evaluation began with a thorough briefing by the test pilots and engineers, and a discussion of aircraft characteristics and programme development. This was followed by two simulation periods for each pilot in an advanced flight simulator with motion and visual systems. In the first, a wide range of Concorde characteristics were explored and flown well beyond the safety margins to illustrate the effects of serious departures from profile. In the second, the aircraft exercise was flown and, in addition, certain procedures (such as two-engine approach) were explored. Cockpit briefings were given before the flight and the result was that they were familiar with the layout and general operation of the aircraft when the flying began.

G-BOAC was engaged on endurance flying, making a long tour of 130 flights from 7 July to 13 September 1975. It is seen here 'resting' between flights at Bahrain. *(BAC)*

The exercise was very comprehensive and covered all the points which they had requested at their meeting with the manufacturers in June, and many others. However, it was made quite clear to the pilots that the programme was not fixed and that they were free to explore other areas should they wish to do so.

No restrictions were placed upon their examination of emergency and failure conditions, within the envelope which had been explored to date by the test pilots. The thrust-to-weight ratio was representative of the conditions anticipated for the production aircraft.

After take-off the aircraft was climbed to 27,000ft and flown at Mach 0.9 while fuel was transferred to allow for supersonic centre-of-gravity changes to be made. Reheat was then selected with full power and the aircraft climbed at 360 knots, reaching Mach 1.0 at 34,000ft and Mach 1.2 at 43,000ft.

After a period of supersonic cruise at Mach 1.2, one engine was cut so that the effect on handling could be observed, and the aircraft descended. At 28,000ft the engine was re-lit, and they were then asked to nominate any other failures which they would like to see. This was called *'failures à la carte'*! At 12,000ft various approach configurations were flown and then a descent was made to 2,500ft for approaches to the ILS on Runway 33L at Toulouse. (On the first day – Pan Am and BOAC – the wind was strong with gusts and was across the runway, a good representative airline day.)

The approaches were flown on 'raw' ILS (no director) and the runway had conventional VASIS (Visual Approach Slope Indicator System). The first approach was flown without auto throttle and ended with an overshoot at 200ft. The second approach represented the worst handling case they were likely to face (an extremely remote case). The flying controls were in mechanical mode, there was no auto-stabilisation on any axis and no auto throttle. The third approach had no failures included, and led to a touch-and-go landing with engine failure at lift-off. The final approach was made on three engines, with a normal full-stop landing using four reversers and brakes.

During the endurance flying, cabin services were provided by crews from a number of participating airlines. Above is a crew from Gulf Air. When flying in the Far East, cabin services were provided by Singapore Airlines. *(Both BAC)*

The pilot's report published later stated: 'For all the flight conditions flown during this first phase the aircraft was pleasant and easy to fly, imposed no excessive workload on the pilot even in failure conditions, and there should be no problems in training airline pilots and engineers to handle the aircraft.'

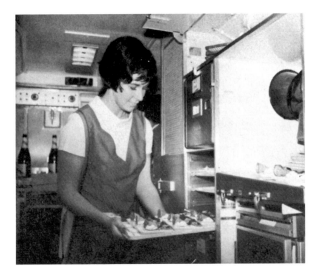

In early May 1970, Under-Secretary of State Alexis Johnson declared that the Concorde programme was progressing favourably, with twelve aircraft authorised for construction; consideration was being given to a 'second generation' Concorde, which would be comparable in size and economic performance to the American SST design.

However, American officials continued to ignore any opportunity for collaboration between the two SST efforts. The totally different design philosophies of the Americans and the Europeans – and the Americans' commitment to being the sole technological and market leader in aviation – precluded any meaningful technical co-operation. Fundamental differences about the importance of the sonic boom and noise issues also kept the programmes apart.

In the spring of 1970 the potential impact on Concorde of American regulations on SST noise and the sonic boom brought formal protests from France and Britain. Ministers objected strongly that the USA was taking abrupt action in proposing to ban civil supersonic flight over its territory and to regulate SST noise around airports. French Transport Minister Raymond Mondon was particularly incensed. Secretary Volpe was told that he had protested 'in the strongest possible language' against the proposed ban. The British also had objected and had filed a less threatening but very positive protest.

That April, the British view was strengthened to Secretary Volpe and FAA administrator Shaffer by Anthony

Above: A Gulf Air hostess in the galley (above) and an Air India steward (below) working the main cabin. (Both BAC)

Wedgwood Benn, the UK's Minister of Technology, at an Anglo-American meeting in Washington. Benn repeated his government's concern over the sonic boom and proposed noise regulations. The American records show that 'he stated he thought it somewhat absurd if we should build SSTs ahead of the rest of the world and then, at the same time, ban them ahead of the rest of the world'.

French concern was reinforced in July, when Henri Ziegler, President of Aérospatiale, called on Secretary Volpe at the Department of Transportation. Volpe repeatedly stressed that premature actions to restrict supersonic flight could seriously jeopardise the future of both Concorde and the US SST.

Throughout 1970, the environmentalists were campaigning for an absolute limit of 100 measured decibels of noise level at take-off and landing in the vicinity of airports, producing practical problems for the airlines, aircraft manufacturers and engine builders, whose engines made more than 110dB.

Apart from idealistic environmental aspects, there were powerful political and economic pressures behind the noise restriction lobby, for the real estate surrounding existing airports could become increasingly valuable for building if the noise was reduced. Therefore, particularly in the American state- and city-owned airports, decibels could literally be measured in millions of dollars of development money. Also it was economically disadvantageous if airports had to be built further and further away from city centres. In 1970, noise control became an important issue of state politics and no one was surprised when New York, with its growing airport problem, led the way.

Raymond Mondon, French Minister of Transport.

With the Boeing 2707 now all but extinct, the Anglo-American environmentalists turned their sights on another SST, which had never even flown at an American airport. Andrew Stein, an aspiring young politician who was chairman of the New York Health Committee, led the charge. Stein, born Andrew J. Finkelstein in 1945, was the last president of the New York City Council and a long-time political leader in that city. He was elected to the New York State Assembly in 1968 and served in that office for nine years. Stein was supposedly seeking to alleviate the sufferings of millions of New Yorkers whose lives, he claimed, were made miserable by the increasing airport noise: 'These machines will make yet more noise and are not yet welcome in our states.'

Andrew Stein's Health Committee hearings were held in a tiny room where the audience was deafened by the noise from a nearby building site. Richard Wiggs flew over to New York to present the case against Concorde at these hearings, which was stoutly defended by the former Minister of Technology, Wedgwood Benn.

Wiggs immediately attacked the man who had once been responsible for Concorde:

New York noise legislator Andrew Stein.

> Mr Benn in fact only represents the builders of the Concorde and that section of the British Aircraft Corporation workers who seem to think they should be granted the privilege of continuing work on the manufacture of a machine which is both a prodigious financial loss-maker and an environmental monstrosity.

When the ex-minister's turn came he pleaded for a rational approach to noise control and told the hearings:

> Our progress towards man's control of machines must start with good decision-making and sound laws, just as it did for our forefathers when they mastered their harsh primitive environment and then later began to eliminate man's barbarity to man.

Tempers flared and harsh words were exchanged when it was pointed out that the current problems were already on such a scale that the proposed Stein Bill would force Kennedy Airport to close because none of the aircraft then flying would be able to meet its noise restrictions. Wedgwood Benn was told: 'Man was not meant to live like an animal, cooped up. He is supposed to open his windows and breathe some of God's fresh air and hear the crickets chirping', and the British team were curtly told by the New Yorker to 'fly the supersonic monster between Britain and Australia so long as you don't bring it here'.

It was not only New York State that started the campaign to ban the SST. The assumption was that it was particularly noisy, particularly nasty and had a special capacity to destroy the environment. With the Boeing SST down, there seemed no chance of Concorde being allowed to land anywhere in the US.

Can we Ban it?

That summer SST director William Magruder asked government departments and agencies three questions. Could the US ban Concorde from American operations? What retaliation might be expected? Would such a ban be wise?

Overall, the view in America was that the FAA could ban Concorde – and its Soviet counterpart, the Tu-144 – for reasons of unacceptable noise, related environmental effects or safety; or that Congress could enact a law prohibiting both aircraft from US airspace. Any such extreme action would provoke retaliatory measures, and would be costly to the US in the long run. If they were to set SST certification noise rules that Concorde could not meet, this would prevent US airlines from operating the machine anywhere in the world, while non-US airlines could in principle fly their Concordes, certificated elsewhere, into the US. A total

ban on Concorde from American airports could turn the USA into a subsonic island in an otherwise supersonic air transport world. Foreign countries might impose reciprocal bans on US aircraft in their airspace and discourage their airlines from buying American aircraft.

The Commerce Department stated a number of measures that could be taken against the USA in the event of a Concorde ban. Purchases of American-built aircraft could be cut; operations of US airlines could be restricted on real or imagined environmental grounds; US airlines could be forced to use alternative, less favourably located airports; and US airlines' passenger service operations could be restricted at airport terminals. Their cargo operations could be affected, including

Amongst the passengers on board the last of the endurance flights was the Archbishop of Canterbury, seen here on the left after landing at London, discussing his flight with (L to R) Alan Beaves of British Airways, Sir Geoffrey Tuttle of BAC and Ken Binning, Concorde Director General at the Department of Industry.

delays in customs clearance; flight quotas could be imposed at busy airports; pressure could be exerted to renegotiate bilateral air transport agreements and compensation could be demanded; and a comparable ban on a US SST – if it was ever built – could be imposed.

The Civil Aeronautics Board (CAB) argued that a ban would violate the bilateral agreements governing air transport between the main nations of the world, such as the Bermuda Agreement between the US and Britain. 'The United States should not ban the Concorde if we expect to operate in a free Bermuda environment. If technology and economics justify a supersonic, and we agree they do, it would be foolhardy to attempt to ban the Concorde.'

The board also made a prophetic comment: 'It is important to recognise the power held by the various local authorities that control airport operations. Bodies such as the Port of New York Authority have great influence over the type of aircraft using their airports, and their support for US national policies should be enlisted.' The CAB went on: 'A ban imposed at this lower level could have equally disastrous consequences abroad.'

The State Department also argued against a ban: 'We do not think that we are in a situation where we must seek to stop the Concorde at all costs.' However, if there was to be a ban, it should be based on legitimate grounds, not on poor economics or competitive impact. The department did not believe that retaliation would be a major problem. However, the Treasury Department thought otherwise and warned that the structuring of general restrictions might be tantamount to an outright ban on Concorde and would indeed incite retaliation – not only against any possible US SST but against US subsonic sales also.

The approach of supersonic airline services to the USA was to be a turbulent passage through unfriendly skies. Normally the process was straightforward: existing international agreements included the mutual acceptance of national airworthiness and licensing standards, and reciprocal agreements on routes. These international agreements were, and still are, subject to relevant national regulations, applied fairly and without discrimination. Hence US approval was required for British Airways and Air France to begin scheduled services by Concorde to that country, and in a completely separate process, a US certificate of airworthiness was required before any American airline could operate the aircraft.

These customarily well-mannered and reciprocal aviation procedures were soon embroiled in a wider storm, as political and environmental arguments, set in the fragile framework of international relations, clouded the normally straightforward resolution of technical issues. The Concorde approval process involved not only aviation authorities but also presidents, prime ministers and the public.

BAC's American subsidiary had looked at the problems of opposition to Concorde in the USA in an internal report in September 1972. They found that anti-SST feeling was still high and suggested that the company should maintain a low profile for the next eighteen months or so and then gradually increase the publicity effort in order to create favourable opinions of the aircraft. Unfortunately, America's SST wounds were too deep and far from healed, and the planned orderly publicity campaign was soon overtaken by an all-out Anglo-French effort simply to ensure survival.

The Nixon Letters

A secret exchange of letters between President Richard Nixon, Prime Minister Edward Heath and President Georges Pompidou in January 1973 later erupted into a major public controversy when their existence and contents were revealed in 1976. The Nixon letters followed Cabinet-level discussion on the single most important Concorde issue in the history of the project, then looming on the horizon: approval for scheduled Concorde services to the US. The immediate question was what to do about the aircraft in relation to noise rules being proposed by the FAA.

Peter M. Flanigan, a special assistant to the president, had noted in November 1972 that 'there are a number of problems facing the Administration with the expected entry into service of the Anglo-French Concorde in 1975. On the one hand, the British and French governments would exert strong pressures to gain approval. On the other hand, rising US congressional and public pressures to ban the Concorde on environmental grounds were expected.'

Flanigan went on to list what he saw as eight problems:

- The FAA wished to issue a notice of proposed rule-making that would progressively reduce the average noise level in US airline fleets; this rule would discourage US Concorde purchases.
- The FAA also had drafted a proposed rule to require SSTs to meet the FAA Part 36 subsonic noise standard; since Concorde could not meet this standard, Britain and France would undoubtedly request an exemption – which in turn would be opposed by environmentalists.

- Concorde would have difficulty meeting FAA requirements for type certification and for operating in US airspace.
- The Environmental Protection Agency (EPA) had drafted a rule governing engine emissions that Concorde might not be able to meet.
- Congress might propose legislation to ban SSTs that exceeded subsonic noise levels; environmentalists would urge the president to sign such a bill, which Britain and France would consider an unfriendly act.
- The CAB insisted that Concorde fares be economic, i.e. possibly so high that few people would use the aircraft.
- Regardless of any federal action, US airport operators could ban Concorde because of local reaction.
- Congress and the public were concerned about the environmental effects of SSTs.

Flanigan listed three options:

1. Seek to support Concorde, by notifying Britain and France of the problems and indicating that the Administration will do what it can to admit the aircraft.
2. Proceed vigorously with US environmental standards and insist that Concorde must comply.
3. Adopt a hands-off attitude, allowing the problems to work themselves out without intervention by the White House.

Flanigan's memo formed the agenda for a December 1972 meeting of the Senior Review Group, comprising the secretaries of state, treasury, commerce and transportation, and the assistants to the president for national security affairs and for domestic affairs.

Prior to the meeting John Volpe submitted his department's conclusions in a paper, which in effect recommended a version of option 3: the FAA should issue both notices of proposed rule-making, without any specific exemption for Concorde. Volpe argued that since the action involved publishing proposed rules, not the adoption of final ones, Britain and France would have the opportunity to seek an exemption during the rule-making process. The government did not have to decide at that moment whether to grant any such exemption.

The Senior Review Group decided otherwise. The DoT would redraft the advanced notice of the proposed fleet noise rule so as to exempt Concorde, directly or indirectly, from its terms. In other words, the Volpe recommendation had been overruled; this decision, the minutes of the meeting claimed, was unanimously approved – as were the decisions on the other seven points under consideration.

The all-important issue of pre-emption – that is, whether a federal decision automatically overrules decisions by states, local authorities and airport proprietors – was touched on at the meeting. The DoT claimed that it had the legal authority to pre-empt state and local noise regulations, but would not seek to do so.

Anglo-French sensitivity on the noise-regulation issue was reflected the same month in letters to Richard Nixon from Edward Heath and Georges Pompidou, and by high-level meetings of officials of the three countries in Washington. Heath and Pompidou both expressed their concern over the likely impact of the proposed rules on Concorde, while an eight-man team of British and French officials discussed the rules and argued for a Concorde exemption with representatives of the FAA, DoT, State Department, EPA and OST.

On 19 January 1973, Nixon was able to reassure Heath along the lines agreed to by the Senior Review Group:

Dear Mr Prime Minister

I welcome your recent letter concerning the problems which the Concorde may face in conforming to proposed Federal regulations on excessive aircraft noise. This is, as we both recognize, an issue of major importance with both domestic and international ramifications.

I can assure you that my Administration will make every effort to see that the Concorde is treated fairly in all aspects of the United States governmental regulations, so that it can compete for sales in this country on its merits. As a consequence of this policy, the Federal Aviation Administration will issue its proposed fleet noise rule in a form which will make it inapplicable to the Concorde. I have also directed officials of my Administration to continue to work with representatives of the British and French governments in order to determine whether a United States supersonic aircraft noise standard can be developed that will meet our domestic requirements without damaging the prospects of the Concorde.

You have noted, Mr Prime Minister, that many aspects of the regulation of civil aviation are in this country outside the jurisdiction of the executive branch of our Federal Government. You must know that the Federal Government's power to influence these aspects, particularly with regard to state and local jurisdictions, is limited. On the other hand, my Administration is committed to principles of non-interference with free and private commerce and non-discriminatory formulation and application of Federal regulations. We will act in keeping with these principles to assure equitable treatment for the Concorde, bearing in mind that it, as well as all supersonic aircraft, raises unprecedented problems of environmental and social costs.

Nixon's assurances were not quite correct. In the instructions given to the FAA the distinction was not between subsonic and supersonic aircraft, which clearly

The flight deck of G-BBDG before being fitted with delivery specification instrumentation. The Canberra visible through the screen is the aircraft frequently used on flight-test chase work in conjunction with the certification programme. (BAC)

would have exempted Concorde, but between aircraft engaged in 'interstate' – that is domestic operations – and 'foreign' or international operations.

In late January 1973, John W. Barnum, DoT general counsel, reported that the British were concerned by this discrepancy, since the proposed rule would prevent US airlines from flying Concorde on such interstate routes as California to Hawaii or Alaska, and New York to Miami. The DoT answer was that the stated concern of the British and the French had been that US airlines should be able to fly Concordes on the North Atlantic routes, which the rule would permit. Barnum advised his department that 'the White House is willing to take the heat from the British and French concerning this domestic applicability to Concorde operations'.

Hands-on Practical Science ...

Meanwhile, on 22 March, during the joint seminar of COVOS (Comité d'Etudes sur les Conséquences des Vols Stratosphériques) and COMESA (Committee on Meteorological Effects of Stratospheric Aircraft) in Paris it was announced that Concorde prototypes 001 and 002 were to take part in a programme of research to improve knowledge of the stratosphere and of the effects of aircraft flying there. COVOS and COMESA were bodies recently set up by the two governments, having official membership but calling in assistance from industry.

Sixty European scientists attended the seminar and discussed work to be done during the next few years to study in advance the possible effects of the numerous daily flights in the stratosphere by civil aircraft, both supersonic and subsonic, in the years 1985–95.

A series of cold-weather trials were flown from Fairbanks, Alaska, using pre-production Concorde 02. (BAC)

The committees agreed that research should be aimed essentially at the following topics:

- better knowledge of the stratosphere's vertical composition in terms of minor constituents such as ozone, carbon and nitrogen oxides, and the numerous chemical reactions occurring between them.
- measurements of cosmic radiation and possible ozone traces in aircraft cabins.
- data on high-altitude turbulence and temperature variations.

Research would be partly in the laboratory, partly by computer models of the stratosphere and partly by direct measurement with aircraft. Prototype 001 was due to make a series of flights in May and June above the Bay of Biscay and the Irish Sea, while 002 would at a later date extend the research over the North Polar area.

By July good progress had been made with the high-altitude sampling flights in support of the international research programme to improve knowledge of the stratosphere.

This was real, practical science, not theoretical 'modelling' in some laboratory. The two Concorde prototypes made nineteen sorties, 001 from Toulouse flying over the South Atlantic and 002, based for the purpose at Prestwick, going northwards to about 72°N. Some flights were made at sunrise and some at sunset.

Three of the sorties from Toulouse were devoted to the programme of the US Jet Propulsion Laboratory, and Robert H, Cannon Jr, Assistant Secretary for Systems in the US Department of Transportation wrote:

> Dr Alan Grobecker has just informed me of the successful Concorde flights made on June 12–16, 1973, on behalf of the US Department of Transportation Climatic Impact Assessment Program (CIAP). Dr Farmer of Jet Propulsion Laboratory and Professor J, Blamont of Centre National d'Etudes Spatiales state that the scientific data acquired by these flights will provide a significant input to the DOT CIAP measurements program and to Aerospatiale atmospheric research efforts. The acquisition of these critically needed data was made possible by the friendly cooperation between Aerospatiale and the US Department of Transportation. I want to express to you and to your management my sincere appreciation for your support and encouragement for the Concorde–CIAP Program.

The results were written up in detail:

> Data gathered by instruments flown on board the Anglo-French Concorde 001 prototype in connection with the US Climatic Impact Assessment Program (CIAP) have provided preliminary evidence that no problems exist with the effect of propulsion efflux in the upper atmosphere.
>
> During tests flown June 13, 14 and 16, a Jet Propulsion Laboratory infrared spectrometer installed on the aircraft indicated that nitric oxide levels in the upper atmosphere did not exceed 1 part per billion and that nitrogen dioxide levels were not over 4 parts per billion. Total flight time during the three exercises was 7hr 17min, with 4hr 22min at supersonic speeds.

CIAP officials said that in the case of both chemicals, the levels were significantly below those computed by theoreticians as being a result of natural phenomena. They also stated that if the data proved correct, there was no foundation for fears expressed by some scientists that increased nitric oxide concentrations brought

All modern aircraft
have to undergo
water-ingestion
tests as part of
their certification
process. Here 002
is seen at Fairford
in Gloucestershire
checking out the
effect of spray from
the wheels entering
the engine intakes.
(BAC)

on by high-flying aircraft would reduce ozone concentrations, increasing solar radiation hazards to earth life.

A CIAP programme official said the findings indicate 'that there is a large (nitric oxide) sink in the lower stratosphere' in which nitric oxides disappear. He said it was not known whether the disappearance was the result of chemical action or simply 'transport' where the nitric oxides would be dissipated by winds.

According to DoT officials, the CIAP/Concorde tests supported data gained by French-sponsored tests flown earlier on board Concorde 001. The French scientific organisation ONERA conducted experiments on flights on 6 June and 9 & 10 July, with five hours, forty-four minutes of flight time, three hours, seven minutes of it at supersonic speeds.

Most of the cost for the CIAP/Concorde flights was absorbed by Aérospatiale, with only basic equipment costs being paid by the US government. The CIAP test flights were flown at about 55,000ft on a route north from Toulouse up the French coast. The IR spectrometer was positioned to peer out the side of the aircraft's fuselage with a field of view from the horizon up to about 100,000ft. According to CIAP officials, the flights also carried an ultraviolet flux instrument designed by Centre National d'Etudes Spatiales, a French laboratory for atmospheric and physical research.

Also during June 1973, a series of tests was made to determine practically Concorde's sonic-boom signature. From an aircraft operating point of view it was important to know as accurately as possible the characteristics of the signature, and in particular the way in which the signature decays to each side of the aircraft's track, so that flights could be planned to avoid public annoyance. *Concorde Flight News* for 23 January 1974 described the tests:

> Theoretical models have been developed to calculate the boundaries of the volume affected by the boom and thus the area swept on the ground, as well as some of the boom characteristics. Numerous test flights have already confirmed the validity of parts of the theory and have clearly demonstrated an attenuation of the phenomenon with lateral distance from the flight path, as also the effects of prevailing meteorological conditions.
>
> The principal Concorde tests have been those in the south of France (operation 'Jericho'), down the west coast of Britain (operation 'Trafalgar'), and

a number of supersonic flights across France from NW to SE. Supersonic flights have also been made over Australia, Iran, Saudi Arabia, African countries and along the English Channel. In these flights it has been possible to establish the characteristics of focused booms occurring during transonic acceleration or during turns at Mach numbers higher than 1, and of those under the track during cruise.

However, one aspect which had not yet been fully explored was the actual extent to which the signatures under the cruising flight path and at a lateral distance might differ. A knowledge of the laws governing the decrease of boom intensity with lateral distance from track would be of the highest interest from an operational planning aspect.

Special tests were therefore carried out in June 1973 along the south-west coast of France in co-operation with the Landes Test Centre (CEL) by aircraft 001. Flights at different Mach numbers and lateral distances from a measuring base were made with the path of the aircraft accurately controlled and recorded by means of the CEL tracking radar. A large array of recording microphones was employed: in all, 130 measurements at Mach 1.3 and 11,900 metres (39,000ft) altitude were obtained, and another 130 at Mach 2 and 15,600 metres, (52,000ft).

Analysis of the results has provided more accurate knowledge of the basic ways in which (a) the overpressure decays and (b) the rise-time increases, with lateral distance from the flight track.

The tests confirm ground observers' subjective impressions that with increasing distance from the aircraft path the nature of the boom phenomenon varies: the bang associated with a rapid build-up of overpressure changes to a dull rumble due to its occurring 100 to 300 times more slowly, while the magnitude of overpressure decreases to about a third. The phenomenon thus loses its specific characteristics and merges into the background of everyday noise levels.

These valuable results extend the knowledge already acquired about the sonic boom and will make it easier to evolve working rules to achieve the best possible standard of operation for Concorde.

... and a Visit Across the Pond

Concorde 02's record flight from Washington to Paris in 213 minutes on 26 September concluded a highly successful 13,000-mile tour to North and South America.

The historic first landing of the Anglo-French supersonic Concorde on Texan soil marked the climax to the dedication of this 17,500-acre world's largest airport. *(Braniff)*

The tour, which brought Concorde for the first time to the United States for the opening ceremony of the new Dallas Fort Worth Airport, followed smoothly and without trouble the plans outlined in the last *Flight News* – the total block time of 19hr 55min being exceeded by three minutes. On its way out Concorde 02 flew the Paris–Caracas route, 4,650 nautical miles between the two capitals, in only 5hr 12min, about half the time required by the fastest subsonic airliners.

So reported issue 54 of *Concorde Flight News* dated 15 October 1973. For this series of flights Concorde 02 was painted in the markings of Air France on one side and British Airways on the other. The tour started in Paris on 18 September:

Taking off from Paris Orly at 09.30hrs, Concorde 02 landed at Caracas Maiquetia Airport at 10.45hrs, Venezuelan time, after a low altitude pass over the airfield. A typical airline-type refuelling stop was made at Las Palmas in a chock-to-chock time of 44 minutes.

Although the great circle route between Western Europe and Venezuela normally calls for a stop at Santa Maria, Azores, Las Palmas airport was preferred on this trip for its existing servicing facilities, in spite of the 15 minutes extra flight time involved.

The distance was 4,650 nautical miles, the block time six hours, twenty-five minutes (including the refuelling stop), sector time was five hours, eight minutes and airborne time five hours, twelve minutes, supersonic for three hours, fifty-five minutes, of which three hours, seven minutes was at Mach 2.

Two days later, on the 20th, Concorde 02 left Caracas for Texas:

At 09.00hrs, on schedule, Concorde left Maiquetia Airport heading for Dallas Fort Worth. Guests on board included Mr Lee Johnson, Vice-Chairman of DFW Airport; Mr Fabrega, Panama's Minister for Public Works; General Berckemeyer, Peru's Director of Air Transport; Mr Acker, President and Senior Executives of Braniff International; Mr Galichon, Chairman of Air France; Mr Ross Stainton, Chief Executive of British Airways; and fifteen US journalists.

The sector time (overhead to overhead) for this flight was 2hr 37min, to which were added 10min for overflying the city of Caracas and 22min for three low passes over the airfield upon arrival at DFW. The final leg between Galveston and DFW overland was flown at subsonic speed in accordance with US legislation.

At exactly 1109hrs local time Concorde 02 touched the runway in the first landing ever made by a supersonic commercial aircraft in the North American continent.

This time the distance was 2,225 nautical miles, the block time three hours, twenty-four minutes, sector time was two hours, thirty-seven minutes and airborne time three hours, nine minutes, supersonic for one hour, forty-eight minutes, of which one hour, twenty-seven minutes was at Mach 2.

The next day two typical operational flights were carried out on the morning of 21 September, carrying as guests officials of the US government and the FAA, the mayors of Dallas and Fort Worth cities, the DFW Airport board members and directors, leading members of the Texan community and the US press:

Both sorties were flown at Mach 2 over the Gulf of Mexico, down to the Yucatan Peninsula with subsonic inbound and outbound legs over the mainland. Concorde again demonstrated its excellent despatch reliability and maintainability.

Sunday 22 September was the opening ceremony for the new Dallas Fort Worth Airport. 'The most beautiful airplane in the world', as it was described by John

Two typical operational flights were carried out on the morning of 21 September, carrying as guests officials of the US government and FAA, the mayors of Dallas and Fort Worth cities, the DFW airport board members and directors, leading members of the Texan community and the US press. Both sorties were flown at Mach 2 over the Gulf of Mexico, down to the Yucatan Peninsula with subsonic inbound and outbound legs over the mainland. Concorde again demonstrated its excellent dispatch reliability and maintainability. *(DFW)*

A commemorative plaque recording this first landing of a supersonic transport in the USA was presented to Erik Jonsson, chairman of DFW Airport, by the Concorde manufacturers. *(DFW)*

Connally, General Commissioner of the Airport Dedication, in his address, took part in the air show that followed the opening of the great new airport. Jean Franchi made a series of six passes in 02 before the thousands of spectators who were impressed not only with the aircraft's beauty but also with its unexpected low noise level and with the absence of engine smoke.

Concorde left punctually at 1400hrs carrying thirty-two passengers and opened the second day's programme of the air show with two low-level passes before heading to Washington DC via the normal airways, at a speed of Mach 0.93.

Concorde by
floodlight was
the star of the
international charity
ball during DFW
Airport dedication
ceremonies, and
the converging
point of thousands
of admirers. *(DFW)*

When Concorde touched down at Washington's Dulles Airport it had proved itself as 'the world's fastest subsonic aircraft'. The actual flight time between the last Dallas flyby and the landing at Dulles was one hour, fifty-eight minutes, a significant twenty-minute gain over conventional subsonic airliners. Guest passengers on the DFW–Washington flight included US Senator Bentsen, Mr R.D. Timm, chairman of the Civil Aeronautics Board, aviation officials from the FAA and CAB, the French and British Ambassadors to the USA and executives of Braniff International.

During the time Concorde remained in Washington, FAA and other top aviation officials had the opportunity to inspect the aircraft. Hundreds of visitors were also invited to have a look at the supersonic airliner. Visitors were brought from the terminal to the aircraft cabin by means of the airport mobile lounge units. Here again Concorde displayed its complete compatibility with present airport facility concepts and equipment.

It was then time for the big finale – Wednesday 26 September, and the first ever North Atlantic crossing by a supersonic airliner. The flight began when pilots Jean Franchi and Gilbert Defer released the brakes of the 389,000lb aircraft at 0746hrs, with Orly Airport a mere 213 minutes away. The payload comprised just over 8 tonnes of airborne test equipment plus thirty-two passengers with luggage. The total crew was ten: four on the flight deck, three flight-test engineers and three cabin attendants.

'We wish to begin services ...'

In the summer of 1974, the British and French governments advised the FAA that the two national airlines wanted to begin scheduled Concorde services to the USA in 1976, preceded by a series of non-commercial, route-proving flights.

The formal process began with letters from Air France and British Airways to the FAA in February 1975, the airlines requesting 'amendments to their operations specifications' to allow them to begin scheduled supersonic services to the US in early 1976. 'Operations specifications' define an airline's aircraft types, airports served, routes and flight procedures, and normally any change was likely to be approved automatically. Specifically, the airlines each sought approval for two flights a day to New York (John F. Kennedy International Airport) and one a day to Washington DC (Dulles International Airport).

Concorde, however, was perceived as being anything but normal. It was the world's first supersonic transport aircraft, and by all accounts its engines would be noisier and would emit more pollutants than those of its subsonic predecessors.

The Americans wheeled out a recent piece of legislation – the 1969 Environmental Policy Act. Under this act, any 'major federal action significantly affecting the quality of the human environment' required the environmental consequences of the action to be analysed in a comprehensive environmental impact statement (EIS). Accordingly, a draft EIS covering the proposed Concorde services was completed and published by the FAA.

The EIS process was not the only federal action to affect Concorde; the draft statement noted that proposed SST noise regulations were expected from the Environmental Protection Agency (EPA). As for sonic booms, the FAA had banned all civil supersonic flight over the US; this rule had not been waived in the past and would not be waived in the future.

Noise test data obtained on Concorde's visits to Dallas Fort Worth, Washington and Boston had confirmed the manufacturers' figures: in common with noise levels of early US subsonic jet transports such as the Boeing 707 and the Douglas DC-8, the Concorde levels were above those specified in Federal Aviation Regulation Part 36 (FAR-36). Concorde's low-frequency noise, causing vibration in buildings, was greater than that of other aircraft. The draft statement considered whether to reject, grant or impose further limitations on the British Airways and Air France applications. Granting the applications was the preferred option. The volume of Concorde operations, and so the environmental impact, would be limited and would not prejudice any subsequent general SST rule-making.

Congresswoman Bella Savitsky Abzug (b. 24 July 1920, d. 31 March 1998).

Public comment on the draft EIS was invited – and received in very large amounts. Written responses were submitted by many, including one from the UK government and an identical one, in French, from the French. In April, the FAA held a series of public hearings in Washington, New York and Sterling Park, Virginia. Strong opposition was evident, including protests from the organised groups that had both contributed to and claimed credit for the cancellation of the American SST programme four years before.

Ken Binning, Concorde Director General at the UK Department of Industry, and Gérard Guibé, Concorde chief engineer for the French side, answered many of the allegations in Washington DC and, a few days later, in New York.

The effect on the stratosphere of the proposed operations was small, they said. Concorde would raise by less than 2 per cent the overall pollution level at Kennedy Airport. The noise level of the aircraft was similar to that of the Boeing 707, DC-8 and VC-10 subsonic jets, and the low-frequency noise of the engines would harm neither persons nor property. The aircraft could comply safely with the noise control regulation of the Port Authority of New York and New Jersey. A noise-abatement procedure to achieve this had already been demonstrated. The airlines had no intention of operating the aircraft during the hours of sleep.

Léoncé Lancelot-Bassou (on the left) and Sandy Gordon-Cumming, aviation counsellors at the French and British embassies in Washington, worked together in the fight for US approval for Concorde services. *(UK Dept of Industry)*

Others attending the hearing disagreed. A group of banner-carrying senior citizens led by Bella S. Abzug, a New York member of the US House of Representatives, was present, as was their right. Representative Abzug said she regarded the Concorde debate as 'a rare opportunity for us to put a halt to blind, senseless technology which is applied at the expense of the general public'. The

British would have regarded her, as they did Richard Wiggs, as a Luddite. Another speaker decided to strike a historic chord. Recalling that in 1775 the lantern signal for the approach of the British was 'One if by land, two if by sea – we have to add another signal – three if by air. Today, we have many Paul Reveres here to warn us of this latest British invasion, this time accompanied by the French. We hope the result will be the same.'

In 1975, members of the US Congress were presented with a summary of the Concorde issue in a report by a Library of Congress analyst, which presented the arguments on both sides. In its discussion of international relations, the report extracted and condensed the controversy in blunt, if somewhat biased, terms, firstly as seen by the Concorde promoters:

> Britain and France are important fellow members of the Western community of nations. Those two nations have invested over ten years of effort and vast sums of money in the development of the Concorde. To ban it now from American airports might result in the collapse of the entire Concorde program, which is in difficulty already as a result of the worldwide economic recession and energy crisis. It would be regarded by Britain and France as a stab in the back, because of the history of the development of FAA's anti-noise regulations. As a way of permitting the 707s and DC-8s to continue to operate after the introduction of FAR-36, the United States (FAA) agreed that FAR-36 would only apply to aircraft applying for certification after 1969. The French and British, who applied for Concorde certification long before that date, regard this as a binding international commitment. Proceeding on the faith that a US commitment was a solid one, they have invested over two billion dollars in their Concorde program. If the United States should revoke its commitment, the act could shake the confidence of any foreign power in future promises or commitments made by the United States. It might also provoke Britain and France into some form of retaliation against the United States, such as banning our aircraft from their air space, or cancelling purchase agreements for US manufactured transports.

Equally, there were valid arguments against the aircraft:

> Why should the American people have to suffer as a result of the bad judgment of the British and French? The Concorde is an enormous white elephant, which should have been scrapped years ago. It is uneconomical, a waste of fuel, and a polluter of the environment. If our action results in cancellation of the program, the British and French taxpayers would thank us for removing this burden from their backs. Retaliation is highly unlikely, since Britain and France need us more than we need them. Anyway, this whole argument is irrelevant. The Concorde should be judged on its merits, and should be banned because of its excessive noisiness, regardless of the nationality of its manufacturers. Why should we allow a foreign aircraft to violate standards to which American aircraft are required to conform?

That Library of Congress analyst distilled the controversy of Concorde in the US to those few lines to reach the heart of the matter – and both sides would use them over and over with variations for the long battle that lay ahead.

Comments for and against the EIS conclusions continued to pour into the FAA following the public hearings. British Airways' US counsel quoted legal chapter and verse to sustain the contention that the airline had the right to operate any properly certificated UK-registered aircraft, including Concorde, to and from the USA, and that no EIS process was required. The British government also made

The view that so many photographers took of Concorde. *(British Airways)*

the point that its participation in the EIS process did not prejudice its rights under international agreements. David Davies, chief test pilot of the UK Civil Aviation Authority, confirmed that the proposed Concorde take-off procedure for Runway 31L at Kennedy Airport – which involved a turn after take-off at a height of 100ft, a relatively low turn by subsonic aircraft standards but feasible for Concorde because of its more precise control – was completely safe.

More Reports from the Americans

The long-awaited scientific report of the US Department of Transportation into the effects of flying in the stratosphere was finally published. At the fourth and final conference of the DoT Climatic Impact Assessment Program (CIAP) at Cambridge, Massachusetts, from 3–7 February 1975, this important document was reviewed by the scientists, including forty representatives from nine countries outside the USA, who had co-operated for over three years in research into the behaviour and pollution of the upper atmosphere:

> The conclusions of CIAP and the courses of action suggested are presented in the Report's Executive Summary, reference DOT-TST-75-50.

> 1. Operations of present-day SST aircraft and those currently scheduled to enter service (about 30 Concordes and TU-144s) cause climatic effects which are much smaller than minimally detectable.
> 2. Future harmful effects to the environment can be avoided if proper measures are undertaken in a timely manner to develop low-emission engines and fuels in step with the future growth of stratospheric aviation. These measures include:
>   a. The development of new engine technology leading to lower levels of nitrogen oxide emissions (which involves a lead time of 10 to 15 years for development, fabrication, certification, and introduction into service of the new engines).

b. Use of jet fuels having a sulphur content smaller than that in current fuels, through the application of state-of-the-art desulphurization processes.
3. If stratospheric vehicles (including subsonic aircraft) beyond the year 1980 were to increase at a high rate, improvements over 1974 propulsion technology would be necessary to assure that emissions in the stratosphere would not cause a significant disturbance of the environment.
4. The cost of carrying out the measures in conclusion 2, including the operational cost of compliance, is small compared to the potential economic and social costs of not doing so.
5. A continuous atmospheric monitoring and research program can further reduce remaining uncertainties, can ascertain whether the atmospheric quality is being maintained, and can minimize the cost of doing so.

The scientific conclusions suggest the following courses of action:
1. Develop, within the next year, a plan for a proper program for international regulation of aircraft emissions and fuel characteristics for whatever stratospheric flight operations may evolve in the future.
2. Accelerate combustion research and engine development programs needed to make stratospheric flight possible with specified nitrogen oxide emission standards.
3. Use low-sulphur fuels. Study the implications of utilizing low-sulphur content aviation fuels for stratospheric flight.
4. Develop a global monitoring system to ensure that environmental protection is being achieved. Continue research (drawing on the monitored data) to reduce the uncertainties in the present knowledge of the stratosphere and improve the methods for estimating climatic change and the biologic consequences.

CIAP also published extensive scientific background notes describing the natural atmosphere, its mechanisms and the possible effects of man-made impurities. These notes also describe the use made by CIAP, in obtaining its data and measurements, of satellites, balloons and aircraft – including Concorde itself. Some of the measurements of key stratosphere trace constituents were being made for the first time.

As a result of all the measurements and the investigations, CIAP states that, of the various chains of potential danger postulated in 1970, only two actually seemed potentially dangerous in the next 30 years – the 'ultra-violet chain' and the 'climate chain'. Both chains, however, could be fully controlled by limiting the injection of pollutants, either by the improved technology already referred to alone, or by also restricting the number and frequency of aircraft flying at given altitudes.

The Ultra-Violet (Ozone) Chain – High-flying aircraft inject (says CIAP) nitrous oxides into the stratosphere. These reduce the ozone which screens out ultra-violet radiation from the sun. An increase in ultra-violet may enhance some biological effects of this radiation on micro-organisms, plants and human skin on earth.

The present smallest change in the ozone which can now be measured is 5 per cent, but a future monitoring system could discern a change of 0.5 per cent over ten years of comprehensive monitoring.

The total ozone reduction effect of the fleets of present-day subsonic aircraft was 0.1 per cent (military aircraft much less), but if the world's subsonic wide-bodied fleet was to increase five-fold and operate 6,700ft higher than today, then the ozone reduction could reach 1.3 per cent.

The ozone reduction which would be caused by a fleet of 100 Concorde-type SSTs in operation for 4.4 hours each day at an altitude of over 16km (54,000ft) would be 0.4 per cent – which was below the minimum amount of change which would be just discernable in ten years of comprehensive monitoring.

If it was decided, therefore, to limit the ozone reduction caused by 100 Concordes to the smallest which could, in the future, be measured (0.5 per cent), no reduction in present-day emission would be required. Any improved engine technology, however, which would, CIAP estimated, require a 5 to 10 per cent addition to the development costs of future engines, could itself reduce future emissions by a factor of 6 or more.

Skin Cancer – The effect of the ozone reduction which might be produced by 125 Concordes was described as the equivalent of 45 minutes more on the beach. Only one in a hundred cases of skin cancer was fatal, and, if the probability of death on the highway was one in ten thousand, then the chances of anyone dying from a half per cent reduction in ozone 'were orders and orders of magnitude less'.

The report, in its section on the natural variability of ozone, says that on a typical day it varies about three-fold over the globe, and 30 per cent between Minnesota and Texas. The distribution in any one locality might see 10 per cent changes from day to day or week to week. 'It is against this background that man-induced changes (such as the 0.5 per cent from 125 Concordes) must be measured.'

The report then deals with the climate chain, and the effects on it of engine emissions of sulphur dioxide and, in lesser degree, water vapour. Sulphur dioxide, after first being oxidised, can react with water vapour to produce solid sulphuric acid particles, and the report states that such particles from present-day subsonic fleets do produce an effect in the stratosphere's 'optical thickness', which, in turn, results in a reduction of global mean temperature. A 10 per cent change in optical thickness, for example, gives a decrease of seven-hundredths of a degree Celsius or one tenth of a degree Fahrenheit in the global mean temperature.

The report says that there could be severe local dislocations in climate by a change of a tenth of a degree Celsius. It considered, however, that any threat from sulphuric acid particles could, if necessary, be countered by present-day techniques for removing sulphur from the jet fuel at a cost of half a cent per gallon.

In contrast with this 10 per cent change, the total world subsonic fleet then was estimated to increase the optical thickness by only 0.5 per cent and 100 Concordes would do so by 0.44 per cent.

DOT-TST-75-50
December 1974

REPORT OF FINDINGS

Executive Summary

**THE EFFECTS OF STRATOSPHERIC POLLUTION
BY AIRCRAFT**

A. J. Grobecker
S. C. Coroniti
R. H. Cannon, Jr.

December 1974

FINAL REPORT

Document is available to the public through the
National Technical Information Service,
Springfield, Virginia 22151

Prepared by
DEPARTMENT OF TRANSPORTATION
CLIMATIC IMPACT ASSESSMENT PROGRAM
Office of the Secretary of Transportation
Washington, D.C. 20590

Clearly this was a huge step forward in countering the attacks from Wiggs, Shurcliff and the like. It brought forth a muted response from Aérospatiale, BAC and their scientific consultants who stated that, in their opinion, the CIAP findings were, in respect of the measures to be taken, over-cautious.

Towards Certification

The year 1975 brought increased efforts in order to gain certification. *Concorde Flight News* in March explained what was happening on the technical front:

Of 5,155 hours to be flown before Concorde receives a full Certificate of Airworthiness more than three-quarters are now behind us. These have contained most of the specific flight tests called for by the mandatory requirements, and the results of these and of the numerous ground tests have lately been converging in a swell of analysis, negotiation and official acceptance.

The last main block of performance data is now coming in from the Madrid trials of G-BBDG. Flying qualities work is now largely completed on F-WTSB. The air intake control system, probably the most important part of Concorde's engineering since it is the heart of the aircraft's 'variable geometry', received its clearance for Special Category C. of A. on 5 March, except for the water ingestion aspect which is in process of conclusion on F-WTSA. Airframe icing tests have been satisfactorily completed by G-AXDN at Moses Lake. The same aircraft has just returned from Nairobi after satisfactory tests demonstrating engine air intake ice safety by sorties into cumulonimbus clouds of the intertropical front. Carbon brake clearance work from F-WTSA tests is going well.

Static structural testing on the ground, and rig testing of the various systems, have long been completed. Fatigue testing of the complete airframe at Farnborough, a continuing commitment, passed a major milestone on 21 January when the requirement for C. of A. (6,800 simulated flights, equivalent to about 15,000 flight hours) was met. The score now exceeds 8,000 flights, and fatigue experience will continue to be amassed on the rig for many years, keeping always ahead of the most-flown Concorde in service by a factor of three.

The Special Category C. of A. is the form of certification to be received by production Concordes 3 and 4, F-WTSC and G-BOAC, before undertaking the endurance, or route-proving, programme this summer. This programme is to be carried out from late May to the end of August on Atlantic, Middle and Far Eastern routes.

A meeting between the French and British certificating authorities and the Concorde manufacturers is to be held at Toulouse at the end of March to review the work remaining for the Special Category C. of A. for these two aircraft. All required tests should be finished by this time and such modifications as may be required will be embodied while the aircraft are in the workshop preparing for the endurance flying. The Special Category C. of A. should be received when they leave the workshop in early May prior to the endurance flying.

Certification of the engine at entry-into-service standard is expected at the end of March.

The endurance flying of around one thousand hours forms the bridge between the Special Category and the Full Cs of A., and the latter duly obtained will qualify Concorde to enter commercial service with British Airways and Air France by the end of the year.

Already, before starting the endurance programme, Concorde has gathered. worldwide experience, carrying numerous passengers from 71 airfields in

41 countries, and flying a total distance of 2.2 million nautical miles, equal to five return trips to the moon. By the end of 1975, Concorde will indeed be the most-tested aircraft in the world.

It was also time to start training crews to operate the airliner. A number of conversion courses for the first team of Air France crews assigned to Concorde began at Toulouse. A group of fifteen captains and flight engineers reported on 17 February 1975 for their ground and flight instruction ready for the endurance and route-proving operation to start in May and for Air France's regular commercial service at the beginning of 1976. They were followed on 3 March by the first group of maintenance engineers and technicians who attended similar courses.

On 15 April, the group proceeded to actual flight training and checkout in production Concorde No 1 in time to complete their qualification during the endurance-flying operation.

Meanwhile, at Filton the first pilots from British Airways started their Concorde conversion training on 3 March. Eight captains and eight senior flight engineers who had begun their course on 10 February were joined at the Filton training centre, run by BAC, by four members of the Civil Aviation Authority.

The extensive route-proving and endurance programme, totalling about 750 flying hours, was inaugurated on 28 May by the third production aircraft F-BTSC, followed later by the fourth aircraft G-BOAC, on the various routes that were to be operated commercially by Air France and British Airways from January 1976 onwards.

Endurance flying formed an integral part of the process of certification, the issue of a type Certificate of Airworthiness being conditional upon the demonstration of a sufficient number of flights covering the range of operating conditions foreseen for the aircraft – weight, altitude, temperature and climatic conditions over typical sample routes with airline participation.

While submitting the aircraft to intense utilisation under real operating conditions, these 750 hours of flying also provided the crews of the two national

Concorde G-BSST surrounded by the usual airport clutter. The machine was retired to the Fleet Air Arm Museum at Yeovilton in Somerset on 4 March 1976. *(BAC)*

airlines with their route qualifications. In addition, it provided the opportunity for various airline adjustments before the public services began, such as schedule finalisation, en route procedure optimisation, maintenance crew routine practice and so on.

For the invited guests travelling on these routes the cabin crews and the ground staff of Air France and British Airways refined the personalised service contemplated by both airlines for future members of the Concorde travelling public.

F-BTSC started the programme with a round trip to Dakar on 28–29 May for the benefit of the international press attending the Paris Air Show, then continued with services to South America and the Near East. As well as demonstrating the operating abilities of the aircraft itself, the endurance programme enabled the airlines to test out their intended maintenance procedures.

With Concorde No 3, F-BTSC, which had been busy since 28 May on the routes to South America, No 4, G-BOAC, now joined the endurance programme on routes to the Near and Far East and to Australia. This aircraft's participation started on 7 July with a daily return service between London and Bahrain, and continued on routes between eight cities with an expected accumulation of 441 flying hours.

An unannounced visit to Gatwick Airport was made by Concorde G-BOAC on 25 June. Three automatic approaches and touchdowns were made at near-maximum landing weight, followed by three climb-outs; as yet, however, no noise complaints were received.

The British Airports Authority automatic noise monitoring unit recorded maximum levels of 96 to 98PNdB on the approaches, well below the daytime limit of 110PNdB. Climb-out readings were even lower, but as these were not standard take-offs from a standing start they are without great significance. Of the six telephone calls made to the airport, one objected to the smoke and five congratulated the aircraft on its low nuisance value, which was taken as positive evidence that, when left alone, public perception was not as bad as the anti-Concorde protesters would have the world believe.

After a slow start, aircraft G-BOAC became fully engaged on endurance flying on Eastern routes, making daily return flights between Singapore and Melbourne.

Concorde had been cleared for using Singapore runways 02 and 20. A number of changes had to be made to the earlier parts of this aircraft's programme; however, 130 flying hours were achieved and the worst delay was two hours on leaving Bombay on 27 July, due to refuelling vent valve trouble. Lesser delays were occasioned by other refuelling snags, air traffic and by passenger handling – typical of the things that route-proving was designed to highlight.

The opening of the Singapore–Melbourne direct service on 2 August easily broke commercial records for this route, almost halving the times of existing services. This also was the first occasion on which the two cities had ever been linked by a return flight in daylight.

On 8 August, Stephen Downes from Melbourne's *The Age* newspaper reported on a trip he made the day before from Singapore:

Just what is it like to fly in a $46 million Concorde superjet?

There is no particular sensation attached to travelling at twice the speed of sound. And the plane's acceleration once in the air is gentle ... there is no feeling of being nailed to the back of your seat.

The Concorde arrived in Melbourne yesterday from Singapore, 4000 miles (6400 kilometres) away, after 3 hours 45 minutes in the air. The subsonic flying time is 7 hours 50 minutes. The Concorde flew faster than the speed of sound – about 660 mph in the stratosphere where it cruises – for 2 hours 43 minutes of the journey. It flew at or above twice the speed of sound – Mach 2 – for 2 hours 22 minutes. At a maximum altitude of 57,000 feet – almost 11 miles – its top speed was Mach 2.04, or 1345mph.

Beyond the 6in by 4in windows – about a third the size of subsonic jets windows – the clouds are a long, long way below. The smaller and therefore stronger windows are to counter emergency depressurisation at extremely high altitudes. The landscape below slips by noticeably faster than in a subsonic jet. And the sky is an unfamiliar indigo – the sort of threatening purple tormented Van Gough [sic] used in his paintings.

The hiss of air from the Concorde's pressurization system is louder than the noise its subsonic counterparts produce. However, the four Rolls-Royce Olympus engines are virtually noiseless from the inside of the cabin – and the sonic boom is left to outsiders to complain about too.

The Concorde left its stand at Singapore Airport at 7.37 a.m. yesterday – 10.07 in Melbourne. It was more a lift-off than a take-off. The ground was left behind with consummate ease. Singapore's skyscraper hotels and the ships in the harbour became Matchbox toys in seconds. Thirteen minutes into the flight and already 80 miles south of the island, flight engineer John MacDonald snapped in the engine reheat switches in front of him, boosting the plane's mighty powerplants to their maximum thrust of 17,260 kilos.

There was a nudge in your spine as you were thrust back into the seat and the Concorde speared its way through the sound barrier. The rest was easy and Mach 2 rolled up in a matter of course.

The Concorde is flown by 13 computer systems – subsonic jets have half that many. The cockpit crew – a pilot, co-pilot and engineer – constantly monitor the systems. Captain E.C. 'Mickey' Miles – the chief officer on yesterday's flight – left the cockpit for five minutes' talk with me during yesterday's ultra-smooth swish through space. He is in love with the Concorde and describes it as an 'incredible technical achievement'. He says it is easier to fly manually than other commercial jets he has flown in a 30-year career with British Airways.

It is not much different 'in principle' from the old, single-engined Royal Navy Swordfish anti-submarine plane – top speed 85 knots – he flew during World War Two, he insists. 'Concorde hasn't got a bicycle on board though ... we used to carry one on the Swordfish to pedal from the plane to the terminal building,' he said.

Flying almost twice as high and over twice as fast as what had gone before was clearly so 'normal', so free from drama. With G-BOAC's landing at London Heathrow on the evening of 13 September, through 30,000ft of cloud and rain, the Concorde endurance and route-proving programme came to a satisfactory end.

Crewing on the routes was shared between British Airways, the official CAA pilots and BAC. Concorde's operating and maintenance base was, as planned, changed during the programme from London to Bahrain, then to Singapore, and finally back to London. These changes, and the monsoon weather conditions thereby encountered, undoubtedly added to the difficulty of the exercise and to the value of the experience gained. It all added to the wealth of knowledge on hand for the certification process.

Many distinguished passengers were amongst the 6,500 carried during the endurance-flying trials. The Prime Minister of Australia flew between Melbourne and Singapore, as did the Premier of Victoria, the chairman and the Managing Director of Singapore Airlines, the deputy general manager and the Director of Marketing of Qantas, and the Vice-President of operations for Philippine Airlines. An Australian sampling Concorde from a different viewpoint was Mr Charles Jones,

Minister of Transport, who travelled to Nullarbor Plain to hear the sonic boom as Concorde traversed the Australian supersonic corridor. He commented, 'Quite frankly the sonic boom would not have satisfied your kids or my grandchildren on cracker night. As far as the sonic boom is concerned, this is a non-event.'

Establishing Other Routes and Market Research

The sales, marketing and government officials had also been working hard, concentrating not only on the American market but also on the rest of the world. On 6 May 1975, France and Brazil executed an agreement permitting Concorde supersonic airliners in Air France markings to land in Brazil on regular scheduled flights.

The agreement was signed in Paris by M. Marcel Cavaillé, French Secretary of State for Transport, and Air Force General Edivio Calvas Sanctos, President of the Brazilian Commission for the Study of International Air Transport (CERNAI). Two statements in the agreement underlined the importance of this event:

> The Brazilian authorities have declared that the introduction of the Concorde supersonic airliner into regular service between Brazil and France constitutes a historic stage in international commercial aviation and will strengthen the links between the two countries. The French authorities have thanked those of Brazil for their welcoming response, and acknowledge the great importance of these strengthened links.

The event was, in fact, the first authorisation ever by inter-governmental document for a supersonic civil aircraft to fly regularly on a commercial route. The scheduled service by Air France Concorde between Paris Charles de Gaulle and Rio de Janeiro Galeão was to start in January 1976.

Guests board one of the prototype aircraft sometime during the certification process. In the background is a Japanese Airlines DC-8.

The commercial divisions of Aérospatiale and BAC conducted a survey at the request of the Concorde manufacturers by Hakuhodo Incorporated of Japan to determine the likelihood of Japanese businessmen flying by SST on important international routes out of Japan.

The main aims of the survey were to determine the elasticity of SST demand in relation to time saved, fare policy and standard of comfort, and SST acceptability in relation to various socio-economic factors and other features of air travel which might have a bearing on the supersonic market.

The principal section of the questionnaire was devoted to establishing the penetration of the SST into the Japanese business travel market on five major routes out of Japan. Respondents were asked to make a comparison between a supersonic service and the subsonic service with which they were familiar. They were shown photographs of the interiors of a subsonic wide-body jet and of the SST, and given details of the seating capacity, and seat size and pitch in both aircraft. The SST was proposed in two possible configurations: single class, with a standard of service similar to first class, and conventional mixed class. For each route on which the respondent had flown – up to a maximum of three routes – the passenger was shown details of the journey time and fare for both subsonic and supersonic flights. Three supersonic fare levels were proposed for each configuration.

On all the routes, the SST journey time was compared with the shortest possible subsonic journey time for the future. In each case this was nonstop, assuming the use of a very long-range wide-body jet, rather than the present-day flight time.

The questionnaire and exhibits, including the journey times, fares and interiors for both types of aircraft, were approved by Japan Airlines before commencing the survey and were thus regarded as comprehensive. Japan Airlines Global Club, the Goshakai (an association of the five major trading houses) and major Japanese companies contacted 261 Japanese business travellers, who were interviewed in Tokyo and Osaka. Each traveller had made business trips in the last three years on one or more of the routes investigated. Total trips amounted to 1,903, of which 374 were in first class and 1,529 in economy class. The sample included travellers who had made between one trip and more than twenty trips in the last three years.

The survey concluded that a substantial proportion of Japanese businessmen would prefer to fly by SST when it came into service. The great majority of first-class business passengers would choose the SST even with fare surcharges of up to 40 per cent. For the proposed fare range, the SST penetration into the first-class market would be very similar for either the single-class or mixed-class SST.

It also showed that many economy-class passengers would be attracted to the single-class supersonic service, and an even greater number to the mixed-class SST. The stimulus effect of reduced journey time would add a further 9 per cent to the SST penetration into the first-class business market, and 4 per cent to the SST economy-class penetration.

The results – which were very similar to what was obtained from the business travellers of the USA in a survey conducted by Market Facts Incorporated in 1972 – were published in *Concorde Flight News* and undoubtedly reached the eyes and ears of American politicians.

The Certificate is Granted

On 9 October 1975, the French government granted the Concorde airliner Certificate of Airworthiness No 78. This official document, issued by the Secrétariat Général à l'Aviation Civile, was formally presented to the manufacturers by

In the presence of
Sir Edward Tomkins,
British Ambassador
to France (left),
Marcel Cavaillé,
France's Secretary of
State for Transport,
proudly displays
the *Certificat de
Navigabilité de
Type* (shown below)
before handing it
to Aérospatiale's
chairman, Charles
Cristofini (centre).
(Aérospatiale)

M. Marcel Cavaillé, in the presence of Sir
Edward Tomkins, the British Ambassador,
and representatives of the French and
British civil aviation authorities.

The speech delivered by the French was
triumphant:

Concorde is now qualified to go into commercial service; Concorde has received its
Certificate of Airworthiness. Recently in
Montreal and in Toulouse I forecast that
certification would soon be granted: since
yesterday, it is a fact.

But what does certification mean?

If it were possible to make a comparison,
I would compare it with the Ministry of
Transport certificate for a motor-car, but
much more difficult and involved because
of the greater complexity of an aircraft
and above all of such an evolutionary aircraft as Concorde. But it is also a solemn
undertaking by the authorities of the
manufacturing countries that a given type of aircraft satisfies internationally
accepted and very strict requirements allowing aircraft of this type to fly and
carry passengers in complete safety.

To emphasise the importance of this most recent Concorde technical
achievement I insisted on delivering the Concorde Type Certificate personally
and officially to the president of Aérospatiale, representing the joint
manufacturers, in the presence of the British Ambassador to France.

Concorde certification is the culmination of a very long process which
started on 29 November 1962 with the signing of the Franco-British inter-
government agreement.

The UK Certificate of Airworthiness was presented by Lord Boyd-Carpenter, chairman of the CAA, to Sir George Edwards, chairman of BAC, in the course of a ceremony in London on 5 December. Attending the ceremony were Gerald Kaufman, Minister of State for Industry, and Lord Beswick, chairman-designate of the proposed British Aerospace Board. This cleared the way for British Airways scheduled flights with fare-paying passengers, which would start with a twice-weekly London –Bahrain service on 21 January 1976. (BAC)

Some people may be surprised that this project, which is the fruit of thirteen years of close and unfailing co-operation between France and Britain, is today receiving French certification only. Actually we have been ready to certificate the aircraft for several days. Our British partners for their part wish to hold their own Certificate over until they have obtained some extra information on the behaviour of the autopilot in certain very special cruise conditions. I must state firmly that this difference in no way affects the safety of Concorde in service. It results only from a nuance in interpreting the scope of a Type Certificate as opposed to that of the various operating regulations.

We thought at one time of waiting for a few weeks so that certification could be granted simultaneously on both sides of the Channel, as was done recently on 29 September for the Olympus engine. After careful consideration and in agreement with our British partners, we decided that there was no valid reason for further delay and that in the interest of the programme it was preferable to grant the French Type Certificate at once.

This event is a very important milestone in the history of the project. In fact it marks our triumph over the technical challenge we faced when the project was launched in 1962; it is the vindication of much hard work, highlighted by some important dates: first flight in March 1969, first supersonic flight in October 1969, first flight at Mach 2 in November 1970, first North Atlantic crossing in September 1973, Paris–Rio and return in a single day on 5 June 1975.

It is the outcome of 5,300 hours of flight including nearly 2,000 hours supersonic, during which the aircraft visited over 40 countries and 70 foreign airports, where the enthusiasm it aroused was often delirious. The most recent visit of this kind was made last week, for the inauguration of the new Montreal international airport at Mirabel in Canada.

Finally, this event is proof that by uniting its efforts and productive capacities the European aircraft industry is capable of achieving the boldest of projects.

Civil Aviation Authority

Engine Type Certificate
for

ROLLS-ROYCE/SNECMA OLYMPUS 593 MARK 610-14-28

This is to Certify that the type of engine, together with any variants, named in this certificate is accepted as complying with the Airworthiness Standards specified in the Engine Type Certificate Data Sheet

[signature]

for the Civil Aviation Authority

Serial Number   SST1   Date   29 SEPTEMBER 1975

Civil Aviation Authority

Aircraft Type Certificate

Aircraft Type Certificate Number: _____ BA 10 ____
(& Type Certificate Data Sheet No.)

Name and Type Designation
of Aircraft: _____ CONCORDE TYPE 1 ____
                    BRITISH AIRCRAFT CORPORATION LTD, AND
Manufacturer: _____ SOCIETE NATIONALE INDUSTRIELLE, JOINTLY ____

It is hereby certified that the type of aircraft named in this certificate is acceptable for United Kingdom airworthiness certification. The basis for certification is stated in the Type Certificate Data Sheet forming part of this certificate. Variants of this type that are acceptable for United Kingdom airworthiness certification are listed in the Type Certificate Data Sheet.

[signature]

for the Civil Aviation Authority

Date of Issue: 4th December 1975 ____

All that remains now is to win the commercial challenge – and this I am convinced will be done. Concorde has cleared many obstacles in the last thirteen years. It will clear the few which remain in its path – whether these are matters of air fares or of landing rights. The next phase begins on 21 January next, with simultaneous entry into the scheduled commercial services of the airlines. This should see Concorde finally established.

Concorde is in truth a collective labour, bringing great honour to tens of thousands of French and British workers, technicians, engineers and administrators who for thirteen years have devoted their utmost efforts to the project and to whom we owe the brilliant technical achievement which we are celebrating today.

I would like to offer my thanks to you especially, your Excellency, for participating in this event. Your presence here symbolises the close co-operation which exists between our two countries, the basis of numerous collaborative achievements. Today's achievement is the most prestigious of all, and bodes very well for the future.

The corresponding British type certificate was issued on the very day that the 2,000 supersonic flying hours mark was passed in the development programme by the UK Civil Aviation Authority. It was presented by Lord Boyd-Carpenter, chairman of the CAA, to Sir George Edwards, chairman of BAC, in the course of a ceremony in London on 5 December. Attending the ceremony were Gerald Kaufman, the Minister of State for Industry, and Lord Beswick, chairman-designate of the proposed British Aerospace Board. This was after additional test flying was conducted to clarify autopilot procedures in special tropical weather conditions.

With all the paperwork complete and under their belt, it was now time to convince the USA.

8

The Coleman Hearing

Issuance of the final environmental impact statement by the US Department of Transport with respect to Concorde service to the USA took place in Washington DC on 13 November 1975. The governments of the UK and France had been advised by the DoT that at this time the US government would not take a position with respect to the application for Concorde service; in fact, issuance of the environmental impact statement would be followed by a forty-five-day period during which the American public would be invited to comment on the statement.

Secretary of Transportation William T. Coleman Jr at a press conference that day explained in detail how he intended to reach a decision on the highly controversial application:

> British Airways and Air France have asked for permission to conduct commercial Concorde operations to and from the United States and have stated that they intend to have six flights per day, four to land at Kennedy International Airport in New York, and two to land at Dulles International Airport, just outside Washington DC. The Concorde is a supersonic aircraft but the applicants have made it clear that all operations over the United States will be at subsonic speeds. The Federal Aviation Administration has advised me that Concorde operations would meet all appropriate safety requirements.
>
> Since this is a major federal action, the FAA prepared and circulated a preliminary Environmental Impact Statement. After public hearings another Environmental Impact Statement is being issued today which treats the environmental issues in a forthright manner.
>
> Prior to making a decision, I thought it would be in the public interest for me to outline the issues as I see them as raised by the Environmental Impact Statement, along with the safety and international considerations and have six hours of argument by those concerned so that these issues can be discussed publicly.
>
> I am publishing an outline of the issues in the Federal Register and I am passing out a copy herewith. As you will note, the date for the public argument will be on January 5th, 1976, commencing at 9.30 a.m. and I will make a decision within 30 days thereafter. The Concorde represents new technology, and as in the case of any new technology, various environmental and other considerations should be taken into account. The Federal Aviation Administration is establishing a special office to handle all public inquiries concerning the Environmental Impact Statement.

William Thaddeus Coleman Jr (b. 7 July 1920 in Philadelphia, Pennsylvania) was the fourth US Secretary of Transportation.

William Thaddeus Coleman Jr was the fourth US Secretary of Transportation, from 7 March 1975 to 20 January 1977, and the second African-American to serve in the Cabinet. He was also a distinguished lawyer who, with Thurgood Marshall, played a major role in significant civil rights cases. Coleman had been appointed the previous year by the Gerald Ford administration.

Viscount Leathers'
enthusiasm to fly
in Concorde was
reflected in his seat
reservation made
in January 1964 –
eleven years before
the inaugural flight
of the airliner. Lord
Leathers is seen
collecting his ticket
from the British
Airways Victoria
Terminal in London
for his 3,515-mile
flight to Bahrain.
Bookings for
regular Concorde
services began on
15 October 1975
in France and Great
Britain. British
Airways reported
that they had sold all
the seats available
on the first seven
flights by the end of
the day.

It was clear that the Concorde decision raised unique questions of public policy. Coleman saw his task as that of achieving the proper balance between technological advances, international relationships and environmental quality. He saw the issues as being difficult, novel and of great congressional and public interest, so he decided to hold a public hearing and to invite comment on the main concerns.

A written submission was made by the British and French governments to the Secretary of Transportation at the beginning of 1976. Realising that this was the crucial preliminary to the forthcoming hearing, the two governments put forward the case for Concorde. They stated that the environmental impact of the machine had been grossly exaggerated by its opponents – Concorde had been subjected to the most thorough environmental scrutiny given to any aircraft, and the results of that study showed that the impact would be small and would be far outweighed by the benefits and important technological and international economic considerations.

Answering specific questions posed by Secretary Coleman, the two governments declared that a negative decision would be discriminatory, as the aircraft met all relevant US and international regulations and the environmental impact had been proven to be marginal. The US had a commitment to the principles of fair treatment and reciprocity. To ban Concorde operations by British Airways and Air France would be widely viewed as a double standard and could lead to reciprocal limitations on US manufacturers and airlines.

At 9.30 a.m. on Monday 5 January 1976 in the Department of Transportation auditorium on Constitution Avenue, Secretary Coleman opened the hearing – the scene was set for a unique confrontation between Concorde proponents and opponents. Coleman patiently listened to seventy interested parties, only occasionally interrupting to clarify points or put specific questions, and he saw to it that it was a civilised confrontation.

The Anglo-French team was led by Gerald Kaufman, Minister of State in the UK Department of Industry, supported by Claude Abraham of the French Civil

Sir Gerald
Bernard Kaufman
(b. 21 June 1930),
a British Labour
Party politician.

Aviation Department, Michael Wilde of BAC, Roger Chevalier of Aérospatiale, Claude Lalanne of Air France and Ross Stainton of British Airways. Their case rested on the argument that the limited number of flights requested would have very little impact on the environment of the US.

There was no national rule that would bar Concorde from commercial service in the US; there was no international standard that the aircraft did not meet. Britain and France were ready to participate in an international programme to monitor and control the many effects on the stratosphere.

Secretary Coleman asked Kaufman and Abraham if they were aware of any agreement between anyone in their governments and anyone in the US that said Concorde had an absolute right to land in the US. No, they were not, they truthfully replied. Abraham went on to stress the importance of US approval: 'The objectives of the Concorde cannot be reached unless we fly commercially to the United States. Service to the United States is essential if we are to realise the benefits of the resources we have invested.'

'The anti-Concorde team will now have an hour of time. The first witness will be Mr Bert Rein, Aviation Consumer Action Project.'

Rein argued that Concorde should be treated as if it was an American aircraft. Its foreign origin should not cause the US to discriminate against it, 'nor should an abstract recitation of foreign relations considerations cause us to discriminate in its favor against the health and welfare interests of our own citizens, and millions of other people throughout the world. Beware the European aerospace challenge; we are dealing here not with a question of biting the hand that has fed us, but really of feeding the mouth that seeks to bite us.'

Similar phraseology was used thirty-five years later by politicians in the Boeing camp during their battle to promote their product and destroy the chances of the Airbus A330 tanker for the US air force.

Dr Maurice A. Garbell, representing cities near San Francisco Airport, had an equally picturesque turn of phrase. He said that the EIS claimed that Concorde would cause no problem in air-traffic control because it would be treated like an ordinary subsonic machine; that was like saying a tiger cub would not claw up the sofa and the drapes, because we were going to treat it as an ordinary domestic cat. Concorde should use military airfields that had special high-speed routes for climb-out and descent.

The anti-Concorde camp was not just confined to the Americans – religious fervour was supplied by the first British anti-Concorde witness, the purple-robed Rt Rev. Hugh Montefiore, Bishop of Kingston-upon-Thames, who was speaking not for his diocese but as President of the Heathrow Association for the Control of Aircraft Noise. 'The noise from Concorde is not hell because, after all, hell goes on forever. It is more like a secular form of purgatory. I can best compare it to the inflamed gall bladder. The pain is intermittent, but it can inhibit speech.'

The arguments ebbed and flowed through the hearing – calm and reasoned points being made by those in favour of Concorde being operated in the USA that were contradicted by picturesque rants coming from those against it. Style and content varied widely from the formal to emotional:

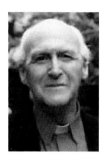

Hugh William Montefiore (b. 12 May 1920, d. 13 May 2005). He was Bishop of Kingston-upon-Thames from 1970 to 1978 and a vehement anti-Concorde protester.

> Whereas, the Fairfax County Federation of Citizens Associations has in the past opposed development of an SST, and whereas this opposition is firmly rooted in concern for the quality of life in the vicinity of Fairfax County airports; and whereas the Department of Transportation is considering granting test flight privileges to an SST; and whereas data has been published which raises severe concern about the adverse noise impact of the Concorde. Therefore, be it resolved: that the Fairfax County Federation of Citizens Associations urges

Secretary of Transportation not to authorize further flights of Concorde SST into Fairfax County airports.

Carol Berman of the Emergency Coalition to Stop the SST put her case somewhat differently:

> We are pleading with you for our homes, for our children, for our lives. I would like to add that the people who live in our area consider themselves Americans, entitled to the same right to life, liberty and pursuit of happiness as our fellow citizens across the land. We believe in government of the people and by the people. That is why we came here today by bus, plane, car, at not inconsiderable difficulty and expense, middle-class, middle-American people. Please show us that it is also government for the people, so that we shall not perish from this earth.

Berman had been a district aide in the offices of Assemblyman Eli Wager and of Representative Herbert Tenzer. She had been vice-chairman of the Nassau County Democratic Committee and was a delegate for Henry M. 'Scoop' Jackson at the 1976 Democratic National Convention in New York City. Berman was elected in 1978 to fill the vacancy in the 9th Senate District caused by the departure of Karen Burstein.

Fewer groups appeared before the hearing to urge approval of Concorde operations. Groups such as the US Council of the International Chamber of Commerce, Citizens for a Better New York, the British-American Chamber of Commerce, and the Committee for Dulles emphasised the business and commercial benefits. The UK-based Campaign for Action on Supersonic Engineering drew a parallel with the acceptance by the British and French authorities in the late fifties of the Boeing 707 and Douglas DC-8 jet aircraft, both of which were novel in design, did not hold British or French certification, were noisier than any previous civil aircraft, lacked nonstop transatlantic range, and required a surcharge on fares.

Individual supporters included John Shatter, former FAA administrator; William Magruder, former DoT SST Director; John R. Wiley, former Aviation Director of the Port of New York Authority, now a visiting professor at MIT; Dr Fred Singer, Professor of Environmental Sciences at the University of Virginia; and Richard FitzSimmons, Director of Advanced Supersonic Aircraft at McDonnell Douglas.

Wiley said he was speaking for the silent majority, whose overall interests were best served when the frontiers of science and technology were encouraged to expand through research and then to be proven by practical operating experience. He said that he was responding to the sad reality that this democratic principle of the greatest good for the greatest number was sometimes overrun by the well-organised expression of a vocal, directly involved minority.

Representatives of the American airlines demonstrated their vested interests by claiming that Concorde would 'skim the cream' off the transatlantic market, with disastrous consequences for the already troubled American flag carriers, Pan American and TWA. It had also been suggested as relevant that the admission of Concorde to the US would spell the end of the dominance of the world aviation industry by American manufacturers, who also deserved protection by their government. Coleman responded:

> Without regard to whether those economic arguments might be true, I have refused to consider either possibility as an element of the decisions I make today – I am, of course, concerned for the welfare of the United States aviation

industry, but I also believe that competition to the maximum extent possible is the best way to preserve a healthy industry. Moreover, the rules of fair competition between US flag carriers and carriers operating the Concorde, as they affect fares, are the direct concern of the Civil Aeronautics Board. That agency is empowered to review fares and to ensure that they are compensatory, and I must therefore leave such considerations to that agency.

Mention had been made on matters regarding the aircraft's fuel efficiency, and there was no doubt that Concorde was less fuel efficient than existing subsonic jet transport aircraft. However, the comparative fuel efficiency would depend on actual load factors; the market, in other words, would ultimately be the best judge of relative fuel efficiency, Coleman noted.

As far as fuel conservation was concerned, the FAA had argued that Concorde should not be allowed to operate into the US, in order to force people to use subsonic aircraft, which would carry more people using less fuel. This was comparable to the introduction of the 55mph limit on American roads, in the interests of fuel conservation. The National Maximum Speed Law in the USA was a provision of the 1974 Emergency Highway Energy Conservation Act that prohibited speed limits higher than 55mph. The original bill was introduced in response to rapidly increasing fuel prices during the 1973 oil crisis. However, although the fuel consumption of Concorde was high, the aircraft offered increased speed as the offsetting factor. 'We have not banned private jets, which average only 13.8 passenger miles per gallon, even though the passenger train may average 190 passenger miles per gallon,' Coleman observed somewhat pointedly. Also, the proposed flights would use only 105 million gallons of fuel a year (most of it British or French), or 0.077 per cent of the fuel used for transport in the US.

Secretary Coleman also declined to accept the argument that Concorde should be banned as a symbolic gesture:

It would be unfair to single out the Concorde as an appropriate symbol of US fuel conservation policy. We did not build it. We will not pay its fuel bills. It would border on hypocrisy to choose the Concorde as the place to set an example, while ignoring the relative inefficiency of private jets, cabin cruisers or an assortment of energy-profligates of American manufacture.

The hearing had enabled everyone who had wished to express a view to do so. All the issues raised in the secretary's pre-hearing questions had been addressed, but the greatest single objection of the opponents had concerned noise. The Concorde issue gave people living near Kennedy and Dulles airports an opportunity to voice their strong feelings about their existing noisy environment, and it was hardly surprising that they and their elected representatives grasped the opportunity.

William Coleman's decision and the exhaustive investigation leading up to it remain an outstanding example of American federal executive action at its best – not only in reaching a fair and prompt decision but also in adopting a clearly defined process and in explaining that process to the American people and the world – and deserves repeating here:

After careful deliberation, I have decided for the reasons set forth below to permit British Airways and Air France to conduct limited scheduled commercial flights into the United States for a trial period not to exceed 16 months under limitations and restrictions set forth below. I am thus directing the Federal Aviation Administrator, subject to any additional requirements he would impose for safety reasons or other concerns within his jurisdiction, to order provisional

amendment of the operations specifications of British Airways and Air France
to permit those carriers, for a period of no longer than 16 months from the
commencement of commercial service, to conduct up to two Concorde flights
per day into JFK by each carrier, and one Concorde flight per day into Dulles by
each carrier. These amendments may be revoked at any time upon four months'
notice, or immediately in the event of an emergency deemed harmful to the
health, welfare or safety of the American people. The following additional terms
and conditions shall also apply:

1. No flight may be scheduled for landing or take-off in the United States before
   7 a.m. local time or after 10 p.m. local time.
2. Except where weather or other temporary emergency conditions
   dictate otherwise, the flights of British Airways must originate from
   Heathrow Airport and those of Air France must originate from Charles de
   Gaulle Airport.
3. Authorization of any commercial flights in addition to those specifically
   permitted by this action shall constitute a new major federal action within the
   terms of NEPA and therefore require a new Environmental Impact Statement.
4. In accordance with FAA regulations (14 CFR #91.55), the Concorde may not
   fly at supersonic speed over the United States or any of its territories.
5. The FAA is authorized to impose such additional noise abatement procedures
   as are safe, technologically feasible, economically justified, and necessary to
   minimize the noise impact, including, but not limited to, the thrust cut-back
   on departure.

I am also directing the FAA, subject to Office of Management and Budget
clearance and Congressional authorization, to proceed with a proposed High
Altitude Pollution Program (HAPP), to produce the database necessary for the
development of national and international regulation of aircraft operations in
the stratosphere.

I herewith order the FAA to set up monitoring systems at JFK and Dulles
to measure noise and emission levels and to report the result thereof to the
Secretary of Transportation on a monthly basis. These reports will be made
public within 10 days of receipt.

I shall also request the President to instruct the Secretary of State to enter into
immediate negotiations with France and Great Britain so that an agreement that
will establish a monitoring system for measuring ozone levels in the stratosphere
can be concluded among the three countries within three months. The data
obtained from such monitoring shall be made public at least every six months.
I shall also request the Secretary of State to initiate discussions through ICAO
and the World Meteorological Organization on the development of international
stratospheric standards for the SST.

Secretary Coleman then went on to address other considerations:

International aviation as we know it today – the reciprocity of rights and
privileges and the widespread exporting and importing of aircraft – is possible
only through adherence to a complicated network of treaties and international
agreements. Unlike domestic law, treaties and international agreements –
because they are not subject to enforcement by any international police power
or to the moral persuasion of a homogenous culture – are delicate and fragile
instruments. Their efficacy is dependent upon the good faith of the parties and
upon the recognition of a greater self-interest that is attained only through

long-term international cooperation. If provisions of international law are strictly construed or applied in new situations only to further some immediate self-interest, the entire fabric of international law is weakened. Obviously, even where a nation acts according to fair and non-discriminatory motives, it must take care as well to avoid the appearance of unfairness or discrimination.

The Concorde represents a 13-year commitment of almost $3 billion by the British and French governments, who are among our closest allies and our best customers of United States goods. Prestige, economic vitality, and employment stability are at stake. Service to the United States on the lucrative North Atlantic market was from the first a substantial element in the Concorde program, and denying the aircraft landing rights in this country could well abort the program. The United States must therefore be very careful, in the interests of our relations with England and France and of the continuation of the free and open use of the established international airways, to be wholly fair and non-discriminatory in making this decision, and to take into account the fact that the decision may in any event be perceived as being unfair and discriminatory.

Although I believe, to the extent one can ever fairly judge one's own actions, that whatever decision I might have made today would have been fairly motivated, a decision totally to deny the Concorde landing rights might easily have been perceived as discriminatory for two reasons. First, the United States would be open to the charge that we treated our own aircraft more favorably than those of foreign countries in regulating aircraft noise. The statutes and historical pattern of aircraft noise regulation, and indeed of most environmental regulation in this country, demonstrate that the promulgation of noise standards has closely followed the development of feasible technology to control noise. FAR 36 was promulgated over a decade after the advent of commercial jet aviation, and 80 per cent of the planes in service today still do not satisfy its standard. The regulation was initially written to exempt temporarily aircraft certificated before 1969, which could not comply, and was amended to cover new versions of those aircraft only after the technology became available. The Federal Aviation Act specifically requires the Administrator of the FAA to consider technological feasibility in promulgating regulations. All feasible steps have been taken to control the Concorde noise and it cannot be modified further to abate the noise levels. Consequently, if we refused to let the Concorde land for noise reasons, the British and the French might well be justified in feeling that the Concorde had been given harsher treatment than we gave our own jets.

Second, the British and French might justifiably feel that the United States was discriminating in its attitude towards stratospheric pollution. There is some risk that even a few Concorde flights may reduce by a slight amount the ozone layer, and that this may cause an increase in the incidence of non-fatal skin cancer. But this is admittedly only speculation. Only recently the United States Consumer Product Safety Commission has denied petitions to initiate rulemaking to ban fluorocarbons, even though the evidence presented would have indicated that the impact of fluorocarbons on the ozone is substantially greater than that of the Concorde. The United States cradles other significant potential sources of stratospheric pollution – military aircraft operations, fertilizers, the space shuttle program – and unless the United States is willing to act against these sources as well, action against the Concorde could well be perceived as discriminatory.

Apart from appearance of discrimination, the British and French might perceive in a negative decision an unfair element of surprise, a defeat of justifiable reliance. No promises have been made to the British or French.

First and last –
*Concorde Flight
News* issued
jointly by BAC
and Sud-Aviation/
Aérospatiale.
Left is Edition 1,
dated 23 June
1969, and right
is Edition 78 from
31 May 1976. This
edition has the
headline 'After Rio,
Bahrain, Caracas …
Now Washington.
Concorde Regular
Services Start on
North Atlantic'.

However, the United States has never promulgated a noise standard applicable to SSTs. In February 1975 the EPA proposed several alternatives, and expressed a preference for the option that would have exempted the first 16 Concordes manufactured and permitted them to land at federally designated airports with approval of the proprietors under specified restrictions. A total ban at this point might well be perceived by our allies as the imposition of a penalty for which they were not given notice. It is true that we would be applying NEPA, but that Act provides little in the way of definite standards which might have put the British and the French on clear notice of precise limits of the amount of noise pollution the United States was willing to tolerate.

Finally, the British and French might well feel that the United States had taken advantage of the benefits of the relatively free and open international aviation structure while being unwilling to pay the costs. The United States has been the chief beneficiary of the agreements and treaties that permit international use of aircraft based on the airworthiness certificate of the manufacturing country. Almost 95 per cent of the commercial and general aviation jet aircraft that have been sold in the free world in the last five or six years have been made in this country. Last year, we exported $2.7 billion in aircraft and aeronautical components – second only to agricultural products in helping to maintain a favorable balance of trade. United States air carriers and aircraft have facilitated commerce throughout the world, opened up new markets for United States products, and created a great many jobs at home. The United States has also been the chief beneficiary of the absence of noise regulations in other nations, for our aircraft – noisy aircraft such as the Boeing 707 and the DC-8 – have been welcomed in the great majority of countries in this world, and have been sold to other countries when our air carriers replaced them with newer, quieter jets. A negative decision could well defeat the British and French effort to enlarge their share of the international aeronautical industry. In view of the history of United States dominance of the aviation industry, it would be quite remarkable if such a decision were not considered to be unfair.

At last sanity and considered reason prevailed, but it was not to last. Coleman's reasoning behind his decision was generally welcomed as fair, honest and comprehensive – but not by all. The anti-Concorde campaigners – working on the principle of if you don't win, appeal – continued their fight. The House Committee on Government Operations had been investigating the Concorde issue, and on

Production examples of Concorde come together. (BAC)

26 May 1976 a joint hearing of subcommittees of that committee and of the House Committee on International Relations recalled Coleman to give further testimony. His leading critics were Lester Wolff and Bella Abzug, who alleged that he had misled Congress and that foreign policy aspects had interfered with US domestic policy-making. In particular, the Nixon letters of 1973 to the British Prime Minister and the French President aroused their suspicion; the so-called 'secret concessions' in those letters, they alleged, were given only after the British and the French had gone to the Nixon White House and extracted them.

Dulles Inaugural Flights

Following the Coleman decision, scheduled Concorde services to the USA began on 24 May 1976, with Air France and British Airways flights into Dulles Airport, Washington DC.

The British Airways flight (BA579) left London Heathrow Airport at one minute past one o'clock in the afternoon (8.01 a.m. Washington time). The commander was Captain Brian Calvert, Flight Manager (Technical) Concorde. Four minutes after Captain Calvert had started to head for the Bristol Channel, Captain Pierre Dudal, chief of Concorde Flight Division and commander of the Air France jet, lifted away from Charles de Gaulle Airport, Paris.

Throughout the 23-mile-a-minute approach to America's eastern seaboard the two Concorde captains were in touch by radio. Then, about 460 miles from the coastline, the two airliners began to slow down, dropping to subsonic speeds 50 miles off shore.

Over Maryland, 50 miles from Dulles International Airport, the two aircraft were just 5 miles apart and under normal air-traffic control supervision as they began the approach to Dulles for the historic landings. The joint approach had been approved by the FAA.

Over 10,000 people gathered to watch the aircraft touch down exactly on time. The British Airways Concorde G-BOAC arrived first, landing at 1153hrs local. Its flight time from London was three hours, fifty-two minutes, of which two hours, forty-two minutes was supersonic. On board were seventy-six passengers, including Edmund Dell, Secretary of State for Trade; Gerald Kaufman, Minister of State for Industry; Lord Beswick, chairman of the Organising Committee of British Aerospace; and Allen Greenwood, chairman of BAC.

The Air France aircraft arrived, as scheduled, two minutes later. Its flying time was three hours, fifty minutes, of which two hours, fifty-three minutes was at supersonic speeds. It was carrying eighty passengers, including Marcel Cavaillé, Minister of Transportation; Claude Abraham, Director General of Civil Aviation; Jacques Médecin, Minister of Tourism; General Jacques Mitterrand, chairman of Aérospatiale; and Gilbert Pérol, President of Air France. The two machines then taxied to the front of the terminal building and parked nose to nose.

Welcoming the aircraft, John Barnum, US Under-Secretary of Transportation, said that these flights 'opened another chapter for your spectacular new aircraft. It has met with ease all safety and technical requirements.'

Edmund Dell said it was a historic day in which Concorde had united the great capitals of the old world with the new. Describing the aeroplane as 'a time machine', he said time had been made not only to stand still but to go backwards. He recalled that the *Mayflower* had made the Atlantic crossing in sixty-six days and nineteenth-century ships took six weeks. He continued: 'The great liners used to take about four days but we took less than four hours. I think Concorde can claim to have captured the blue riband of the Atlantic.'

Marcel Cavaillé, French Minister of Transportation, said that 'the people of Great Britain and France have given the best of themselves to produce this splendid achievement. They are today happy and proud to see this aircraft entering regular service between both nations' capitals and the capital of USA.'

The first departures of the Concordes from Dulles the next day were comedic in content, but provoked a flurry of protest, accusations of cheating and a diplomatic incident!

The two parallel main runways at Dulles designated for Concorde operations are aligned along compass headings of 010 degrees and 190 degrees – roughly north–south. When used for a take-off or landing to the north they are known as runways zero one left and zero one right; when used in the opposite direction the same strips of concrete are known as one nine left and one nine right. On 25 May, both Concordes were expected to take off from runway zero one left, but a change of wind direction forced a change to the opposite runway direction. News cameras and mobile noise monitors were hurriedly moved from zero one left to one nine left, where the Air France machine took off first. The French captain elected to boost power – and therefore noise – by keeping his Concorde's engine afterburners on, in order to gain height rapidly before passing over the town of Chantilly. Norman Todd, captain of the British Airways Concorde, elected to use runway one nine right after being advised by air-traffic control that 'all the TV and cameras are set up for one nine left takeoff'. Co-pilot Brian Calvert, who was handling radio communications on that flight, told ground control that one nine

Joint arrival at Dulles: on the left is British Airways' G-BOAC; on the right is the Air France Concorde.

right was preferable for community noise reasons. Accusations of cheating and evading the noise monitors followed and the British Ambassador was summoned to explain the crew's actions.

In the 26 May congressional hearing, New York representative James H. Scheuer accused the British of not following the rules. Captain Calvert was later to write; 'The FAA knew we would use this runway as often as possible, simply because its departure route took us over fewer communities. Secretary Coleman was embarrassed and issued a public rebuke, but no harm was meant – we were simply doing our best.'

It seems that looking down from the flight deck of Concorde G-BOAC as it took off from runway one nine right on the inaugural service from Dulles, the crew perhaps noticed the angry US officials and media crews who were up to their waists in poison ivy at the end of the runway.

9

The Battle of New York

The Coleman decision may have enabled British Airways and Air France to begin supersonic services to Washington with little delay, since Dulles Airport was operated by the FAA, but the decision also ramped up the anger and frustration of the anti-Concorde movement. They quickly turned their attention to John F. Kennedy Airport, which was operated by the Port Authority of New York and New Jersey, which chose to delay Concorde services there very much indeed. Though the reason was simple – politically, the authority did not wish to appear to be imposing more aircraft noise on the long-suffering residents of New York City – the legal issues were complex.

One of the key questions concerned whether a federal decision should overrule, or pre-empt, a state or local one. Coleman had been careful in the wording of his decision to leave this question open.

Another issue was the division along national lines within the Concorde team over the best strategy to adopt. The French did not want to force action by the port authority, arguing that more time should be taken in reasoning with them and, especially, trying to bring political pressure to bear on them from federal and state government officials. They did not want to precipitate a negative decision by the port authority, and they did not want to risk losing a law suit.

The British thought otherwise – that with the Coleman decision, the federal government had done as much as it was going to do on the Concorde approval issue. Neither the outgoing president, Gerald Ford, or the president-elect, Jimmy Carter, would risk offending voters in the key state of New York, and since the federal government had so far escaped any liability in airport noise litigation, there was an inclination within the FAA and DoT not to interfere. Among the active Concorde opponents were Governor Hugh Carey of New York, leaders of the state legislature, and the mayor and city council of New York City. The port authority was not going to oppose the state governor on a question affecting a New York airport, especially as it was the airport proprietor who would be liable to noise damage claims. The governor of New Jersey, although well disposed toward Concorde, would not interfere in something that primarily affected New York. Opposition to Concorde was an easy, no-cost option for the politicians and for the port authority.

None of that was likely to change without some form of litigation, a time-honoured way of breaking political log-jams in the USA. A federal judge's decision could let public officials off the hook. Conveniently, the port authority could face no possible liability for noise damage and its political masters could face little criticism for obeying a court order – hence the British conclusion that the route through the courts was the one to take.

The Concorde team advised the port authority that British Airways and Air France intended to begin Concorde service to Kennedy Airport on 10 April 1976. The aim was to force it to act and, if landing rights were denied, immediately to challenge that decision in the federal district court. Accordingly, a letter from the airlines was delivered to the port authority board for consideration at its 11 March meeting, whereupon the board responded by adopting the resolution to ban:

> Resolved, that the Port Authority deny permission to operate any supersonic aircraft, including the Concorde, at Kennedy International Airport, until after at least six months of operating experience has been evaluated, after a report on such experience has been made to the Board and pending further action thereon by the Board.

This triggered the long and costly process of gaining access for Concorde to New York. The authority's noise limit for Kennedy was 112PNdB, and the board knew that the two airlines claimed that Concorde could meet that requirement. However, it claimed concern about the aircraft's low-frequency noise and the 'expected aggravated community response' to it. Also, New York governor Hugh Carey had signed proposed legislation that would direct the port authority to refuse entry and so the board directed its aviation director to analyse six months of Concorde operations at Dulles, Heathrow and Charles de Gaulle airports.

In challenging the ban, the legal action initially taken by the airlines was lukewarm. At French insistence, the lawyers filed only a bare complaint seeking a declaratory judgement and an injunction. They would not take the normal actions – such as seeking a summary judgement – that would lead to a prompt decision. This warning shot was fired on 17 March 1976, when the two airlines filed their complaint in the district court and the matter was assigned to Judge Milton Pollack. More than a year passed before the case came before Judge Pollack – by which time the USA had Jimmy Carter as its new president and Brockman 'Brock' Adams as the new Secretary of Transportation.

The testing was now complete – no more endurance flying, no more performance trials like here in South Africa – it was time to get Concorde into service. However, the New York Port Authority did everything to put obstacles in the way. *(BAC)*

The court case was the port authority's reaction to a telegram sent on 7 March 1977 – three days before the authority was due to make its final decision on Concorde – by Charles Goodell on behalf of the French Minister of Transport. 'The airlines reaffirm in the strongest possible way that it has been indisputably demonstrated by the manufacturers' tests at Toulouse and Casablanca that Concorde can meet the Port Authority noise regulations for operations at Kennedy Airport as they are applied to all other aircraft.'

Both airlines were convinced that the noise impact could be further reduced by concentrating their take-off operations on runways three one left and two two right at JFK Airport, at weights significantly lower than maximum, and stood ready to discuss these new procedures further with the authority, which immediately grabbed the opportunity to announce an indefinite postponement of its Concorde decision to allow further consideration of the proposed noise-abatement procedures.

Secretary of Transportation Brockman 'Brock' Adams (b. 13 January 1927, d. 10 September 2004).

The fight for New York rights was conducted in the courts and on the streets. Four court cases were needed to decide the complex legal issues involved: two district court cases, known colloquially as Concorde One and Concorde Two, each followed by an appeal.

Out at JFK Airport, what *The New York Times* called the 'Foes of the Concorde supersonic transport' gathered in some 600 cars to drive around the airport for nearly three hours on 17 April, vowing to shut the airport's operations if the British-French airliner was introduced there.

Concorde One began on 11 May 1977 before district judge Milton Pollack. British Airways and Air France asked the court to declare the ban invalid, claiming that the port authority ban conflicted with international treaties and illegally invaded an area of regulation that was pre-empted by the federal government. The port authority responded by asserting that in the absence of a specifically stated federal pre-emption, it had the right to investigate the noise of Concorde at Kennedy and in the meantime to exclude the aircraft from operating there.

It was a question of federal supremacy, ruled Judge Pollack. A 1968 addition to the 1958 Federal Aviation Act established the federal government's responsibility for noise abatement, though the FAA could delegate authority to regulate noise to local airport proprietors. Actions taken under this were subject to any overriding federal action, must not impose an undue burden on interstate or foreign commerce and must not unjustly discriminate between different categories of airport users.

Judge Milton Pollack (b. 29 September 1906, d. 13 August 2004) was known for enforcing strict deadlines on counsel, forcing cases either to settle or to go to trial, and other judges sometimes referred cases to him for this purpose.

Since 1951 the port authority had operated a regulation stating that no jet aircraft should land at Kennedy without permission. William T. Coleman, Transportation Secretary, had considered but rejected full federal pre-emption of aviation noise abatement, believing that the control of aircraft noise must remain a shared responsibility among airport proprietors, airport users and governments. Airport proprietors were in the best position to assess a local noise problem and to determine how to respond to it, but were not in the best position to judge the effect of a noise-reduction proposal on national and international air transport systems. The federal government was obliged to ensure that airport actions to meet local needs did not conflict with national and international purposes. Federal action would, under the supremacy clause of the American Constitution, invalidate local action where the two schemes of regulation were in conflict.

Judge Pollack went over the statutory aspects of the Coleman decision in detail. He stated that the secretary had statutory authority for his decision, and it was not necessary for him to state specifically that he was pre-empting any regulation of the port authority, whose only noise regulation was the one requiring the permission of the authority for jet aircraft to land at Kennedy. He also stated that the subject of the port authority resolution was noise around Kennedy, and the authority had stated that its role was limited to the question of whether Concorde could meet that noise criteria. Coleman had concluded that noise and other environmental impacts were not significant reasons for denying limited operations, that the environmental cost was outweighed by the benefits that would accrue to the American people from observing at first hand the application of the technology and obtaining actual noise data during the trial period.

Judge Pollack concluded that the port authority resolution conflicted with the federal decision, and so the resolution must give way under the supremacy clause of the Constitution. The port authority resolution was void, and the two airlines were entitled to the injunction they had sought. The judge added that the other ground on which the airlines had argued their case – that of conflict with international treaties and agreements – was not relevant since the proposed services were 'experimental tests'.

More protests happened again on 15 May, when hundreds of slow-moving cars stopped traffic on the main circle road at Kennedy Airport for two miles at 6 o'clock that evening. This was followed by extra police manpower and a fleet of tow trucks being assigned to the area in and around the airport to cope with another traffic-clogging motorcade by opponents on 22 May.

Not unsurprisingly, the port authority appealed against Judge Pollack's decision, the appeal being heard at the beginning of June. This hearing introduced a new factor into the case, not because of anything the plaintiffs or the defendants said, but because of a point made in an *amicus curiae* (translated as 'friend of the court') brief submitted for the United States by the acting assistant attorney general. *Amicus* statements may be made by anyone with an interest in the subject of the case; on this occasion they were filed for Friends of the Earth and other organisations, governments, municipalities and individuals. The *amicus* brief for the United States had been requested by Chief Judge Irving R. Kaufman, and it was to prove pivotal in the Concorde approval process.

Judge Kaufman said that the port authority took pride in its tradition of noise regulation. The two airlines claimed that Concorde could meet the Kennedy standard and sought to prove this in actual operation there. The Coleman decision

had recognised the right of the port authority to refuse landing rights to Concorde. Secretary Coleman, his successor Brock Adams and President Carter had all affirmed that the Coleman decision did not pre-empt the port authority's right to exclude Concorde on the basis of a reasonable,

Chief Judge Irving Robert Kaufman (b. 24 June 1910, d. 1 February 1992). Apart from his landmark Concorde decision, Kaufman was known for presiding over the espionage trial of Julius and Ethel Rosenberg and imposed their controversial death sentences. He also presided over the deportation hearing of John Lennon and rejected the government's attempt to deport him from the US to England based upon his having pleaded guilty in England to possession of hashish. After a widely publicised hearing, Kaufman found that Lennon had been singled out for deportation for political reasons and allowed him to remain in the US.

non-discriminatory noise regulation. Kaufman said, 'We need not tarry long over the issue that heretofore has occupied center stage in this litigation.' Judge Pollack's argument that the Coleman decision pre-empted the conflicting exercise of power by the port authority was 'untenable and erroneous'. The Coleman decision was never intended to deprive the port authority of the right to impose reasonable noise regulations for the use of Kennedy by Concorde.

However, a point was raised in the *amicus* brief: that the port authority's delay in evaluating Concorde's operating experience and in taking further action was reasonable. Thirteen months had elapsed since Concorde operations had begun at Dulles. 'Implicit in the federal scheme of noise regulation, which accords to local airport proprietors the critical responsibility for controlling permissible noise levels in the vicinity of their airports, is the assumption that this responsibility will be exercised in a fair, reasonable and non-discriminatory manner.' Nevertheless, that point was not a matter for the appeals court, as the district court had not considered it.

The *amicus* brief for the United States 77-7237 of 25 May – after arguing that there had been no federal pre-emption – stated:

> We do believe that the Port Authority is obligated to conduct its proprietary determinations in a reasonable manner and one that is not unfair or discriminatory. There is evidence that this is not the case. Specifically, the Port Authority has ignored its own resolution of 11 March 1976, to assess and report in a timely fashion upon Concorde noise as that data became available from operations elsewhere. Also, it has given no reason why the Concorde is not acceptable under standards generally applicable to other aircraft operating at Kennedy.

The brief concluded:

> The Port Authority may have exercised its proprietary powers in such a manner that its ban against the Concorde could not survive judicial scrutiny. We believe its actions have been unfair, dilatory, arbitrary and unreasonable.

The regulation of aircraft noise had traditionally been a co-operative enterprise, Judge Kaufman continued, involving both federal authorities and local airport proprietors. However, the scope of the port authority in this enterprise was limited: the authority's power was simply to promulgate reasonable, non-arbitrary and non-discriminatory regulations to establish acceptable noise levels. The port authority accepted that its power to set noise rules was subject to the proviso that the rules must be reasonable.

Kaufman concluded that US treaty obligations were relevant. Equal treatment of domestic and foreign air commerce was the touchstone of the complex network of agreements regulating international aeronautical traffic, of which the US was a major beneficiary. The two airlines argued that the port authority's ban was not a valid and enforceable regulation under the bilateral agreements; it was an ad hoc measure directed solely against them and preventing them from demonstrating that Concorde was environmentally acceptable. If the ban was to be found arbitrary and capricious, it would raise the serious question of its compatibility with American treaty arrangements.

So, the result of the appeal was a reversal of Judge Pollack's ruling that the port authority ban was pre-empted by the Coleman decision, but the new question – whether the thirteen-month delay in promulgating reasonable SST regulations represented unfair discrimination – was passed back to the district court to decide.

Democratic politician
James Joseph 'Jim'
Florio (b. 29 August
1937). Florio
(above) was the first
Italian-American to
become governor
of New Jersey, and
his shouting match
with American police
officer and politician
Mayor Francis
Lazarro 'Frank' Rizzo
Sr (b. 23 October
1920, d. 16 July
1991) (below)
became something
of a highlight of
one of the court
hearings.

Judge Kaufman was in no doubt about the urgency of the matter. While understanding the pressures that had been brought to bear on the authority by the interested governments, the state of New York and segments of the public, he urged the port authority to 'conclude its study and fix reasonable noise standards with dispatch'.

Throughout the summer of 1977 the protests against Concorde continued building more and more upon the foundations created by Shurcliff, Wiggs et al. On 5 July stuntman Jerry Hewitt was seen hanging from a balloon piloted by Ronald Di Giovanni during a flight over Queens as a way of making their protest about Concorde. It seems that the pair took off at about 8 a.m. near Flushing Airport and were chased by police helicopter to St John's University, where they landed on the football field. Di Giovanni was issued summonses for unauthorised landing, unauthorised advertising (it seems they had a 'Ban the SST' poster hung from the balloon), flying over congested areas and reckless endangerment.

The next day Representative James J. Florio of New Jersey called Mayor Frank Rizzo of Philadelphia 'a prime candidate for the bad neighbor of the year award' for suggesting that Concorde should land at Philadelphia International Airport. Even the Soviets weighed into the debate, when TASS, the Soviet press agency, accused the port authority of maintaining a 'deliberately hostile, discriminatory and intolerable attitude towards the Concorde'.

In Concorde Two, held in August, the district court's reappraisal of the port authority ban concentrated on the detail of the authority's actions. There emerged what could only be called a damning account of time-wasting and inconsistency in dealing with the Concorde question. The court ruled in favour of the airlines, on the basis of the following findings as outlined by Judge Pollack.

Basically, the port authority's avowed purpose in imposing its ban was to have an opportunity to set noise standards that would apply to supersonic transports. It had not done so. Instead, the ban had been extended indefinitely, ostensibly to permit further research and analysis. Meanwhile, Concorde was being deprived of a chance to prove itself environmentally acceptable at Kennedy.

The court went into some detail on the characteristics and measurement of aircraft noise. Psycho-acoustic measures, such as perceived noise decibels, took into account the different perceived noisiness of different frequencies. Measurements reflected the frequencies and the duration of the sound; such levels could be plotted as noise contours around a specific airport to show an aircraft's noise 'footprint', so allowing comparisons to be made between different types of aircraft. These so-called single-event measures demonstrated the noise made by a single take-off or landing, but a further measure could be applied to indicate the noise experienced over a given period.

One such measure was known as the noise exposure forecast (NEF). NEF contours enabled the incremental effect of additional noise, say that caused by four Concorde flights a day at Kennedy, to be seen in the context of the existing level of noise at that airport.

At the time of the authority's ban, the FAA's final environmental impact statement had presented single-event and NEF contours which gave a comprehensive picture of the likely noise impact of Concorde at Kennedy Airport. The EIS also covered likely vibration effects. Thus a vast quantity of relevant scientific data was already available. Since then, the port authority had engaged two consultants: Dr Karl Kryter of Stanford Research Institute, a psycho-acoustic expert, to assess the validity of the EIS; and Dr Aubrey McKennell, a British social psychologist, to survey the reactions of people living near Heathrow Airport. Kryter had taken measurements and recordings at Kennedy, Dulles, Heathrow and Charles de Gaulle airports and had developed a 'vibration rattle index' which could relate low-frequency vibration to noise levels. However, there remained the problem of 'additivity' – how could the combined annoyance of noise plus vibration be calculated and compared for different aircraft? In February 1977, he told the authority it could not; further research was needed.

On 7 March, the airlines requested permission to present to the port authority new Concorde operating procedures, specifically designed to reduce the aircraft's noise impact at Kennedy. This immediately caused the authority to delay further a decision on Concorde. On 1 April, the British and French airlines and aircraft manufacturers submitted a written report on the new procedures and their predicted effect, including NEF contours showing almost identical noise footprints for Concorde and the Boeing 707-320B. At the request of the port authority, BAC and Aérospatiale sought FAA confirmation that the report was technically valid.

On 14 April, the FAA confirmed that the Anglo-French analysis was technically sound and that, if the assumptions were borne out in practice, the indicated noise reductions would be realised.

Kryter was apparently assigned to assess the impact of the new procedures. On 7 July, he presented his supposedly final report to the port authority board, but there was some uncertainty about the assessment. The board reviewed the reports of the two consultants; according to the minutes of the meeting, the reports showed that the proposed Concorde operations could be expected to result in 'significant annoyance and complaint activity'. The vibration rattle index was being further studied, but more research and analysis was needed. Thus the board resolved to continue to enforce the ban on Concorde operations at Kennedy.

Judge Pollack summarised the port authority's activity since March 1976. The authority had been 're-ploughing old ground and doing re-reviews of scientific and theoretical data previously available'. Its consultants had undertaken vibration tests at Dulles and Kennedy airports and community-response tests at Heathrow. It had had monthly federal reports on Concorde operations at Dulles and reports of the NASA vibration studies. These reports had yielded no index by which vibration could be measured as additive or unique in terms of the noise spectrum. The port authority had confirmed that Concorde could meet the 112PNdB noise regulation at Kennedy. It had no evidence that the community effects of the limited test operations as federally authorised were rationally unacceptable or that the operations would appreciably worsen present conditions. Secretary Coleman had found that low-frequency vibrations would be slight, brief and barely perceptible, presenting no danger of structural damage and little possibility of annoyance. The research that Kryter and McKennell had undertaken for the port authority appeared to be redundant and irrelevant.

> The conclusion is inescapable from the evidence presented to the Court, and the Court finds that the Port Authority has no intention of taking the responsibility of setting the present or another noise standard applicable to the Concorde. Its failure and excessive delay in doing so are unreasonable, discriminatory and unfair and an impingement on commerce and on the national and international interests of the United States.

Under the circumstances, Judge Pollack concluded, the ban on Concorde's transatlantic services into and out of Kennedy was an undue interference with the achievement of congressional and national objectives. The airlines were entitled to proceed at Kennedy under the existing regulations. The port authority regulations of 11 March 1976 and 7 July 1977 were unlawful and void. That appeared to be clear enough: the seventeen-month delay by the port authority was unreasonable, discriminatory and unfair.

It was not at all clear to the port authority, however. Its chairman, Alan Sagner, immediately declared the authority's intention to appeal the decision.

The Second Appeal

Between the arguments placed before the appeals court trio of Chief Judge Kaufman and Judges Walter R. Mansfield and Ellsworth A. Van Graafeiland on 19 September 1977 and their published decision ten days later, the Carter administration published a notice of proposed rule-making for the operation of supersonic transport aircraft.

Transportation Secretary Brock Adams announced also that pending the issuance of permanent SST noise regulations, the Concorde operations at Dulles would be allowed to continue. The administration also continued to support the proposed trial Concorde services into Kennedy Airport, subject to court action.

Giving his decision in the appeals court, Kaufman was highly critical of the port authority. He noted that it had been advised over seven years previously that Concorde services were desired at Kennedy. The Director of Aviation had replied that SSTs would 'be required to meet the same noise levels as will be demanded of subsonic aircraft'. The Concorde manufacturers were well aware that its noise posed a serious problem and had spent almost $100 million on noise abatement. Tests had shown that the aircraft could consistently meet a standard of 109PNdB. NEF contours considered by Coleman had indicated that the impact of the proposed Concorde services would be negligible, but he recognised that a testing period of actual Concorde operations was necessary; raw data alone could not forecast community response. 'The 16-month demonstration ordered by Coleman was thus a crucible in which to assay the subjective attitudes of airport neighbors and our willingness to fairly assess the issue of supersonic transportation.'

Kaufman commented that while technicians strove to project scientifically the community response to Concorde noise, local leaders on the political scene lobbied to prevent the aircraft's use of Kennedy. At the Coleman hearing and again before the port authority's operations committee, New York State Commissioner Raymond Schuler had conveyed Governor Carey's unqualified opposition to Concorde. The impact of these actions on the port authority commissioners was not known, but the authority's ban followed soon thereafter.

Above: James Earl 'Jimmy' Carter Jr (b. 1 October 1924) served as the 39th President of the United States. His administration published notification of rule-making for the operation of SSTs. Carter was one of five presidents – the others being Kennedy, Johnson, Nixon and Ford – who had dealings with Concorde.
Right: Governor Hugh Carey on the left, and Raymond Schuler, Commissioner of Transportation. Both men were opposed to Concorde entering New York.

When the authority's consultants reported in March 1977, Kryter noted the unsolved additivity problem, but the port authority refused to fund any further research on it. 'Thus it is not at all clear to us how the port authority intends to solve this additivity dilemma, if indeed it ever expects or wants to do so,' the chief judge noted.

McKennell reported that his Heathrow study on the whole was inconclusive. Although the port authority's March 1976 ban had been set to apply for up to six months, the authority ultimately established 10 March 1977 as the date by which it would reach a definitive decision. Much relevant information was available by that date, but the authority had responded to the airlines' further submission by postponing a decision until 'a later date'. It was not surprising that the airlines told the port authority that their patience had run out.

In tracing the port authority's response to the Concorde One case, Kaufman recalled that on 7 July the authority had indefinitely extended the 'temporary' ban imposed sixteen months earlier. It had now grasped another excuse for non-action; it would await a final federal compilation of Concorde data, due in late September. This was puzzling in light of the authority's repeated rejection of earlier federal studies favourable to the aircraft. Even more perplexing, since the work of its consultants had ceased four months earlier, was its statement that 'a vibration rattle index is being further studied'. On 15 September, Transportation Secretary Adams declared that it was unnecessary to define a vibration rattle index before taking regulatory action on new noise standards and indeed had reported that Concorde vibrations were no greater than those induced by such subsonic aircraft as the Boeing 747 and the Douglas DC-10, both of which had been flying into Kennedy for several years with no apparent rattle problem. Thus the 23 September decision that the existing sixteen Concordes could fly into thirteen US cities, including New York, involved no further vibration research. The chief judge continued:

> The law simply will not tolerate the denial of rights by unwarranted official inaction. If ever there was a case in which a major technological advance was in imminent danger of being studied into obsolescence, this is it. There comes a time when relegating the solution of an issue to the indefinite future can so sap petitioners of hope and resources that a failure to resolve the issue within a reasonable period is tantamount to refusing to address it at all. The same is true of studying the question in such a manner that the issue will disappear by sheer frustration or the assumption by another institution – in this case the courts – of the task of deciding a charged dispute whose resolution otherwise is the duty of the agency. The hour is at hand for the Port Authority's indefinite ban on Concorde flights to be recognised as an abdication of responsibility. The airlines should no longer be forced to suffer the consequences of such illegal delay.

The appeals court had urged in the Concorde One case that the port authority should expeditiously establish reasonable, non-arbitrary and non-discriminatory noise regulations at Kennedy. Kaufman continued:

> This it has not done. Rather, the Port Authority has steadfastly refused to accord landing rights to an airplane that is capable of meeting the rule that has consistently been applied to all other aircraft for nearly 20 years – 112PNdB.

Accordingly, the chief judge ruled that the court confirmed the order of the district court in dissolving the port authority's ban, but left it open for the authority to adopt a new, uniform and reasonable noise standard in the future.

Not every point in the chief judge's announced decision was unanimous. In a minority comment, Judge Mansfield, while agreeing with the main ruling to confirm the abolition of the port authority's ban, did not agree that the port authority had acted in bad faith. He concurred that a continued ban could not be justified, not because the authority was at fault but because 'there comes a time when the hourglass runs out and even a public agency must "fish or cut bait". That time has now passed.'

The port authority was still not convinced. In a last-ditch attempt to postpone 'fishing' a while longer, it appealed to the US Supreme Court to allow the ban to remain. The Supreme Court refused. The port authority in a news release announced that Chairman Alan Sagner had expressed 'extreme disappointment' at the news. The authority's obligation to develop and promulgate new noise regulations remained, he said, despite the Supreme Court's decision, which finally cleared the way for Concorde services to New York to begin on 22 November 1977.

10

Epilogue

In hindsight, Concorde was a combination of brilliant technical achievement and economic failure. The two governments' 'captive' airlines, having been allowed to write off the capital cost of the aircraft, went on to make operating profits with their Concordes. Their customers were buying the time-saving convenience and the service that the aircraft were providing. That point is important, and one that has been swamped by all the strident talk of environmental and noise pollution.

Some Americans – and not just the manufacturers – were very keen to go ahead and build SSTs. Others were determined to do all they could to kill them off by using fair means or foul.

It is clear from the located documentation that Concorde started to die as a viable project from the moment Robert McNamara became part of the Kennedy administration – a process that was strengthened when he was appointed to head up the President's Advisory Committee under Lyndon Johnson. At that moment he decided to kill off the US SST, which set in motion a process that ensured Concorde could never succeed commercially. McNamara also killed off the B-70 Mach 3 bomber that could have been used as a basis for an American SST and, through manipulation of funding with the World Bank, also ensured the death of the UK TSR-2 strike aircraft. Indeed, it has been argued that by killing off the TSR-2, McNamara forced the entire Olympus 593 engine development costs – that would have otherwise been in the defence budget – on to Concorde, the share of which would otherwise have been minor.

It is also clear that the playboy President Kennedy – intoxicated with his own power and self-perceived abilities in facing down Nikita Khrushchev over Cuba and inspiring NASA to shoot for the moon – took a step too far in declaring that the Americans would then go for a Mach 3 airliner. This reinforced the idea that was already in the minds of the American aviation industry and all their politicians that the USA alone was capable of producing such a machine and that the rest of the world was incapable of producing a supersonic airliner. This created a mindset of a far too inflated opinion of their own abilities and a far too derogatory view of the rest of the world's aeronautical industry.

Despite the arrogance of their own superiority, the Americans were determined in their own paranoia to learn all they could about the activities of their 'rivals'. It should not be but somehow it is surprising to discover hard evidence that the CIA were spying not only on their enemies, the Soviets, but also their allies, the British and the French. This is all the more remarkable in that most of the material they obtained from western Europe was publicly available. Such was the paranoia of the time that even then the intelligence services and those making up the President's Advisory Committees still refused to believe what they had discovered. Much of this was fuelled by the corporate mindset of those within the Boeing Aircraft Company – which, if anything, has got worse over the years. Again, one only has to look at the rhetoric spewed out by their 'supporters' on

Capitol Hill (and something that was never contradicted by the company) over the recent saga of the USAF tanker replacement.

The whole subject of supersonic transport aircraft – American and otherwise – became bogged down in a quagmire of opportunistic vested interest politics, rabid environmentalism and truth distortions. Much of this was picked up by 'happy hippies' intent on cracking the smooth silhouette of American materialism. This early spark of 'rage against the machine' – a fiercely critical attitude, which brewed sloganistic left-wing rants against corporate America, cultural imperialism, social inequality and government oppression – was stirred up and manipulated by Shurcliff, Wiggs et al. and rapidly picked up by the media. The money-hating flower children were, paradoxically, the very product of wealth. These self-indulgent hippies could only drop out because others did not; because others stayed behind to run the store, pay their taxes and run the world.

The question of whether or not Concorde could be or was a commercial success became a self-fulfilling prophecy. It was not a success in the broadest sense of the term because it was never allowed to be.

Despite the many millions of words written by the pro- and anti-Concorde groups, one aspect is often overlooked: passengers were buying tickets from Air France and British Airways because they wanted to fly Concorde. Compared with the number of passengers flying on subsonic airliners, the number of Concorde passengers was very small, but Concorde fares were high compared with subsonic airliner fares. Neither of those points detracts from the fact that Concordes were serving a valid part of the air transport market. To that extent, the Concorde achievement is more 'real' than the achievement of the US Apollo space programme. The supersonic airliner was meeting a proven need. It is that very point that proves without a shadow of a doubt that there was a commercially viable market for supersonic travel, despite the claims of the doom-mongers.

The End of an Era

When Concorde was retired it was the end of an era or, as television presenter and journalist Jeremy Clarkson said when he stepped off the aircraft for the last time, 'One small step for man, one giant leap backwards for mankind'. Most of the aircraft went to museums or were put on display, which allowed Clarkson to make another telling point: 'It seems strange going to a museum to see the future!'

While on the subject of museums, it amuses me that three surviving airframes are on display in the USA, the country that did all it could to kill it off: G-BOAD at the Intrepid Sea, Air and Space Museum in New York; F-BVFA at the Smithsonian's Steven F. Udvar-Hazy Center at Dulles Airport, Virginia; and G-BOAG at the Museum of Flight in Seattle, Washington. I am sure that for every day it was in service, Concorde coming into land and taking off from JFK and Dulles must have stuck in the throat of the anti-Concorde protesters – and to have one of the survivors preserved at Boeing Field, King County International Airport, just outside Seattle, the home of the Boeing Aircraft Company, is certainly sweet justice after all the political infighting that originated from there!

Perhaps, though, the final word should go to George Banks, who did much of the menu planning for British Airways' Concorde services for many years – this was indeed gourmet and glamour in the sky:

> There are just not enough superlative adjectives to describe the Concorde. What, after all, can I say that has not been said before? The most beautiful aeroplane ever designed, the ultimate in speed specification, an aircraft with grace,

elegance and élan. Everyone's ultimate dream was to be on board as she soared gracefully into the sky .

How many people have said to themselves: just once, please, just once let me be on board, and I was no different, longing to fly the supersonic queen of the skies, the flagship of British Airways and Air France, all those years ago when I was with British Caledonian Airways at Gatwick.

There was always excitement on Concorde. A Texan man got engaged on this flight and asked the crew if they would put the huge diamond ring he had bought in a glass of champagne to present to his girlfriend as he proposed. She said yes of course!

Managing the menu planning for Concorde was a delight but not without its pressures. My colleague Colin Synnock who had previously managed the Concorde menu portfolios already had a very efficient menu process in place for Concorde, when I took over, with five different menu rotations operating from London to New York, Washington and Barbados.

The last ever passenger-carrying Concorde service BA002 operated on 24 October 2003 from New York to London. Pages were written about it in the newspapers and thousands flocked to Heathrow to see it land. On board there was not a free seat, and stars on board included the actress Joan Collins, the model Christie Brinkley and Sir David Frost.

The beautiful specially designed menu card for the last flight, designed by British Airways design services department, was finished in silver grey set off with a luxurious double grey tassel. One of my own food visions for Concorde presented way back in Vienna in June 2000, 'Lobster Fishcake with Bloody Mary Relish', was on the final menu, and I was thrilled to hear it mentioned twice on BBC2 television! On Sky News Sir David Frost praised my lobster fishcakes and said they were delicious! British Caledonian was also not forgotten as one of the Cabin Services Directors on this flight, Miss Tracey Percy, was originally a British Caledonian cabin crew member. The Concorde finished in style with the last flight serving three wonderful champagnes specially chosen by our expert Wine Manager Peter Nixson. Only the use of plastic cutlery on the final flight instead of the beautiful Conran-designed cutlery marred an otherwise perfect finale for Concorde.

I will always feel enormously privileged to have been given the opportunity to plan the menus and food products for the British Airways Concorde, which for me will always be a high spot in my career. I do feel that catering and flying on Concorde was my ultimate dream come true.

Bibliography/
Research Sources

Boeing Aircraft Since 1916, Peter M. Bowyers (London: Putnam, 1966).

Bristol Aircraft Since 1910, C.H. Barnes (London: Putnam, 1964).

Clipped Wings: The American SST Conflict, M. Horwitch (Cambridge, Massachusetts: MIT Press, 1982).

Concorde Flight News Issue 1 dated 23 June 1969 to Issue 78 dated 31 May 1976 – Aérospatiale/BAC.

Concorde: New Shape in the Sky, Kenneth Owen (London: Janes, 1982).

Concorde: The Case Against Supersonic Transport, Richard Wiggs (London: Ballantine/Friends of the Earth, 1971).

Concorde: The Inside Story, Brian Trubshaw (Stroud: Sutton Publishing, 2000).

Concorde: The Inside Story, Geoffrey Knight (London: Weidenfeld & Nicolson, 1976).

Concorde: The International Race for Supersonic Passenger Transport, John Costello and Terry Hughes (London: Angus & Robertson, 1976).

Crosswinds: An Airman's Memoir, Najeeb Halaby (Garden City, NY: Doubleday, 1978).

High Speed Commercial Flight: From Inquiry to Action, J.P. Loomis (Columbus, Ohio: Battelle Press, 1989).

High Speed Commercial Flight: The Coming Era, J.P. Loomis (Columbus, Ohio: Battelle Press, 1987).

Jetliners in Service since 1952, John Stroud (London: Putnam, 1994).

Legend and Legacy: The Story of Boeing and Its People, Robert J. Serling (New York: St Martin's Press, 1992).

Of Comets and Kings, Sir Basil Smallpeice (London: Airlife, 1981).

Project Cancelled, Derek Wood (London: Macdonalds and Janes, 1975).

Project Horizon: Report of the Task Force on National Aviation Goals, Federal Aviation Agency (Washington: GPO, 1961).

S/S/T and Sonic Boom Handbook, William A. Shurcliff (New York: Ballantine/Friends of the Earth, 1970).

Soviet SST: The Technopolitics of the Tupolev-144, Howard Moon (New York: Orion Books, 1989).

Stuck on the Drawing Board, Richard Payne (Stroud: Tempus, 2004).

Supersonic Cruise Technology, F.E. McLean (Washington DC: NASA, 1985).

The Aeroplane and Astronautics, various editions, 1956–64.

The Battle for Concorde, John Costello and Terry Hughes (Tisbury: Compton Press, 1971).

Wings Across the World, Harald Penrose (London: Cassell, 1980).

Central Intelligence Agency, Langley, Virginia.
Citizens' League Against the Sonic Boom Handbook, held in the Institute Archives
    and Special Collections of the Massachusetts Institute of Technology Libraries
    in Cambridge, Massachusetts.
Congressional Quarterly Weekly Reports.
FAA Historian's Office – including the records of the FAA Office of Supersonic
    Transport Development, National Records Center.
Federal Reporter, Federal Supplement and United States Reports.
NASA History Office, Washington DC.
The National Archives, Kew, London – including papers from the groups AIR,
    AVIA, DCA, BT, CAB.
Papers of the US Court of Appeals.
Papers of the US District Courts.
Papers of the New Jersey Legislature.
Papers of the Port of New York Authority.
Papers from the Public Relations Department, British Aircraft Corporation
    (Operating) Ltd.
Papers of the US Department of Transportation.
Presidential Library of John Fitzgerald Kennedy, Boston, Massachusetts –
    including the President's Advisory Committee on Supersonic Transport, the
    National Security Files, the President's Office Files and the White House
    Daily Diary.
Presidential Library of Lyndon Baines Johnson, Austin, Texas – including the
    Vice-President Files, the President's Advisory Committee on Supersonic
    Transport, the National Security Files, the President's Office Files and the
    White House Daily Diary.
Public Papers of the Presidents of the United States – John F. Kennedy, Lyndon B.
    Johnson, Richard M. Nixon, Gerald Ford and Jimmy Carter.
The SST – a General Description, September 1969. The Boeing Company
    Commercial Airplane Group, Supersonic Transport Division.
The Supersonic Transport: Hearings before the Subcommittee on Priorities and
    Economy in Government of the Joint Economic Committee, 92nd Cong.,
    2nd sess., 27–28 December 1972.
The US National Archives, Suitland, Maryland.

Index